SHADOW PAINTER

A PRACTICAL HANDBOOK FOR PROPHETIC AND WORSHIP ART FOR THE CHURCH IN OUR GENERATION

Laurie A. Stasi

SHADOW PAINTER

Printed in the United States of America

International Standard Book Number:

978-1-888081-85-5

For more information email: stasiart@gmail.com.
www.shadowpainter.org
Facebook Page: The Shadow Painter

Published by
GOOD NEWS FELLOWSHIP MINISTRIES
220 Sleepy Creek Road, Macon, GA 31210
Phone (478) 757-8071

Thank you, Abba,

For speaking to your children

And rising up Prophetic Artists

For Your use in our generation

Thank you for guiding in the

Preparation of this book.

Let it be to Your glory.

I also want to thank my husband,

Paul Stasi, for his love and support,

And always encouraging my

Gifts and creativity

Special thanks to Amanda Flowers

And Nichole Ryder for the use of

Their artwork and their assistance

And support of prophetic art.

TABLE OF CONTENTS

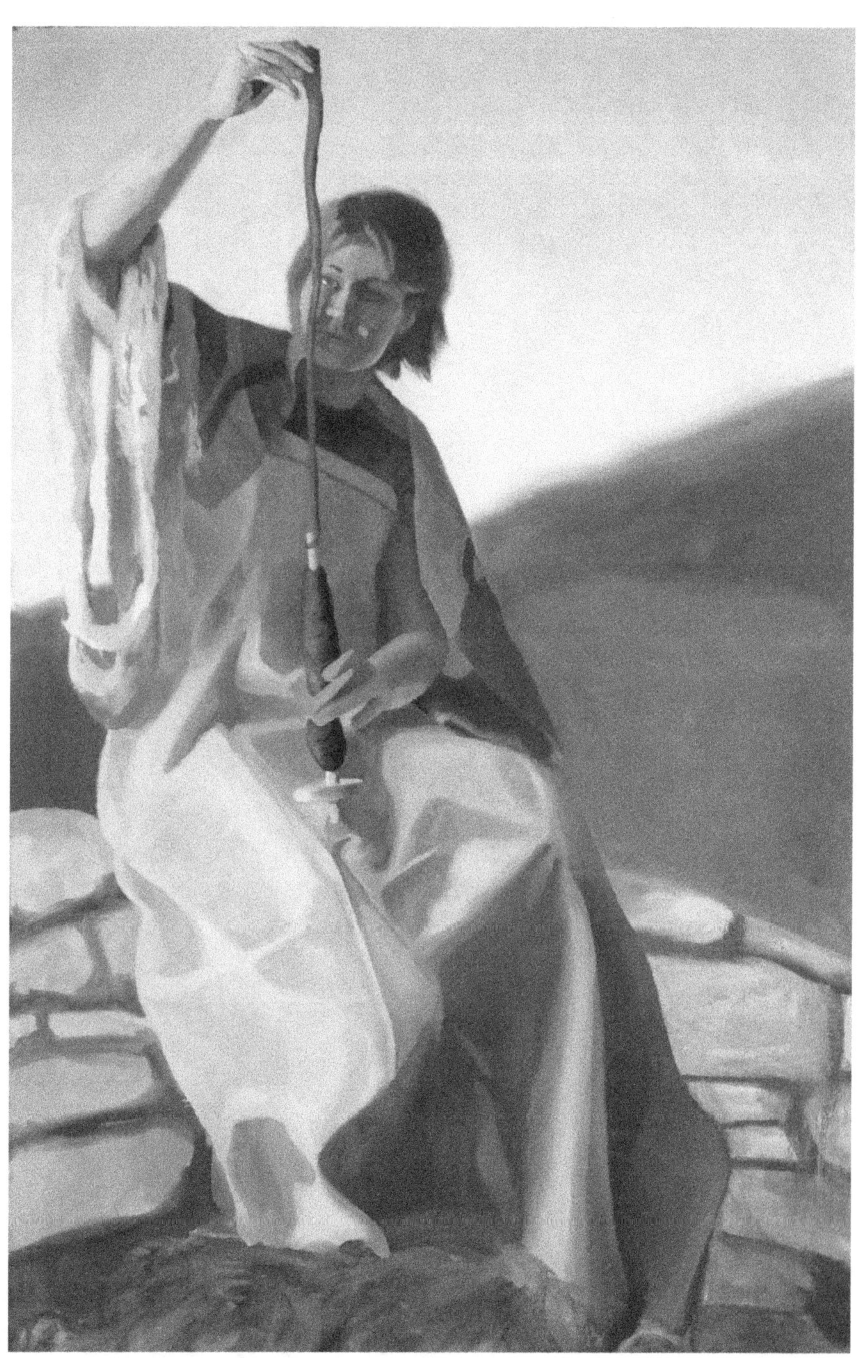

"Return of the Arts" from Exodus 35 by Amanda A. Flowers

INTRODUCTION

We live in a generation that is seeking more of the Lord and of spiritual things. Many are receiving revelation from Him. Countless individuals from all Christian denominations hear from God, may have dreams, visions or even trances. Some of these people feel called to demonstrate what they have seen or heard in their creative art. These individuals we now call, "prophetic artists."

The aim of this book is to help prophetic artists in every area of art to understand the vast possibilities in doing art for God. *Shadow Painter* includes 33 types or categories of prophetic art, 29 exercises, and 24 Bible Study topics to develop your prophetic artistic gifting.

Shadow Painter will also help others in the church understand what prophetic art is, and why God wants the body of Christ to embrace the Father's gift of creativity and His revelations from heaven. This book will encourage artists in the lifestyle of the prophetic, and give helpful direction in hearing from Him and translating their visions into their art form.

The Bible gives us solid understanding of the prophetic and the arts. *Shadow Painter* stands on scriptures to present topics related to art, imagination and creativity. Christian artists should know what the Lord says related to these subjects so they can be the most effective in their callings as artists.

I pray that as you read this book, God will anoint your creativity, and you will find more ways to use the arts for the Lord's glory. Whatever your field of study, weather it be the visual arts, music, cinema, calligraphy, banners, photography, dance, writing, drama, etc., *Shadow Painter* will give you information that will stretch you and help you grow in your creativity. In writing this manual I frequently put information in context of visual art, but please apply the principles to your creative medium.

The Lord has precious revelation He wants to release to our generation. He has prophetic guidance and wisdom He wants to impart to His children. I pray that churches will embrace the arts, and the artists in their calling as they release a message from heaven. I encourage artists to fearlessly go forward with the message they have received, empowered by the Holy Spirit.

The world has had an evil grip on the arts for too long. Its time we take them back and offer the arts as a sweet sacrifice to our Savior. *Shadow Painter* will give direction and guidance and together we can create for the Lord's glory, releasing His messages from heaven.

CHAPTER 1

PROPHETIC ART

Suddenly, from His hand there is a flash of light, and multiple explosions. Planets spin and find their resting place in the order and design of the cosmos. This is scene one from the book of all time; it is The Creator miraculously forming the splendors of all of creation. So begins the Bible. The first thing we find out about Almighty God is that He creates. Soon after that it tells us that we are made in His image; the image of the God of creativity. In the last book of the Bible John wrote about God's creativity as he stood before the throne. The four living creatures cry out to the Creator:

> *"You are worthy, our Lord and God, to receive glory and honor and power, for you created all things, and by your will they were created and have their being." NIV Rev. 4:11.*

God created all things for His "will," or pleasure and purpose. He also gave us the ability to create for His pleasure and purposes. It is in our DNA. We create and make a beautiful world around us, by designing fashionable clothes, decorated cakes, building skyscrapers, creating suspension bridges, sculpting topiary gardens, etc., all because of the flow of the Creator through us.

God desires our creativity in all areas to glorify Him. Man usually creates for function, or aesthetic pleasure of man. We should create the world that ought to be, a place that is worship to our Maker. We are born creative, but much of our creativity is forfeited. Pablo Picasso said, "Every child is an artist. The problem is how to remain an artist once he grows up." The enemy, satan, (I refuse to capitalize his name) comes to steal this precious gift because he is jealous of it. We are in continual struggle with the enemy over the arts. They are a gift that we must use to worship, as Ray Hughes said, "Creativity should not be our escape from the mundane. It should be the core of our expressed worship," (Hughes).

Worship is the highest purpose for the arts and our creativity. The second highest function of the arts is to release a prophetic statement, a message from the Lord. The arts may also demonstrate the character of Jesus or a word from the Bible. Through our creativity, we may display things in heaven as God reveals to it us, or share the Father's heart with others through something as personal as a prophetic word for an individual. When God speaks, something within us is stirred. Our spirit testifies to truth of the message that is given us. People who see or hear true prophetic art may be challenged or changed in their inner being. The Holy Spirit will use prophetic art to draw people closer to the heart of the Father.

Prophetic art at its simplest form is a message from God. Just as the prophets in the Bible were sent to carry warnings, instruction, and revelation from Him, so Prophetic Art is to do the same. It is a gift from God. Artists can bring a rhema word, an image of hope to someone in particular, or a message that visually stays in the person's mind like a sermon. It can be a call to war, or like a banner it can signal the troops. God wants to use the arts as a form of communication to the body of Christ. I will discuss each purpose in further detail in Chapter four.

> *"Follow the way of love and eagerly desire gifts of the Spirit, especially prophecy." 1 Cor. 14:1.*

We are supposed to "eagerly desire" the special gift of Prophecy. It is a treasure of revelation from God and is extraordinary and powerful. The prophetic and prophetic art ministers God's love to individuals, churches and nations. The Father desires to communicate and have relationship with us, and the prophetic contributes in this dialogue with Him.

The title of this book, *"Shadow Painter,"* refers to the fact that we can see into the heavenly realm and take a picture and are able to paint a shadow or reflection of the things in heaven, and things to come. As artists, craftsmen, musicians, writers and creative people in dozens of areas, we are able to see what God wants to release for this time in history and we can display God's heart through our creativity and talent. It is a privilege to be able to go boldly before the throne of grace, receive from the Lord and release the kingdom here on earth. This generation of Christian artists is developing these gifts through the power and revelation of the Holy Spirit.

The Bible says, "Without vision, the people perish." Without spiritual vision we die, but having revelation from the Father gives life to His people. It keeps them moving forward in His direction and purpose. This can deeply impact church bodies as they receive revelation and run with the vision. For centuries, the prophetic was asleep in the church; even now too many individuals and churches get off track of God's plans because they don't listen to His voice. Worse yet, they begin to follow the plans of man or the flesh. The prophetic word of the Lord can help them accomplish the destiny of their church by keeping them on task. The goal of prophets or prophetic artists is to release what they are seeing or hearing from the Lord. This may also confirm what others are getting from the Lord.

How do you know if you are called to be a prophetic artist (whatever the media)? The prophet Jeremiah said;

> *"His word is in my heart like a fire, a fire shut up in my bones. I am weary of holding it in; indeed, I cannot." Jer. 20:9.*

If you are called, there will be something within yourself that you cannot continue holding in. You will be frustrated until you let it out. If you stop doing your art you will be miserable. Life will seem dull and meaningless because you are not walking in your calling. The devil may even give you depression because of this emptiness. We all have to be true to the talent and word of the Lord within us. Some may struggle for years in finding the right way to release what they have growing in their bellies. I pray that the truths you read in this book will resonate with your spirit and help release the Lord's fiery message within you. What a joy it is to create for the Master and be His message and light bearer.

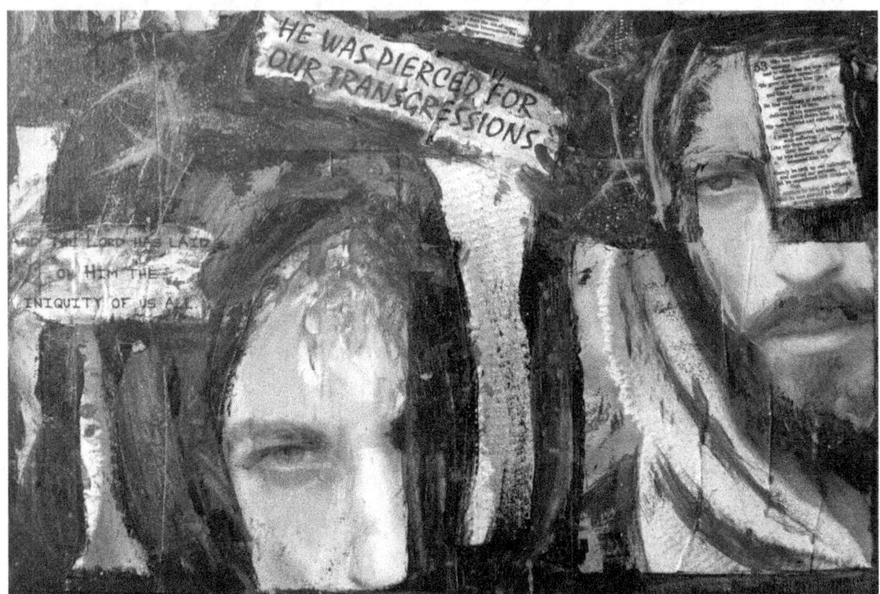

"Isaiah 53" by Laurie A. Stasi

There are numerous people doing prophetic art in this generation. For many within the church, there is still the question about what Prophetic Art is, and more importantly, what is its purpose. I hope artists and non-artists alike, who are really questioning, will find this information interesting and helpful.

In the Old Testament, the people who had visions from the Lord were called 'seers'.

> *"Formerly in Israel, if someone went to inquire of God, they would say, "Come, let us go to the seer," because the prophet of today used to be called a seer." I Sam. 9:9.*

It was, and is very common for the Lord to give messages to His people in visions, visitation, trances or dreams. We can "see" a message from the Lord. While in prayer, many Christians can have an image flash into their mind. This is a short vision. Sometimes it is longer and may be like a video clip. God loves to speak to His children. It's a little like getting an email from the Lord with a picture in it, or a video. Our loving Father is sending us "pics." Some Christians may spend time in prayer and fall into a trance. We read about this kind of revelation in the book of Acts. In this state, we become unaware of our physical bodies and surroundings, and deeply delve into what God is showing us. We may even feel like we have left our body completely. Paul wrote:

> *"And I know that this man—whether in the body or apart from the body I do not know, but God knows— was caught up to paradise and heard inexpressible things, things that no one is permitted to tell,"* 2 Cor. 12:3-4.

The Father spoke to His people in the Bible in many diverse and creative forms. We have a God who is Elohim, Creator, and He is limitless in His ways to speak to us and get our attention. In another chapter, I will spend more time discussing the different ways we receive from God. In the Bible, we have seen Him in a fire by night, cloud by day, in a burning bush. He also uses a variety of forms of creativity to share His messages: poetry, songs, and art, even music videos just to name a few.

When Moses went up the mountain to talk with the Lord, God displayed Himself with thunder and lightening and terrified the people and they wouldn't dare come close. He spoke verbally through His prophets, but He also used the prophets in dramatic, visual ways. God used performance art, having Ezekiel act out different dramas to deliver the message to His people. Prophetic art is the release of a message or revelation from God to others, and can take many forms.

Another aspect of prophetic art is worship. A piece of artwork, painting, sculpture, dance, or drama can bring worship and glory to the Lord. There were many examples in the temple, objects that pointed to Jesus as Savior. They brought glory and worship to the Father. They displayed His splendor. Creating them was an act of worship. David wanted to build a house for the Lord out of his love for God. His act of worship was making the plans to build the temple. David also danced before the Lord, in joy and celebration in pure adoration of God. Dance is a beautiful form of worship, delighting the Lord. All of the arts need to be purified to use to honor and worship God. We need to reclaim the creativity that the devil has stolen, and bring it to the glory of God. It should all be for the display of God's splendor.

The act of painting art can be a prophetic action; it can release God's word or purpose to the natural realm. It can be like a key that opens up the door from heaven. Prophetic art can include all the art forms, and should never be limited or put in a box. Ray Hughes once said, "We need a generation that doesn't know a box." God wants us to expand our creativity, not limit it. The only limitation to put on prophetic art is holiness; which means we make art that does not promote sin. (For example, we don't want to bring the viewer into lust, greed, temptation, or unjustly offend.)

There are many purposes for prophetic art, let the Lord speak to you and guide you to create for His glory. Help your church embrace creativity. Be an Esther for your generation. She hid her identity for a season, but then, with prayer and fasting, took a stand for God's plan and His people. Listen for God's timing, and make a stand. Let your art be a voice.

CHAPTER 2
THE MISSION OF BEZALEL

When I did a study on the Holy Spirit throughout the Bible, I was surprised to find that the first person who was ***filled*** with the Holy Spirit was not a priest, prophet, king, worship leader, poet, or musician. It was an artist/craftsman named Bezalel. Prior to him, there were people in the Bible that the Spirit "came on," but being "filled" is the Hebrew word "male`" which means: "to be filled, fullness and with abundance." God chose Bezalel for a special assignment that required the fullness of the Holy Spirit.

> *"Then the LORD said to Moses, 'See, I have chosen Bezalel son of Uri, the son of Hur, of the tribe of Judah, and I have filled him with the Spirit of God, with skill, ability and knowledge in all kinds of crafts- to make artistic designs for work in gold, silver and bronze, to cut and set stones, to work in wood, and to engage in all kinds of craftsmanship.'" Ex. 31:1-5.*

The first time a subject is mentioned in the Bible, there is particular significance. As a visual artist, I have questioned God many times why He filled Bezelel with the Holy Spirit before anyone else. Bezelel crafted the furnishings of the tabernacle, and constructed the place of habitation of the Lord. In some ways, he is a reflection of Elohim, who is the Creator of the heavenly tabernacle (we are all supposed to be a reflection of our Father).

Under the anointing of Holy Spirit, Bezelel fashioned the Tabernacle implements guided by the Spirit who imparted beauty and glory. Bezalel fashioned the earthly ark of the covenant,

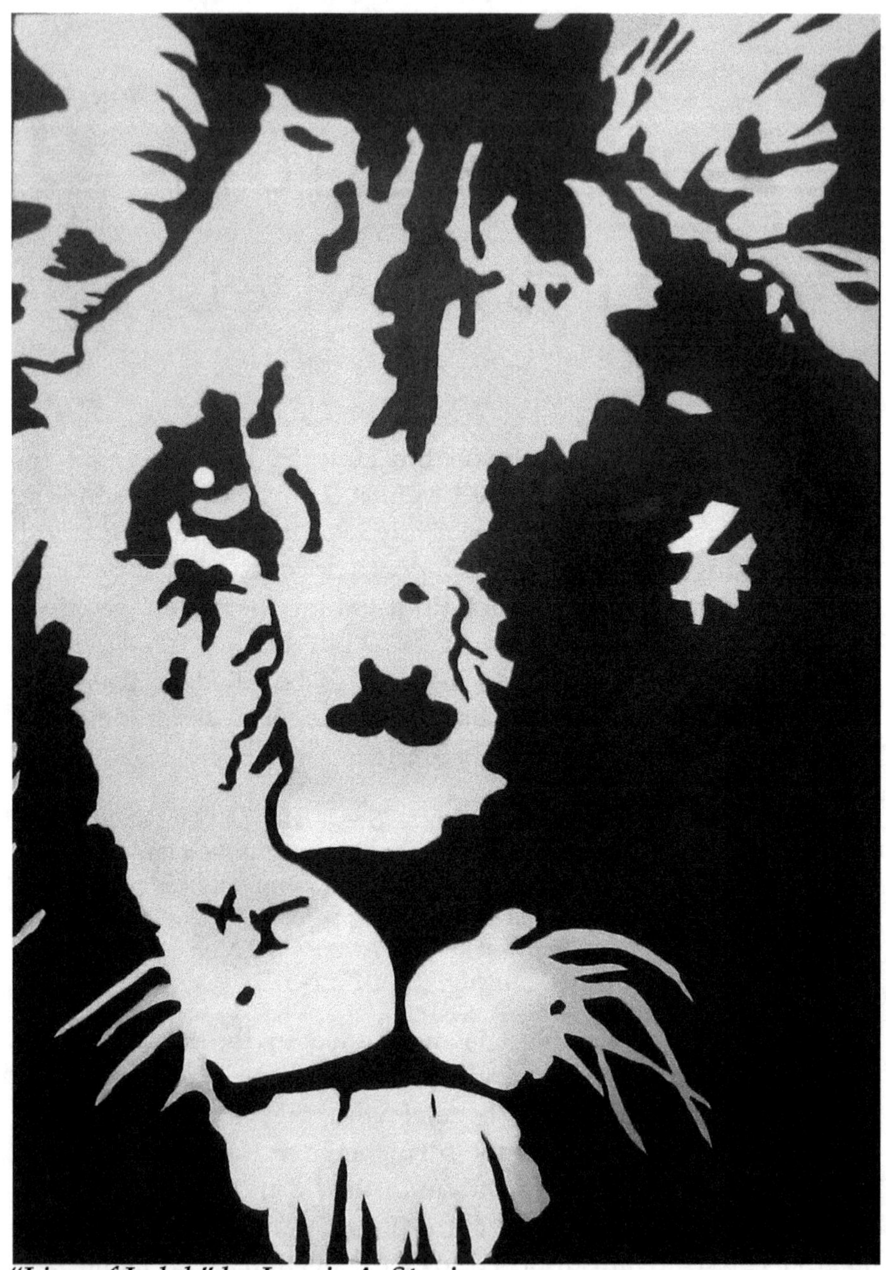

"Lion of Judah" by Laurie A. Stasi

which of course is just a simple human replica of the majestic heavenly one. The Tabernacle is also a copy and shadow of what is in heaven. Everything Bezalel created was under supervision of Holy Spirit and guided by Moses, as instructed by God, following the pattern that was given to Moses on the mountain (see Hebrews 8). In Revelation, John saw the heavenly temple. It exists and is more real than anything here on earth.

Bezalel means, "in the shadow of God." The shadow is a place of protection in the Lord. David said, "Hide me in the shadow of Your wings," Ps. 17:8. The wings were a picture of a bird covering it's young and protected them. It also represented the wings of the angels that overshadowed the Ark of the Covenant. Bezalel lived in the shadow, the place of God's presence. This is where all Prophetic artists should dwell, close enough to hear the heartbeat of our Father.

We have a supernatural covering, as Bezalel did. His name, in the shadow of God, also reminds us that Bezalel created shadows, which are copies and forms of the original in the heavenly realm. As prophetic artists, we are "shadow painters."

Bezalel's assistant, Oholiab means "Father's Tent." This makes reference to the tabernacle that was "the tent," which was the dwelling place of God the Father, the tabernacle they both worked on as craftsmen. Both Bezalel and Oholiab were commanded to teach other artists and craftsmen. As artists, we are all called to study our craft, and then teach others and share the information the Lord has given to us. These men were chosen to create a portable dwelling of worship for the God of the Israelites. The Lord took their assignment very seriously, and He dedicated an enormous amount of space in the Bible describing the Tabernacle and Temple in great detail because if its importance to His heart.

The earthly temple was no longer needed after Jesus completed His mission at the cross. We have become the earthly temple of the Holy Spirit. We are all filled with Holy Spirit and can reflect the heavenly temple with our creativity. We can all glorify the Creator. When the Spirit leads us, it will be natural for the presence of God to be on our art. People should be drawn to it because it reflects the God we serve, heaven, the sacrifice of the cross, and the heavenly tabernacle.

In Israel, they have re-created the silver utensils, implements and furniture for the next temple. I believe this is a prophetic sign in the natural that it is time to restore the arts to God's glory. I pray that our generation takes back the mountain of the arts and creativity and let it glorify our Awesome Mighty God!

God gave Bezelal wisdom, understanding, knowledge and craftsmanship. I believe it was a special manifold, or multicolored wisdom that the artist was given. In Chapter three, I will discuss this special wisdom. Bezalel was assigned to the creation of the beautiful implements for the tabernacle. These were a type and shadow of things to come. He was given revelation of the heavenly items to create their copy here on earth. This is what it is to be a prophetic artist. We can see the source, the originals in heaven, and bring a replica of them to earth to facilitate in worship, prophecy and interceding, or create a shift in the spiritual realm.

The earthly tabernacle was created for us to encounter God. He inhabited it for the sake of our relationship. The heavenly prototype was much better, but he came down to this man-made structure out of His love for us. Now we can encounter the God of the universe anywhere.

Bezalel was given wisdom (chokmah in Hebrew), also interpreted as skill. It was the same wisdom spoken of about King Solomon:

> *"All the earth was seeking the presence of Solomon, to hear his wisdom which God had put in his heart." 1 Kings 10:24.*

King Solomon exhibited great wisdom and creativity, and the Queen of Sheba commented about it. She came to test him with difficult questions to test his wisdom. She also mentioned his wisdom in relation to the house he built, the food and the presentation of his table with servants, and his stairway. Wisdom from God encompasses the creative way we present our houses, our food presentation and architectural design elements. It flows into all our art and creative projects. In the next chapter we will discover some more amazing facets of the Spirit of Wisdom.

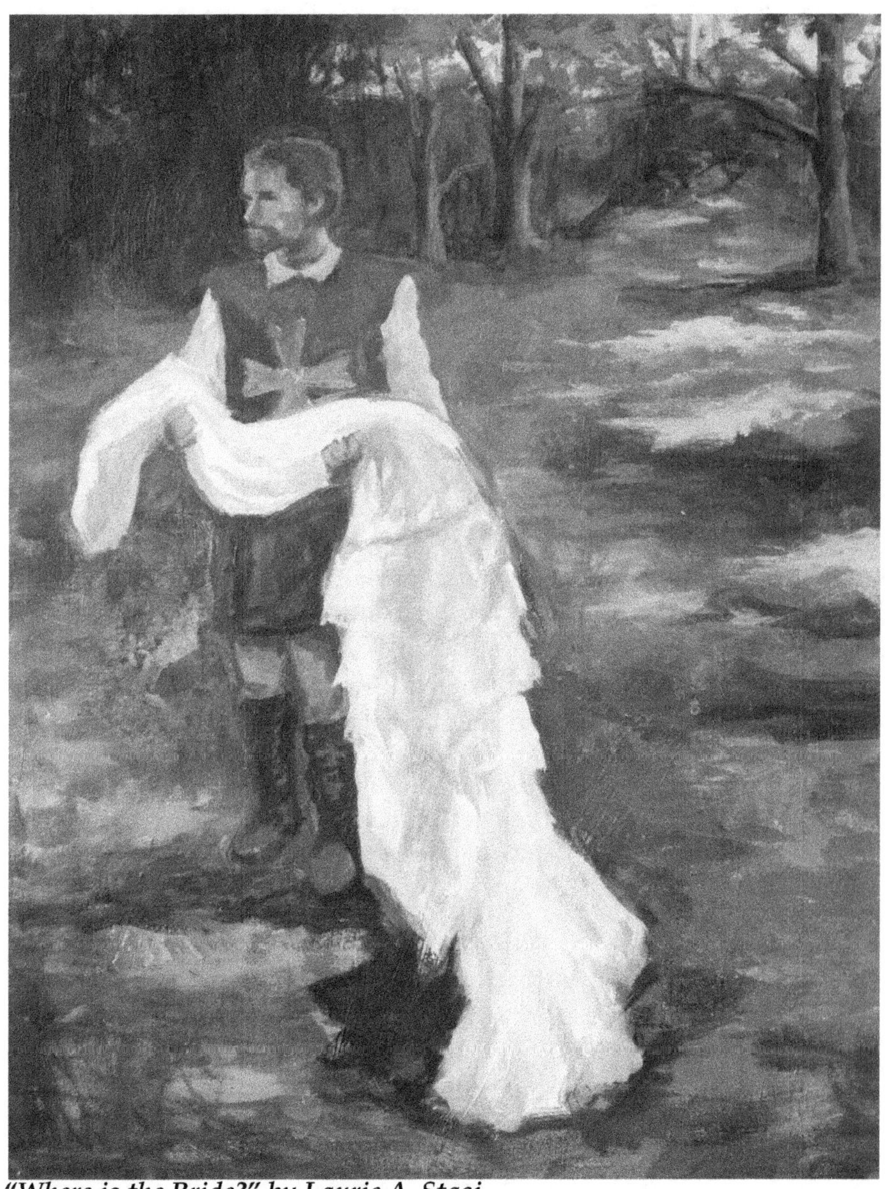

"Where is the Bride?" by Laurie A. Stasi

CHAPTER 3

THE MYSTERIOUS SPIRIT OF WISDOM

As artists, we are given skill and ability from God to create for Him. The Hebrew word "craftsman," was used in Exodus to describe the artisans who worked on the temple. As we work skillfully and creatively with talent, we are using wisdom. When we use the word wisdom, many think of an earthly wisdom, or someone wise or knowledgeable with insightful answers. The word "wisdom" in Hebrew is "chokmah", meaning; "skillful, wisdom, wisely, wit." It was used interchangeably in the Bible for wisdom or creative skill. The first time wisdom is recorded in the Bible, it is referencing skillful people in the act of creating the garments for the priests. They were given the spirit of wisdom to create:

> *Ex 28:3-4 "You shall speak to all the skillful persons whom I have endowed with the spirit of wisdom, that they make Aaron's garments to consecrate him, that he may minister as priest to Me." NASU*

Remember, the Spirit of Wisdom was given by God to create, to fashion the garments and articles for the Tabernacle. This was a creative wisdom (there are many types of wisdom). In Proverbs 3 it says, "By wisdom the Lord laid the earth's foundations," which demonstrates that God used creative wisdom to fashion the earth.

The priestly garments were made by this creative wisdom. You can imagine the skilled weavers and embroiderers using their skill, bringing together the colorful threads to honor God. Aaron dressed in this beautiful attire and was consecrated as a priest to minister to the Lord. That means, the creative product, the garments, contributed to ministering to God. The Bible tells us that Aaron was not presentable to God without the garments, created by artisans with the spirit of Wisdom. Prophetically, this is a picture of the creative wisdom that will make the spiritual mantles (garments) for the end time priestly generation.

In 1 Kings we read about the man who was the craftsman for the temple named Huram.:

> *"King Solomon sent to Tyre and brought Huram, whose mother was a widow from the tribe of Naphtali and whose father was from Tyre and a skilled craftsman in bronze. Huram was filled with wisdom, with understanding and with knowledge to do all kinds of bronze work. He came to King Solomon and did all the work assigned to him." I Kings 7: 13,14.*

Similar to Bezalel, Huram was chosen and filled to create. Here in 1 Kings 7 it tells us that he was filled with wisdom, understanding and knowledge. These are the gifts of the Holy Spirit for creativity. As artists, we can ask to be filled like Huram and Bezalel, "Lord fill us with Holy Spirit, Wisdom, Understanding and Knowledge for our creative assignments."

Wisdom from God is the fire of our creativity. Through it we get revelation from the Lord, it mingles with the inspiration of creativity, and then blossoms into beauty. Wisdom is Christ in us, feeling His heart, seeing things as He sees. It is the glorious majesty and beautiful perfection of heaven released through us. Through His Wisdom, we can see the sounds, scents, and colors of heaven, and release God's magnificence in our art form. As a Christian artist of any art medium, you need God's Wisdom.

> *"His intent was that now, through the church, the **manifold wisdom** of God should be made known to the rulers and authorities in the heavenly realms, according to his eternal purpose that he accomplished in Christ Jesus our Lord," Eph. 3:8-11.*

This verse is about revealing the manifold wisdom of God. This word, 'manifold' means, "multicolored." The original Greek for manifold is polypoikilos, which has a very artistic word meaning; "much variegated, marked with a great variety of colors, of cloth or a painting, much varied, manifold."

We know in this chapter, Paul was referring to the Jew and Gentile coming together in the variety of colors, acknowledging their differences. But we can look at "multicolored" in the broader sense, and if we took a little liberty and re-wrote the Ephesians verse for artists from the original Greek, it might look like this:

His intent was that now, through the church, the creativity of a great variety of colors created with artistic skill as wisdom of God, should be made known to the rulers and authorities in the heavenly realms, according to His eternal purpose that He accomplished in Christ Jesus our Lord. (Eph. 3:8-11 My paraphrase from original Greek and Hebrew).

The implications of this verse for a visual artist are very powerful. It would appear to mean that creating artwork (and other creativity) through Wisdom of God would be revealed to the rulers and authorities in the heavenly realms. Artwork can have impact in the heavens with an eternal purpose! That is profound spiritual art!

> *"We do, however, speak a message of wisdom among the mature, but not the wisdom of this age or of the rulers of this age, who are coming to nothing. No, we speak of God's secret wisdom, a wisdom that has been hidden and that God destined for our glory before time began. None of the rulers of this age understood it, for if they had, they would not have crucified the Lord of glory." I Cor. 2:6-8. NIV*

There is a 'wisdom,' quite possibly a spiritual creativity or skill, or a spiritual power that is a secret wisdom hidden from before time. God destined it for our glory. It is so secret and mysterious; Paul doesn't go into detail to explain it, except that it was purchased through our crucified Lord. He goes on to say,

> *"No eye has seen, no ear has heard, no mind has conceived what God has prepared for those who love him" but God has revealed it to us by his Spirit. For the Spirit searches all things, even the deep things of God," I Cor. 2:9 NIV.*

Holy Spirit, our dear friend, reveals the deep mysteries of God to us. How amazing and incredible! This is so mysterious that no one has seen or heard anything like it before! I pray that this secret wisdom will be revealed to us, and specifically to artists through Holy Spirit. Paul goes on in verse 16 to give us a clue, "For who has known the mind of the Lord that He may instruct him? But we have the mind of Christ." We can have a link to the mind of Christ and download from Him such mysteries, wisdom and knowledge that far exceed human intelligence. As we apply this wisdom, it has profound effect in heaven and on the earth. What a mysterious gift.

We receive Wisdom from our Father in heaven. He releases it to us here, and we create. It then is released back to Him in heaven, opening the heavens, interceding as art, and manifests the kingdom here on earth. We know that we can bind or loose things in heaven. This principle is one of the keys of the kingdom. We have to believe that our creativity has spiritual purpose and power. God can anoint it, and use it for His eternal purposes. We need to get these principles into our spirit. There is a hidden creative power in wisdom, which God wants us to understand. There is an eternal purpose in releasing this wisdom.

Ezekiel 28 tells us about the devil and his attractiveness. He was adorned and covered with beautiful stones and full of wisdom:

> *"'You were the seal of perfection, **full of wisdom** and perfect in beauty. You were in Eden, the garden of God; every precious stone adorned you: carnelian, chrysolite and emerald, topaz,*

onyx and jasper, lapis lazuli, turquoise and beryl. Your settings and mountings were made of gold; on the day you were created they were prepared. You were anointed as a guardian cherub, for so I ordained you. You were on the holy mount of God; you walked among the fiery stones." Ezekiel 28:12-14.

He was an amazing creation of beauty, anointed and ordained as the cherub who covers on the holy mountain. But satan corrupted his gifts:

"Your heart became proud on account of your beauty, and you ***corrupted your wisdom*** *because of your splendor. So I threw you to the earth; I made a spectacle of you before kings," Ezekiel 28:17.*

Satan was given a gift of wisdom. It was creativity, skill, a beauty and splendor and he ruined it. Some believe that satan was the only creature given the ability to create besides God. Satan despises our creative gift. He tries to destroy our creativity, especially when it is linked to the prophetic word of the Lord.

The beauty that adorned satan is now reserved for the Church. She is adorned in gemstones of beauty and creativity to prepare herself for her groom. Jesus will look on the Bride and declare how beautiful she is. She will be dressed in white and gleaming in splendor. When Jacob's servant found Rebekah for Jacob, she was given jewelry as a promise and security from her intended groom. It was like an engagement ring, a promise of the coming wedding. Jesus gave Himself and the Holy Spirit as security for our union. He gave the greatest gift ever, His own shed body to seal the deal for the Bride of Christ. He paid the bride price or dowry. I think the manifestations of jewels in meetings are demonstrating this "engagement ring" for His bride. He wants her to be adorned for the coming wedding.

"How beautiful are your feet in sandals, O prince's daughter! The curves of your hips are like jewels, the work of the hands of an artist." SS 7:1.

We are the Bride, whose hips are adorned and beautiful like jewels. These gems are "the work of the hands of an artist."

We are adorned with beauty and ability to create, similar to satan's ability before his fall. Women are designed with hips to carry their young. We, like Bezalel and Oholiab are supposed to teach and encourage others to grow up and mature in their creativity. We carry them in the process, until they are able to walk on their own. This process is beautiful, like the jeweled hips in Song of Solomon.

The Bible gives us other examples of this. The sons also are compared to ornaments:

> *"Lift up your eyes and look around; all your sons gather and come to you. As surely as I live, declares the Lord, "You will wear them all as ornaments; you will put them on, like a bride." Is. 49:18*

That verse states that each son of God becomes an ornament or beautiful gem to be worn, like a bride.

> *"For He has clothed me with garments of salvation and arrayed me in a robe of righteousness, as a bridegroom adorns his head like a priest, and as a bride adorns herself with her jewels." Is. 61:10*

I was surprised to find that the Hebrew word "jewels" (Kelly, 3627), is the same word used for "utensils" and furniture" that were made for the tabernacle in Exodus by Bezalel. As we are adorned with beautiful jewels as the bride of Christ, we are like the tabernacle utensils and furniture that had purpose and function for service. We are the temple of the Holy Spirit, and He makes us useful and beautiful. The artists and craftsmen made the utensils, and artists now have the assignment to adorn the bride with utensils of creativity and beauty for serving and ministering. We will see more creative miracles as we are adorned for our King.

Artists, musicians, and craftsmen are given the gifts of wisdom, skill and beauty, and many fall into the same path as Satan. His great downfall was pride. Be careful with the great wisdom and creativity that God gives you, not to see yourself as magnificent in your own doing. All glory needs to go back to the Father as we minister and create in humility.

In Proverbs it tells us that the fear of the Lord is the beginning of wisdom. Our skill and creativity will be enhanced when we learn what it really means to fear the Lord. God has

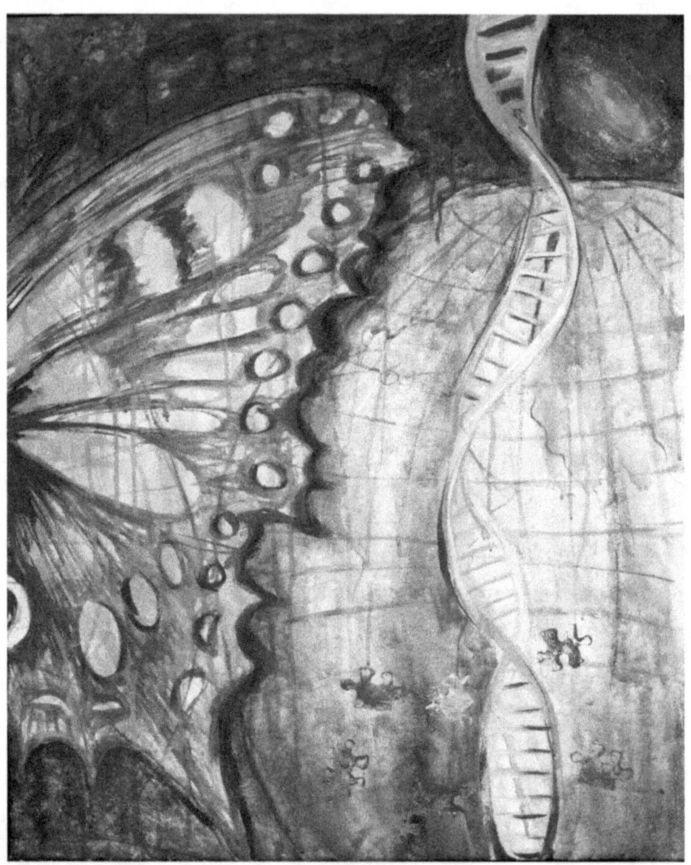

"Grand Design" By Laurie A. Stasi The world has evidence, proof of God's creative authorship in natural patterns and design. We see it in the beautiful simple patterns on a butterfly's wings and in the complexity of DNA.

chosen to give us creativity. He has made us in His image. We must not squander the gift or abuse it. We need to treat it as holy, and live with a fear of the Lord and He will pour creative wisdom into our lives.

The artistic things Bezelel, skillful crafts-men and women made were used in the temple as holy objects. What we create for the Lord is holy. There is a difference in the art we create for the world, for success or income, than the art we create for His glory and with the prophetic anointing. We need to ask the Lord where He wants the art to go, and obey Him. We need the right frame of mind to create for the Lord:

> *"Now set your heart and your soul to seek the LORD your God; arise, therefore, and build the sanctuary of the LORD God, so that you may bring the ark of the covenant of the LORD and the holy vessels of God into the house that is to be built for the name of the LORD." 1 Chron. 22:19*

This tells us to, "set your heart and soul" (get them ready), "to seek the Lord." Our hearts must be pure and holy to create for Him. We need to seek Him above all other things. We need to set ourselves apart from the world, and be sanctified in Him.

In Chronicles there is a clue to the difference between artistic creativity, musical creativity and talent:

> *"Chenaniah, chief of the Levites, was in charge of singing; he gave instruction in singing because he was skillful." 1 Chron. 15:22.*

This musical skill, in Hebrew "biyn," which translated means Chenaniah as chief singer could: "perceive, discern, understand, know, observe, mark, distinguish, consider, had discernment, insight, and understanding." It also includes intelligence, and the ability to teach or share these things with others. This ability is prudent and we see it exemplified in the best worship leaders. It is different from the word and gift of "wisdom." Many worship leaders may also have the gift of the prophetic and weave it together with their "skillful" abilities. A select few may also have the creative gift of wisdom, the ability to create through their talent. Human wisdom is different from wisdom from the Spirit:

> *"We have not received the spirit of the world but the Spirit who is from God, that we may understand what God has freely given us. This is what we speak, not in words taught us by human wisdom but in words taught by the Spirit, expressing spiritual truths in spiritual words..." 1 Cor. 2:12,13 NIV.*

We need to separate from human wisdom, the spirit of the world. This means we need to set ourselves apart from the darkness and the world's thinking. Some artists have been exposed to the world's art, messages and philosophies. They have been exposed to its corruption and sinfulness. If that is the case, they need repentance, a cleansing, and awareness of being set apart in the form of consecration. Don't be polluted by the world. This verse tells that the Spirit instructs us, telling us the deep things of God. Allow Him to guide you in your projects. The Spirit of God freely gives, and you can release His will into your art. It is not a natural thing, it is spiritually discerned. What a privilege to hear the thoughts of God. He even tells us things to come. Once we are really submitted to His holiness, we get to have the mind of Christ guiding us, leading our creativity, directing our poetry, music and brush strokes.

God is so incredible. In our love walk with Him, He reveals secrets! He tells me things and I am shocked by what He says or shows me. Occasionally, in a dream I have watched top government officials making key decisions in a conference room. God can show us things going on in the natural. We can intercede about that event, and even create art or do prophetic actions related to it. When we are prophetic artists for the Lord we get the inside scoop.

God promises if we lack wisdom we should ask Him, and He will give generously. His wisdom develops your skill in your art, writing, music, etc. He instructs you and gives you knowledge. Let Him be your teacher. He can guide you into creativity that has not yet been seen on the earth. He gives witty inventions, new ideas, and concepts that are a mystery from heaven.

> *"No eye has seen, no ear has heard, no mind has conceived what God has prepared for those who love him – but God has revealed it to us by His Spirit. The Spirit searches all things, even the deep things," 1 Cor. 2:9.*

God has revealed it to us, by His Spirit, wow. God reveals things we haven't seen before, heard before, or even our minds conceived. The very deep things of God are whispered to us. What a sweet thing to be in relationship with the living God of the universe!

Press in and go deeper with God. As prophetic artists, we need to understand all these mysteries and flow in them. Our art is a great tool in the body of Christ and will reveal the deep mysteries as God. Consecrate yourself and contend for the manifold wisdom of God.

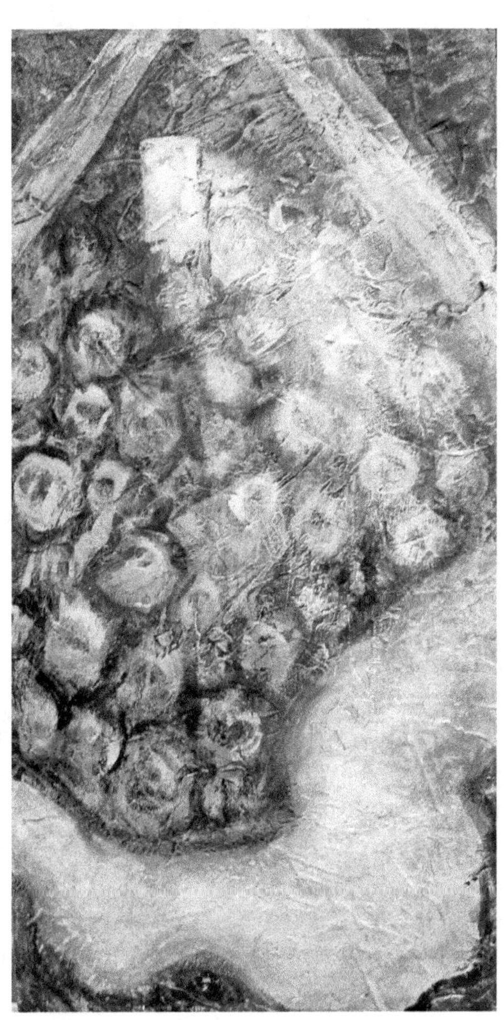

"Revival River" By Laurie A. Stasi

CHAPTER 4
33 CATEGORIES OF PROPHETIC VISUAL ART

The following chapter is a list of 33 types and categories of Prophetic Art and includes examples. It is not intended to be an all-inclusive list, because the Father will continue to increase creativity and ideas.

#1 CREATING UNDER THE INFLUENCE OF HOLY SPIRIT

This type of prophetic art is done while painting and we let Holy Spirit direct all choices of paint, strokes, form and colors in the moments we are painting. There are many artists who paint during church services who are expressing prophetic art in this way. This may be done without a vision or image, just letting the Holy Spirit orchestrate the art. The results are abstract and free. They may express; images, emotion, color from heaven or the very heart of God. It is important to allow yourself to feel Holy Spirit's lead and His anointing, and surrender yourself and your thoughts to allow Him to flow through you. Sometimes, it can be almost trance-like, where you are not conscious of making mental choices of color etc., but are completely led.

In music, this is done with improvisation under the anointing. Many now "sing in the spirit," hearing a tune and words from heaven and release it in song. This could also be done with rap for those individuals who have their art so fine tuned that they can just flow with rhyming words to the anointing. They are able to creatively release a message from heaven.

#2 A SACRIFICIAL OFFERING OR AN ACT OF WORSHIP

This type of prophetic art is very similar to painting in the spirit, but the intent of the heart is totally engaged in worship. It is a giving mode, not receiving. The final results shouldn't matter to people around us. It is an offering of worship to God. You may paint from an image from a vision, or it may be free flow of painting in the Spirit. This is the highest form of prophetic art. It is an act of love. This, of course, can be done in music, or any other medium. I prophetically sing in my kitchen while unloading the dishwasher, purely as an offering of worship. Some things we create are for God alone. They are a fragrant worship offering.

The Greek word in the New Testament for worship is "proskyneo." It can mean to kiss the hand, as a token of reverence. Another meaning is to fall upon the knees and touch our forehead to the ground. We can let our creativity become kisses of adoration and bowing in surrender to Almighty God. We can put our gifts before Him as an offering of love.

I once saw a vision of a pomegranate, and the Lord showed me that it was about intimacy with Him and His desire for me. Soon after this, I was asked to paint at a small worship meeting and felt I needed to paint the pomegranate. I set up in a back corner, which is uncommon. Usually prophetic artists are near the front. But I was not painting this one for the audience to receive a message; I was painting as a gift to the Lord. It was the most incredible time with Jesus. I could not stand; I kept getting rocked by God. I painted pomegranates as my gift to Him, painting in pure love.

David spontaneously danced when the ark was being brought into Jerusalem. His dance was a pure act of worship. He was filled with celebration as the Spirit overcame him with joy.

We can paint in the spirit without any earthly paint. Just use your spiritual eye and reach for heavenly colors and paint in the heavenly realm. This painting is recorded in heavenly galleries. It feels much like play, and the Holy Spirit loves it. You are painting by faith for the Lord. Sometimes we have to learn how to come like a child. This is a good exercise for prophetic art groups to break off rigid thinking and become kids again.

Some art is to draw others into worship. The act of performing the art is a creative form that allows the process itself to become a performance and corporate worship to the Lord. Art can be executed in many creative ways. My husband and I were given tickets to see Trans Siberian Orchestra. They present music with extravagant presentation of: lights, visual images, smoke and fire. It is a wonderful experience in creativity. The way we present worship can be an extravagant experience to glorify the Lord. He is worthy of splendor and spectacular display.

#3 USHER IN GOD'S PRESENCE

We can usher in God's presence with our prophetic art. We know the Bible says that He inhabits the praise of His people. He also rested on the Ark of the Covenant in the Holy of Holies, a piece of artwork and beauty made by human hands. He could have made it Himself, but he commissioned Bezalel to do it. God will never again fully inhabit a piece of earthly material, but His anointing and presence can be on objects. In the New Testament, even pieces of cloth could carry the anointing. It says,

"God did extraordinary miracles through Paul, so that even handkerchiefs and aprons that had touched him were taken to the sick, and their illnesses were cured and the evil spirits left them," Acts 19:11,12.

Artwork, banners and flags can carry the anointing and presence into a meeting, and even bring the Lord's healing power. Artists should anoint their canvases, flags, or supplies, and believe that the Lord consecrates them as holy. Use anointing oil, and set them apart for the Lord. We should also prepare our hearts and cleanse ourselves to be His priests and prophets in executing our art. We should be anointed while we paint, and the paintings will retain God's presence. I believe as prophetic artists walk this out, their representational or abstract paintings can hang in secular places, and the people in that environment will sense the presence of the Lord, and may even be healed.

#4 ADORNS THE BRIDE-PRIEST

Art reflects us, as His bride, fully adorned in gemstones and beauty like the tabernacle was, dressed for her groom. We are the temple of the Holy Spirit. When we create for His glory, He sees us as beautiful and it gives Him joy. He wants us to be adorned magnificently, and He wants artists to be part of adorning His bride, who are also His priests. Let us look again at Exodus 28:

"You shall make holy garments for Aaron your brother, for glory and for beauty." Exodus 28:2 (NASB)

God said that the purpose of the garments was for beauty and glory. Why would God have wanted to give glory to priests? It was His temple, shouldn't the glory all be His? God wants his servants adorned delightfully. All the glory given to His priests reflects glory back to Him. When we get glory, it is given to the Lord. It also unifies us with the Lord. Jesus prayed,

> *"I have given them the glory that you gave me, that they may be one as we are one— I in them and you in me—so that they may be brought to complete unity. Then the world will know that you sent me and have loved them even as you have loved me." John 17:23,24*

This verse shows that the glory also proves to the world that God loves us. This is His display, like the banner over us is love.

The skillful persons, artists, were endowed "with the spirit of wisdom," to make the garments. The artists of our generation will be endowed with the Spirit of Wisdom of the Holy Spirit, to adorn the Priestly Generation. When the priests are consecrated, they will dress in the beautiful, striking spiritual garments inspired by God, bringing glory to them and to the Father!

Artists must contribute to getting this generation ready. Our prophetic messages and release of creativity will be part of the process necessary for the priests to be prepared.

#5 REVEALS GOD

One purpose of Prophetic Art is to reveal the knowledge of God. It is Him speaking through the art. It is to glorify Him. This art creates intimacy for both the artist, and the audience. We receive the message, but even more importantly, we encounter the message giver, the Lord. We can experience His presence, just as in the temple they saw the Shekinah glory glowing from behind the veil. They encountered the Table of Showbread, and the Lamp stand. All these visual things ultimately drew them into the presence and knowledge of the Lord. We can display the nature of the Lord in visual images. He is the Strong Tower; He is our Good Shepherd. In this art, we come to a deeper understanding of His traits, and then encounter Him through that revelation.

#6 HONOR OUR CREATOR

Prophetic art can reflect God's creation, and honors Him as Creator. In Genesis He formed the world and revealed His name as Elohim. Many artists paint nature, displaying the heavens and the earth, which brings the viewer closer to the God of all living things. This type of art draws us into worship by showing the splendor of creation.

> *"For since the creation of the world God's invisible qualities—his eternal power and divine nature—have been clearly seen, being understood from what has been made, so that people are without excuse." Rom. 1:20.*

Nature itself testifies about God and His "Invisible qualities-his eternal power and divine nature." It is a testimony that people cannot escape, that God is our awesome Creator and He has eternal power. Making art that captures God's creation is a testimony. There are amazing photographers who travel the world and take photographs of places and people we would not encounter in our life. It took my breath away when I saw a photograph of Niagara Falls in January, frozen in icy splendor. Bjorn Jorgensen's photographs of the Northern lights are incredible, the green glow reminds me of the emerald rainbow. We worship the Creator, and are thankful for the photographer. There are many nature photographs from space that remind us that our God is the awesome author of all creation. The Lord is the original designer; everything else is a copy. We can learn from Him as The Master Craftsman. When we create this art, it testifies to His awesome, creative power.

#7 TO PLEASE GOD

Prophetic art gives God pleasure. He enjoys the act of creating. In Genesis, He looked on what He had created, and said, "It is good." He rested to enjoy what He had fashioned. I think He savors our creativity and gets pleasure from it too. We are, after all, made in His image. It is the same as when your child brings you a colorful painting he made, and you hang it on your refrigerator. You enjoy seeing him create, and you are pleased that he enjoyed doing it.

I have felt the Lord's pleasure while painting. His love starts to wash over me like warm water, and sometimes I cannot stand. I 'feel' His approval. Whether you are a beginner or have been painting for 20 years, God takes pleasure in your various forms of creativity.

#8 REVEALS GOD'S LOVE FOR US

Symbolism of objects in prophetic artwork can reveal God's love for us. Read in Song of Solomon how He compares His beloved with palm trees, and "lips like scarlet thread . . . temples like a slice of a pomegranate behind your veil . . . ." (SS 4:3). Pomegranates, palm trees and scarlet threads were also used in the temple. Each is a symbolic message of the Lord's love for us. If we visually painted the Book of Song of Solomon, it would be a collection of the most beautiful, love paintings. They would reflect the undying love of the king for his bride.

One of the artists who paints during our evening services, frequently creates a picture of Jesus that reveals His love for us. God uses His prophetic art to touch people in a different way. It is a valentine from the lover of our soul.

God's Word is the book of love for us. We can see this love visually, and some artists may be called to focus on this theme in their art. Maybe you are a calligraphy artist who captures the beauty of the Word and can deliver God's love message. However we display it, His love has no bounds and it ministers to others as we remind them of His great love for us.

#9 SHOW GOD'S POWER

Prophetic art can display or present God's power. Moses was given this instruction, "But I have raised you up for this very

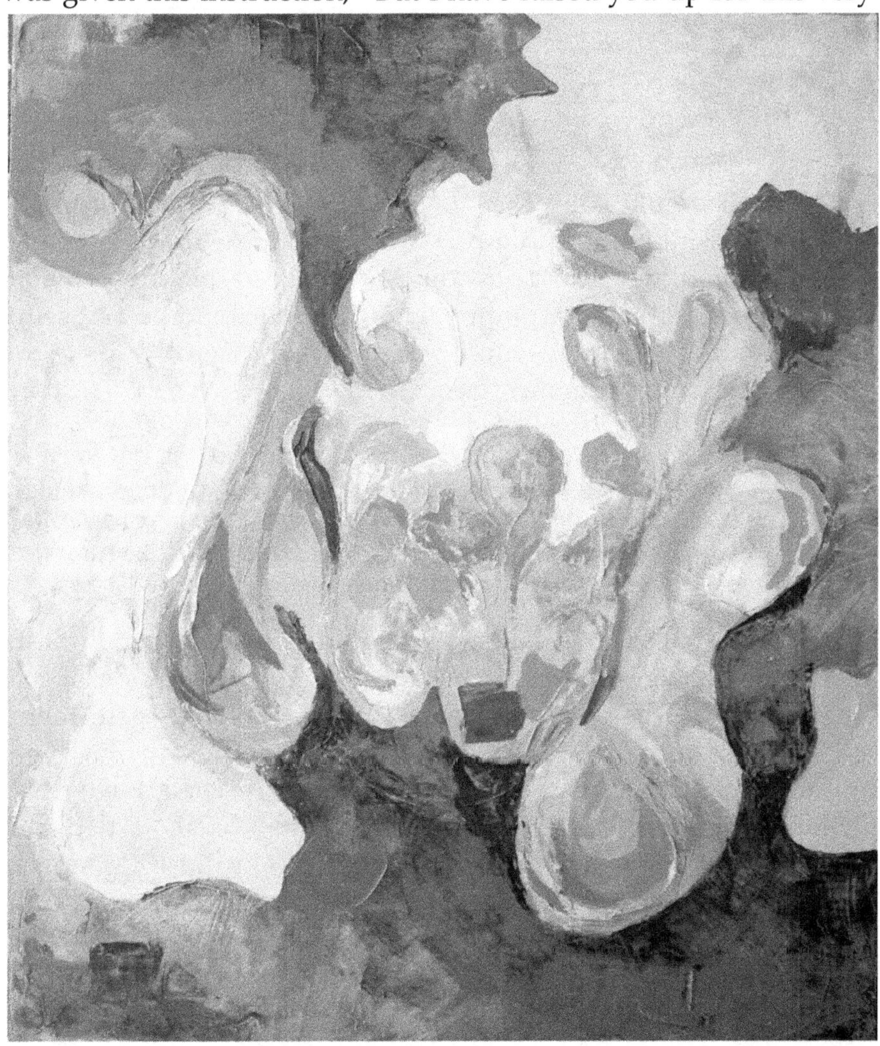

"Song of Songs" by Amanda A. Flowers

purpose, that I might show you my power and that my name might be proclaimed in all the earth," Exodus 9:16. When Moses set up the tabernacle, it was a man-made structure and craftsmen made the objects, yet God came and inhabited it. His power and glory were evident in the cloud by day and the fire by night. God can display His power through a song, or a spiritual presence on your created art.

#10 BRING UNITY

God wants to bring unity using prophetic art. I asked the Lord what I should paint for our "Burning Heart" church service for the following Sunday. Our leadership told me that the theme was 'the anointing.' I had several days to get a picture of what God wanted me to paint. I immediately felt it should be on Psalm 133. I think this Psalm is a message of what the Lord wants to do through prophetic art in meetings:

> *"How good and pleasant it is for brothers to live together in unity! It is like precious oil poured on the head, coming down on the beard, running down on Aaron's beard, down upon the collar of his robes. It is as if the dew of Hermon were falling on Mount Zion. For there the Lord bestows his blessing."*

From this verse, I knew I should paint the high priest. Shortly before the service, I took a nap, and saw a vision of the breastplate of the high priest with the colored gemstones brilliantly shining. The picture widened, and I saw the high priest's face. Then, to my surprise, Jesus' hand reached down from the heavens and touched his forehead. Aaron looked startled and I was also very startled and suddenly awoke. I did a few quick sketches and found some resource pictures to help me with proportions and perspective. I went to church, and painted the high priest, his breastplate, and the hand of Jesus coming down and touching his forehead.

After I painted one of the leading church intercessors came over to me and said she had been praying for the service earlier that afternoon. She prayed for Jesus to come in the meeting, to touch our foreheads and anoint us as His priests. God had been guiding us both on how to intercede and release His will for that gathering. She was amazed that my painting was the same as her prayer.

I believe the artists (and intercessors) can get the picture of what God wants to release, and show or diagram it for the people. The purpose of this type of picture is to draw everyone into unity of that vision in a specific meeting.

"How good and pleasant it is for brothers to live together in unity." These are occasions when artists should have opportunity to explain what God is showing them. Prophetic art can bring the meeting into unity, a focus of vision that will release the Lord's will. Often, though, people do not understand what the artist is painting, and do not connect with it. Once we are drawn into unity, it releases the anointing. "It is like precious oil poured on the head, coming down on the beard, running down on Aaron's beard, down upon the collar of his robes." There is great power in unity.

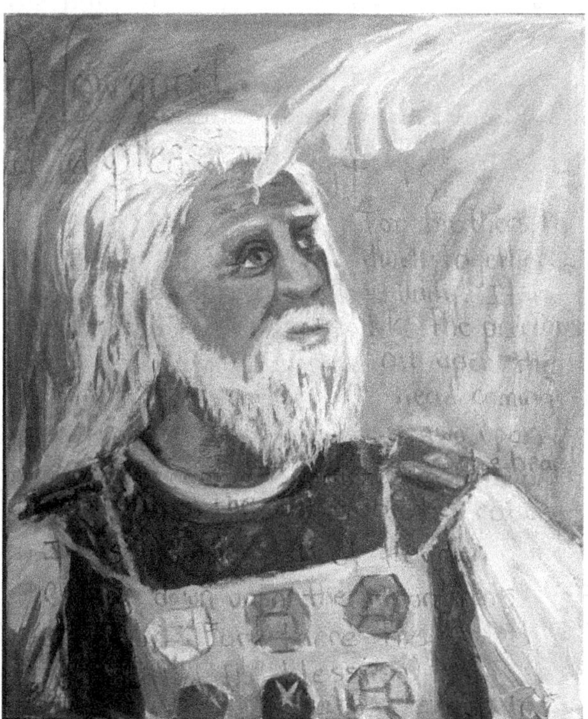

In the early church, they were of one accord. They were in complete unity in worship and prayer. This ushered in the presence and power of the Holy Spirit. I believe that unified vision is one of the keys of the kingdom. If the church is unified in a prophetic focus, God can tell them what they are to hunger for, what should be the focus, and their hearts can unify and ask God to release it. There can be a prophetic theme that the Lord wants to draw people to understand in worship. A painting or worship theme can bring unity and focus to the people so that in their unity they get synergy. This unity increases the strength of the worship, and they will see the intent God had for the meeting being poured out. I have been to revival meetings where the hearts of the people who came were so hungry for God, that it was easy to get into unity together. Everyone's vision was the same and they all pounded on heaven to release the glory. We were then shaken by God's powerful presence poured out on us.

Imagine if everyone realized that God wanted to personally touch him or her as individuals and anoint them as priests that evening when I painted Aaron. What if they opened up their hearts to God, and received that anointing. Sometimes, God wants to use art to focus the audience to receive His gifts.

The colored gemstones on Aaron's breastplate also reminded me of a colorful palate of paint. I believe that visual artists can be a type of high priest. The high priest would petition the Lord with the Urim and Thummim. We don't know what they looked like, but they may have been objects like dice that would indicate "innocent" or "guilty" or a "yes" or "no" answer to questions. They were connected with the breastplate, maybe stored within it. They were referred to as light and perfections, or revelation and truth. Talmudic rabbis and Josephus believed that light shone through the stones of the breastplate, and revealed an answer from God. I believe that we can reveal a prophetic word from God, and give His revelation through the colorful, full spectrum of the creative arts.

#11 INSPIRED BY A DREAM, VISION OR TRANCE

Nichole was asked to paint in church. The night before, she had a dream of pink and brown circles on three canvases. She didn't understand the meaning, but painted it. Two separate individuals came after the service and told her that it represented blood magnified, as if under a microscope. It was a symbol of Jesus' atoning blood, "magnified."

Sometimes "we know in part and prophesy in part" (I Cor. 13:9). Nichole didn't know the meaning of the dream, but others did. It is similar to when someone prophesies in church and another has the interpretation. Sometimes the artist is waiting for someone else to contribute the spiritual explanation.

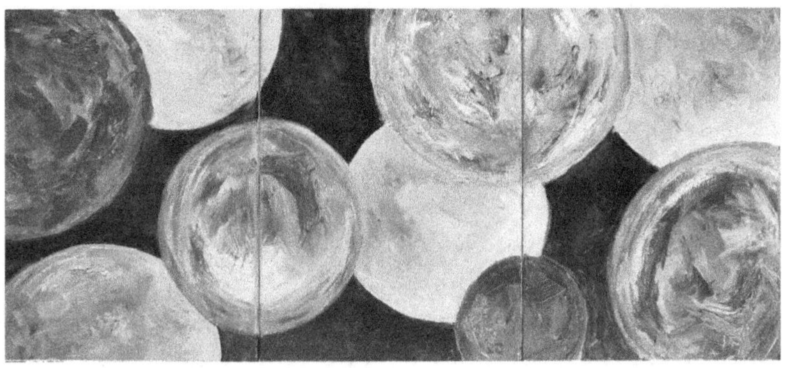

"Blood Magnified" by Nichole A. Ryder

Creative people over the centuries have received songs, inventions, medical treatment, book ideas, direction for their lives and answers to difficult creative problems through their dreams. God speaks to us in our dreams, and He can release creative wisdom and messages to us through them. In Chapter 7, will cover more about the many ways we hear from our loving God.

William Blake was an artist who had open visions of people standing right before him, and he painted them. As we meditate on the Lord, we can receive still pictures, or moving visions. Not all visions are supposed to be painted or to be shared with everyone. Some of our visions or dreams are personal messages for our family or ourselves. We need to use discernment and hear the instruction of the Lord on which ones to paint.

#12 A MEMORIAL STONE

Prophetic art can be a memorial to the Lord. A memorial stone can be a visual representation to others of what God has done. Jacob rested on a journey and fell into a deep sleep. His head was resting on a rock as he encountered the Lord:

> *"When Jacob awoke from his sleep, he thought, "Surely the LORD is in this place, and I was not aware of it." He was afraid and said, "How awesome is this place! This is none other than the house of God; this is the gate of heaven." Early the next morning Jacob took the stone he had placed under his head and set it up as a pillar and poured oil on top of it." Gen. 28:16-18.*

Jacob was in a place of a spiritual portal. He realized it, and said, "Surely the LORD is in this place." He called it a gate of heaven. Sometimes we may find a place that is an open heaven. As we see in this verse, we can create a marker, a sculpture or memorial artwork to commemorate what the Lord has done there. It may also take us back into the encounter with the Lord that was in that place. The art or song may be a portal or a gate of heaven. We can use prophetic art to honor the Lord's encounters, and keep the flow of heaven open in that place or in the memory of that spiritual experience.

When the Israelites crossed the Jordan and in other similar events, they were told to build memorial stones, or altars. The purpose was to honor what God had done and proclaim that He is the Deliverer. It became a place of worship and remembrance. When we look at what He has completed, it reminds us He can do it again. Art can be a visual reminder of crossing over from one event in our lives, or our ministry, to another. Every time we look at it, we celebrate our incredible God. In a place of amazing miracles, we look at the art thinking and meditating on the fact that that God can repeat His goodness and our heart cries, "God, do it again!" I recently watched a video of the story of a boy raised from the dead after 24 hours. The video as prophetic art, leads us into worship of the Lord in what He has done. It also makes us cry out, "more Lord," as it builds our faith to see God bring resurrection to other people whose lives were cut off by the enemy. Our prophetic memorial art can do the same.

The Father instructed His people to set up memorials, and to keep the feasts as memorials. It is part of His system to keep our minds on the things He has done out of His love for His people. Through the memorials we remember Him and His power. I love art based on the festivals and I am convinced that the Lord loves it also. Any art that constantly reminds people of His love, His deliverance, miracles, His guidance, or salvation is a memorial to Him. It testifies of Him and glorifies Him. It allows us to ask Him for a repeat performance in our lives.

#13 TELLS A STORY FROM THE LORD

Some prophetic artwork may be a message in story form from the Lord. It can be a progression of revelation. It could be executed in a series by an artist, or by a group of artists, each doing one piece. It could be a book that is illustrated with prophetic pictures. The new Christian movies that are being created are a great example of this prophetic art. We recently watched "October Baby," a film that touches on the issues of abortion and adoption. It is very pro-life, and will bring healing to many who have gone through these experiences. God can release whole stories through prophetic revelation.

Another example of a prophetic story from the Lord is the book series, "The Final Quest." I was deeply changed by these books written by Rick Joyner. They were written based on Rick's encounters with the Lord and are somewhat similar to "Pilgrim's Progress" by John Bunyan. They are a prophetic allegory for the church of today. Prophetic artists and writers need to be faithful and follow through to write and illustrate these amazing stories from the Lord. They touch people's lives with the messages given from the heart of the Father.

Becca Eisenburg, from the School of Prophetic Arts in Kirkland Washington, has prophetically written and developed a six-piece monologue drama for women in the trafficking trade. The Lord downloaded prophetic details of individual's stories, how they got into trafficking and how the Lord will rescue them and bring their restoration. The actors perform the drama and believe they are prophesying even as they practice. The actions become intercession and prophecy for the change in the lives of these women. The Lord prophetically directed Becca as she let Him guide her in writing the script. More writers should be inspired and directed by the Lord and He will use them in incredible ways. The School of Prophetic Arts has a class on Prophetic Writing, as well as other classes.

#14 INSPIRED FROM SCRIPTURE

Some prophetic art is to reflect God's Word and to honor Him as The Living Word. Art throughout history has been used to illustrate and show people the stories of the Bible. In history, there were many people who were illiterate, and art was created to teach the Bible stories to them. Today, we see very complex pieces of art that expound upon certain verses, taking us deeper into their mysteries using visual form. Calligraphers design the very words of God with beauty that is anointed with praise. The Word is a delight to us:

> *"I meditate on your precepts and consider your ways. Open my eyes that I may see wonderful things in your law… for I delight in your commands because I love them." Ps. 119:15,18, 47.*

Anointed artists visually display the Word, bringing delight to us, and to the Father. You may meditate on a verse or Biblical theme, and create something from the revelation you receive from it, either abstract or literal. Kirk Bennett has a book, Revelation through Meditation, that teaches us to meditate on a verse for extended periods of time. It is amazing how much revelation we can receive from meditation. The deeper we dig, the more God reveals.

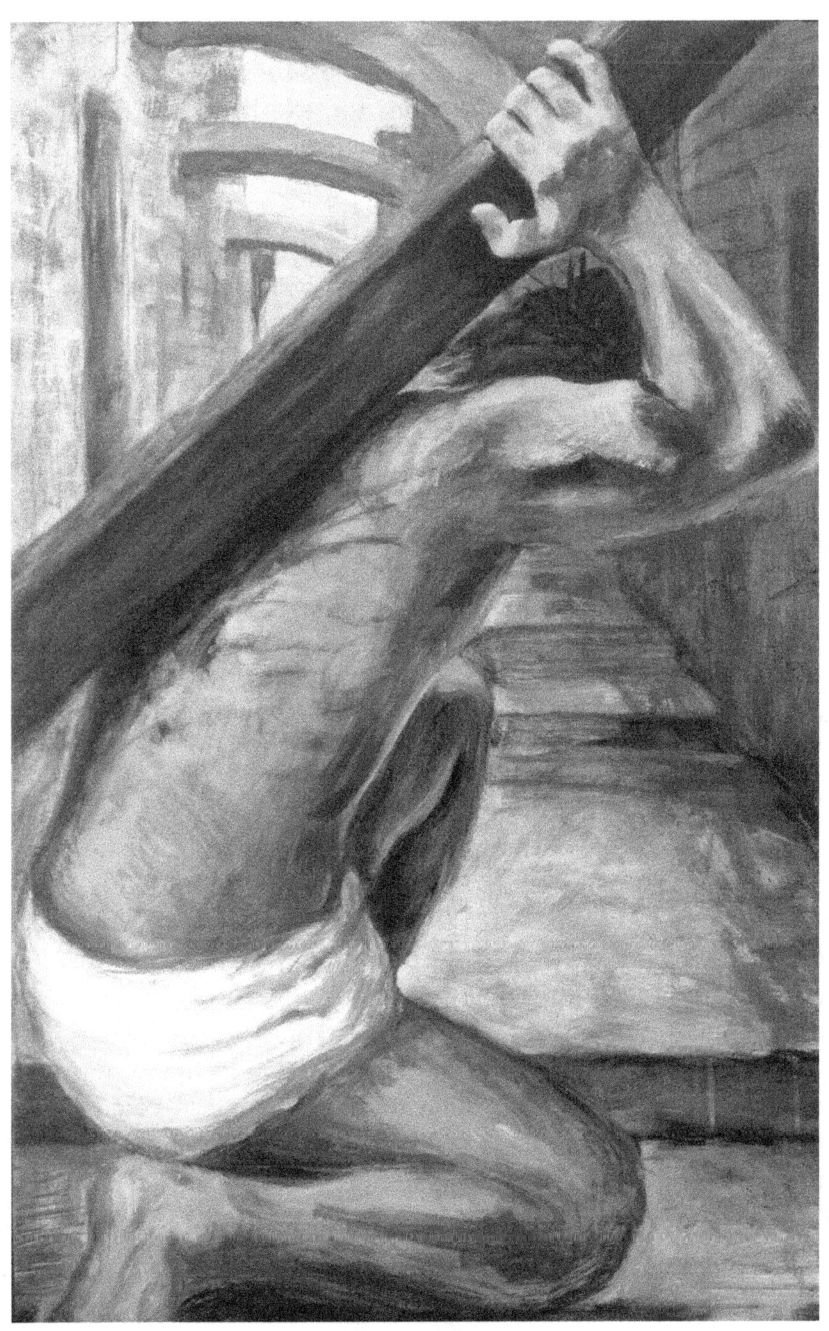

"Take Up Your Cross" By Laurie A. Stasi

This scripture, prophetic revelation can inspire a painting, calligraphy, song, poem or book. Besides focusing on a single passage, you can focus on a theme, for example, the blood of Jesus. Many songs have been written on this theme. Other examples would be; grace, forgiveness, Jesus as the light of the world, or unity in the body. Study some verses on particular theme and meditate on them, asking the Lord for a visual representation. Then let the Lord take you on a journey of creativity releasing the revelation!

#15 COLLABORATIVE ART

Several people can work on the same piece or project together. We are the body in unity through the Spirit. Musicians work together in this way and can flow in the spirit together. Visual artists do not normally think of unity in our creativity. It stretches us when we are challenged to work together. God can bring people together to do amazing performances and projects together. I have listed more in a section further in this book in chapter 12, in the art assignments.

You could take it a step further and get radical and very multi-media. Think of what we can learn from the Blue Man Group. Incorporate live collaborative art and worship spontaneously in sweeping motion! Imagine drums, multiple easels, paint flying, lights pulsing, and artists in movement. They could be switching paintings as the beat increases with rhythm and energy. The Spirit and power vibrates through their expression, paint on paint, image on image, and revelation on revelation. I think this would be fun to do in an open outdoor field event where it could get messy. If someone does it, please invite me.

#16 CONCEPTUAL ART

God speaks in concepts and parables and these should be included in prophetic art. In the Bible a pile of rocks became a monument to what the Lord has done. The concept behind the pile made it a tribute to the Lord. Rocks themselves mean nothing. In modern conceptual art, it is the concept or meaning that is important in the art or object. I visited a modern art museum and saw a chair that was placed upside down on the floor. Close by was an artist statement, describing what the chair placement represented. The artist's ideas were the important artistic contribution; the chair was a prop to represent the idea. Encyclopedia Britannica explains conceptual art this way:

> "Conceptual art, also called post-object art or art-as-idea, artwork whose medium is an idea (or a concept), usually manipulated by the tools of language and sometimes documented by photography. Its concerns are idea-based rather than formal." (Britannica)

And Sol LeWitt, famous conceptual artists once said,

> "In conceptual art the idea or concept is the most important aspect of the work. . .The idea becomes a machine that makes the art." (Sol LeWitt)

Our God is very symbolic in His language to us. Dreams are presented in symbolic ways to make us ponder engage us to get us thinking. Conceptual art puts a demand on the viewer to think. Why is that chair upside down? What is the artist trying to say? I would love to see galleries and museums filled with conceptual art that has hidden messages from God. Our Father loves word puns; it actually makes Him laugh! He enjoys making us contemplate. Jesus reminded the disciples that the people were, "ever seeing but never perceiving." He wanted to challenge the disciples to think about and ponder the parables. Conceptual art is under-used in the church; most people don't even know what it is. What a great opportunity to make them think about the things of God.

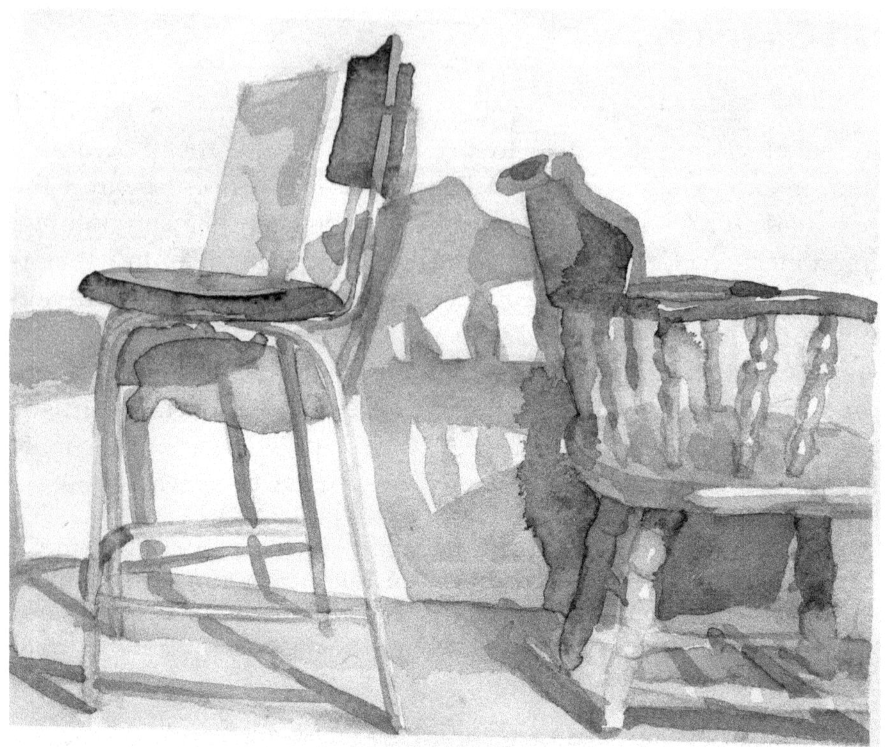

"Chairs" by Amanda A. Flowers

#17 PERFORMANCE ART

Prophetic performance art can be done with painting, sculpting live, or a physical performance or drama. It can be a prophetic act that is carried out by doing Spirit-led actions. It may be a message for the corporate church. Ezekiel and other prophets did prophetic actions that were a message for the Israelites. Here we see some actions, which Ezekiel was required to do in front of the people:

> *"Now, son of man, take a block of clay, put it in front of you and draw the city of Jerusalem on it. Then lay siege to it: Erect siege*

works against it, build a ramp up to it, set up camps against it and put battering rams around it. Then take an iron pan, place it as an iron wall between you and the city and turn your face toward it. It will be under siege, and you shall besiege it. This will be a sign to the people of Israel.

"Then lie on your left side and put the sin of the people of Israel upon yourself. You are to bear their sin for the number of days you lie on your side. I have assigned you the same number of days as the years of their sin. So for 390 days you will bear the sin of the people of Israel." Ezekiel 4:1-5 NIV.

Prophetic performance art is when we act out directions from the Lord. He may tell you to do this in the form of a skit or as Ezekiel was told, to build a sculpture and act out the instructions with it. Ezekiel drew the city of Jerusalem on a tablet, just as we would draw a diagram. The Lord uses diagrams and other visual media as prophetic action and demonstration for the people.

The art world has used performance art for decades, but I have yet to see this used in a church setting, other than in dramas. In the art culture, there are performances on the streets, in malls, in museums, or theaters, which are artistic dramas of performance art. Britannica gives us a definition to the world's idea of performance art:

> "A time-based art form that typically features a live presentation to an audience or to onlookers (as on a street) and draws on such arts as acting, poetry, music, dance, and painting. It is generally an event rather than an artifact, by nature ephemeral, though it is often recorded on video and by means of still photography." (Britannica.com)

Performance art is in direct communication with the audience. One secular example of performance art is by French artist Orlan. She went into museums and lay on the ground and measured off lengths of herself on the floor. She said that it was like an animal marking its territory. Maybe in the spiritual world she was laying claim to the art museums in the evil realm.

Some of the world's performance art uses music or spoken word. One Buddhist artist, Stefan Laug, went into the woods and installed strings of lights on the ground in beautiful spiral forms. He spoke out defilements of the Buddhist religion, and then performed the Buddhist, "global prayer" in this performance space. Christians can create a similar worship space and speak what God is prophesying over the land. We have authority in the spiritual realm and can take back what the enemy is stealing!

Many of the world's performance art has become highly offensive. Much of it includes nudity or sexual perversion. One artist wanted to videotape people dying and was trying to recruit individuals to volunteer. Christians should be led to do performance art for the Lord's glory and purposes, and tear down those demonic strongholds of evil art.

At an outreach for the homeless in Jacksonville, I did a painting during worship. I wrote words on a canvas, "adulterer, addict, rejected, prostitute, hopeless, depressed," and other words that our audience would relate to in their lives. Then I painted over it, covering up the past, and I created a picture of Jesus holding a lamb. I wrote, "You are loved." Before I was even finished with the painting, a homeless man came up to me and asked if he could have the painting. Many artists are now doing this type of art as performance. It can be very effective in community outreaches.

Some performance art may be temporary and created for the moment, with no lasting product. Buddhist monks create a type of art called a sand mandala. They use colored sands and make ornately designed patterns that illustrate the principles of their religion. The monks work on them for several weeks. When they finish, they ceremonially remove it in sections and then place the sand in a nearby river. They believe the temporary nature of this art expresses doctrinal belief in the transitory nature of material life. The art is quite beautiful, and draws a lot of attention. They were requested to come and do a sand mandala in a college here in Jacksonville. It bothers me that the Buddhist religion is easily accepted into our schools through their mandala art. The monks release their beliefs into our atmosphere and students become accepting of their false religion. Christians should be invited do art in local colleges releasing the prophetic and the power of God through revelation to people the Lord loves. We need to be creative and proactive as Christian artists.

Performance art has a meaning, or concept, connected with action. God wants more creative Christian people willing to do this type of art. It could even be short activities on busy street corners. Some actions cause people to stop and think. One secular example was a woman who stood and cut her long hair off on a public city sidewalk in a business area. Then she proceeded to shave her head bald. People stopped, watched, and wondered what she was up to. Her assignment was to draw a crowd.

I think God could have Christians do actions that would bring conviction, or a thought process that would lead the crowd to a revelation from the Lord. This form of art is very Biblical. Ezekiel's prophetic actions as performance art probably drew quite a crowd. He was asked to shave his head and divide his hair on scales. Then he was told to burn a third of his hair and scatter the rest to the wind. You can read more about it in Ezekiel 5. The Lord used his actions to demonstrate a prophetic message. God can use artists who are surrendered to His purposes to create this type of dramatic art.

#18 ART THAT CALLS FOR A RESPONSE

There may be social issues that can be addressed in a prophetic painting or art project. It may bring conviction in the viewers. This type of prophetic art stirs the hearts of the participants. It may be a call to action. It may be about social issues like abortion, or the father's heart calling us to repentance. The process is to give information that incites a response. In the secular world, we see art used as propaganda. During the World Wars they had posters, and news updates designed to encourage patriotism and positive attitudes toward the military and the war.

Art was used to influence their hearts toward a purpose. It stirred them to respond. This type of prophetic art can do the same. It may be a video to help starving children in Africa. It can unify and rally people towards God's objectives and His heart. Revelation leads to application.

#19 INTERCESSION

There is a story that came out of Bethel Church, in Redding, CA. During a meeting they had a prophetic artist paint. The following night, someone got the news that a tidal wave was heading toward Figi. Everyone immediately began praying. They felt they should pray that a wall would be put in the way of the tidal wave. It was then that someone went in the back and pulled out the painting from the night before. It was a painting of a tidal wave with a wall in front of it, and an island on the other side! They prayed with increased faith after seeing this image, and soon got word that the tidal wave had disappeared!

In this case, the art increased faith in God's plan to disperse the tidal wave. Any time there is a word from the Lord, it establishes vision and focus. It builds faith in the participants. It connects us to the will of heaven, and our intercession releases the kingdom. The painting itself may help manifest the vision from the spiritual realm into the natural realm, with prayer and faith.

Elaine Zink, a friend of mine from church, had a vision of two French Huguenots. She saw and felt what they were feeling as they walked through a marsh. Suddenly, they were killed. She felt the Lord tell her to paint it. We live in Jacksonville, Florida where the Huguenots landed and built a fort in 1562, before any other group came to settle in America. They fled religious persecution in Europe and were slaughtered in Jacksonville by the Catholic Spanish. Our church later had a conference with a group of French Huguenots for reconciliation with Spanish Catholics.

Her painting was part of the message of the Lord and guided intercession for this meeting.

A number of years after this conference I moved to Jacksonville and the Lord also gave me a dream of the Huguenots. He guided my husband and I to go to a place for intercession regarding the bloodshed there. At that place, my husband and I both had open visions of the martyrs looking on that place, Fort Caroline. It reminded me of the verse,

> *"They called out in a loud voice, "How long, Sovereign Lord, holy and true, until you judge the inhabitants of the earth and avenge our blood?" Rev. 6:10.*

That morning, the pastor randomly brought up the Huguenots in his sermon. At the night service I painted the vision I had for our church. I also included an image of the Huguenot cross. Our lead worship leader came to the meeting wearing the same cross. The Lord wants to use prophetic art for intercession and unified focus regarding things that lay on His heart and He uses many ways to show us and confirm His vision.

Painting, calligraphy, music, dance or poetry can be released as a prayer. For example, a painting can be done in the Spirit where the very actions of applying the paint become a prayer. It can also serve to draw others to focus on that prophetic message of prayer and call their Spirit deeper into intercession for it. Once, when I was in the prayer room in Jacksonville, I saw a vision of a high cliff with houses on it. The ground was shaking and the houses were going to fall. I sketched it in my journal and I prayed for God's mercy in this situation. The next week in Christ Church, in New Zealand, there was an earthquake and I watched the TV coverage. They showed the same cliffs, and the camera zoomed to the earth below, where houses had fallen and lay in a crumpled heap.

Sometimes we get a vision for us or the body of Christ to intercede. We can draw quick little sketches to share the images with other to help guide in prayer. Prophetic art doesn't always have to be neat and polished to do what God sent it to do.

As prophetic artists we come boldly to the throne of grace to connect with the Father's heart for intercession. There may be artists who find prophetic intercession is their main calling. They may sit at Jesus' feet and listen to His heart and "see" His direction for intercession and can sketch it out. There should be this type of intercession artist in the International House of Prayers (IHOPs) and prayer ministries to partner with the other prayer warriors and share what God is revealing.

#20 A LADDER TO ACCESS HEAVEN

We can access the kingdom of heaven through prophetic art. I did a series of ladder paintings I received during worship, as visions, or in dreams. I know they symbolize going up and down the ladder as in Jacob's dream, and receiving revelation from heaven. We have access to the heavenly realm, and our art may be a type of "Bethel."

I have felt the presence of the Lord while painting, and know that there are those who receive visions during meetings who access portholes into spiritual realms. In one meeting, I remember seeing a doorway, and I asked the Lord to take us through. Then the worship and anointing intensified corporately. I saw a stairway and another doorway, and asked to go through again. The worship again, went up a level. This happened many times, until I saw and heard the great cloud of witnesses worshiping the Lord. Many people in that meeting said they heard the angels singing, but I believe they heard the great cloud of witnesses that I had seen in the vision. Maybe there were others who saw something similar to what I had seen in that meeting. We were unified in seeking the Lord, asking to go higher.

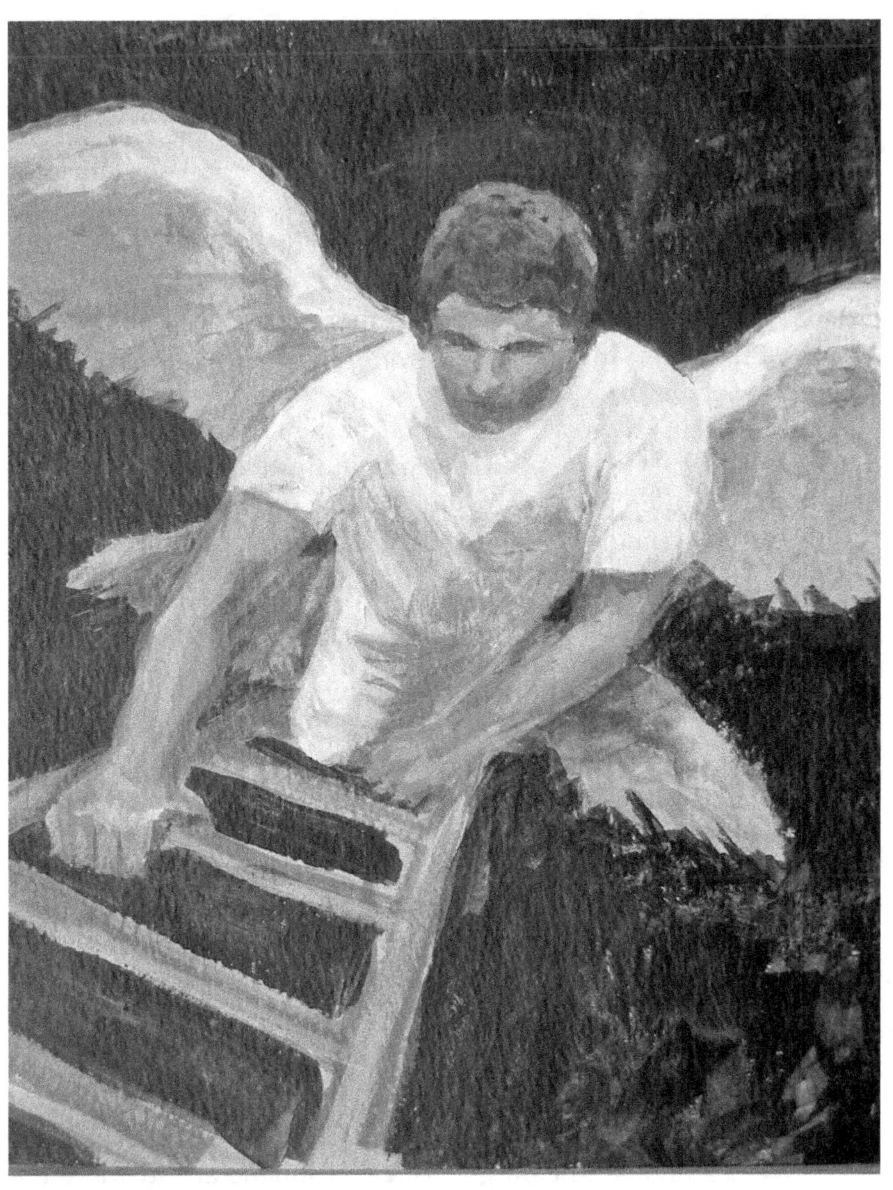

"Angel Ladder" By Laurie A. Stasi

We might be able to display the visions and bring everyone corporately to that same place. We long to get to the throne room, and to stand in the awesome presence of the Lord.

He wants us to come boldly. The art may be a message from the Lord to show us the way.

Art can be a portal or a spiritual place for some viewers. In viewing one of my paintings, a woman had a "spiritual experience" that made her cry when she meditated on the message from God that the painting carried. It was an image of Jesus carrying His cross through the streets of Jerusalem. She had an open vision and felt like she was standing there with the crowd surrounding Jesus, and she could hear and feel the surroundings. She was deeply moved by God's presence viewing the art. Obviously, this is a God-given experience that we cannot make happen, but when we consecrate our art, and ourselves and listen to Him guide us as we paint, we can participate in opening "ladders" or "portholes" in the spiritual realm and heaven.

#21 A STATION IN A PRAYER ROOM OR MEETING

This prophetic art is a visual cue for people to pray for their government, or other specific places or people. Examples would be pictures of Washington D.C. or Jerusalem. It could also be government leaders, or orphans. As we hang this art in a place of prayer it becomes a focus for the intercessors. There could be an entire wall of images that is a collage of images for prayer focus.

#22 HEALING ART

We can release healing through prophetic art, just like the serpent on the pole in the desert. If God told us to make an object to have people look on it and be healed, would we do it? Would our religious spirit kick in, and not submit to the request? The Serpent on the pole was a type of the cross, and symbolic of Jesus hanging as a curse on it. The Israelites didn't know they were prophetically looking at Jesus and accessing His healing power. In

God, there are no time limitations. It was as if they were right there at the cross and looking through a time portal. It says, "When anyone was bitten by a snake and looked at the bronze snake, he lived," Num. 21:9 NIV.

The same God, who forbade the Israelites from making any graven image (and worshiping it), commanded them to make an image. The purpose of the serpent on the pole was to access Jesus. God was not afraid to give this sculpture to help his people. His only stipulation was, do not worship the object. As soon as the Israelites worshipped it, the Lord told them to destroy it (2 Kings 18:4). The same principle applies to any art that is worshiped; it must be destroyed. It has become an idol.

If God chooses to let an object draw people to the picture of Jesus as healer, and be healed based on that revelation, then let it happen. Just as there were no time limitations for the Israelites to access the healing of the cross, we have no time limitations either. We can stand at the foot of the cross accessed through a piece of art and be healed. I hope and pray that God would allow this. The greater question is, would people want to worship the object? The prayer for the artist should always be that this never happen, and if it does, commit to destroying the artwork.

Through art we can access the cross, and all the gifts of God. It is almost like a time machine, and we can go back in time and be there and receive forgiveness, healing, deliverance, cleansing or salvation. Of course, we do not need the art to access these things, but God brings healing through many sources. It may be through your pastor, through taking communion, through reading a scripture, through a person praying in faith, or through art, music, poetry or dance. The same anointing that brings us in contact with the cross can be delivered through different means.

I once saw a vision of a strange cell arrangement and felt like painting it. The next week a friend described her disease and it was specifically what I painted. God can show you specifically someone's ailment to release healing. The art is a point of contact, and to increase faith.

#23 MINISTERS TO THE SPIRIT

The prophetic arts can bypass our human intellect and minister directly to the person's spirit. One Biblical example is found in 1 Samuel 16:14-23:

> *"Now the Spirit of the LORD had departed from Saul, and an evil spirit from the LORD tormented him. Saul's attendants said to him, "See, an evil spirit from God is tormenting you. Let our lord command his servants here to search for someone who can play the lyre. He will play when the evil spirit from God comes on you, and you will feel better."*
>
> *So Saul said to his attendants, "Find someone who plays well and bring him to me."*
>
> *One of the servants answered, "I have seen a son of Jesse of Bethlehem who knows how to play the lyre. He is a brave man and a warrior. He speaks well and is a fine-looking man. And the LORD is with him."*
>
> *Then Saul sent messengers to Jesse and said, "Send me your son David, who is with the sheep." So Jesse took a donkey loaded with bread, a skin of wine and a young goat and sent them with his son David to Saul.*
>
> *David came to Saul and entered his service. Saul liked him very much, and David became one of his armor-bearers. Then Saul sent word to Jesse, saying, "Allow David to remain in my service, for I am pleased with him." Whenever the spirit from God came on Saul, David would take up his lyre and play. Then relief would come to Saul; he would feel better, and the evil spirit would leave him."*

When David played the lyre for King Saul, his music was able to minister directly to Saul's spirit, bringing peace to him as he was tormented by demons. Art in every society touches people on a spiritual and emotional level, even when they don't realize it. We have the ability to bring God's perfect peace and touch a place within other people that moves them in their spirit. It may be a song, a photograph that connects with people's spirit, a painting, or a variety of other mediums that brings a positive emotional response and settles their spirit.

The illustrator, Norman Rockwell was able to connect on another level with people's experience and relationships. He had the ability to present pieces of life that felt familiar to everyone and it touched them emotionally. We can also do this with the Holy Spirit's lead, and create things that people identify with in their spirit.

We are spiritual beings, and heaven is a spiritual place. We, as prophetic artists can tap into heaven's reality and release it through creativity. We have to be in tune with the Spirit and learn to be in a place of rest. When Jacob rested his head on a rock for the night, he was open to the spiritual things of God. He was able to receive a heavenly vision through the angels who were sent by God as they traveled to and from heaven on the ladder.

Through Jacob's rest, he gained spiritual understanding. Through our rest we can minister to others out of what we ourselves have encountered. Our natural man can block the flow of spiritual things, so we have to learn to make our flesh submit, and then we can release the things of the spirit. David ministered to Saul out of his spirit from a place of relationship and peace in God. Jesus told Nicodemus in John 3, "Flesh gives birth to flesh, but spirit gives birth to spirit." As you are able to birth your creativity from your spirit, your artwork will minister to the spirits of others and some people will not even understand what hit them.

#24 PROPHECY

Prophetic art is used to prophecy and to give a message from God. Prophetic art speaks in the now moment, a word for a church, a person, a city, a particular region, or a generation. It is revelation as part of God's dialogue with us because of His great love and our personal relationship with Him.

One of my instructors at a secular school (who was into New Age), told our class, "An artist is a prophet for their generation." She didn't mean it in a Christian or godly way. She was emphasizing that the world's artists are radical, pushing change against the culture. They are willing to go where the rest of civilization is not ready to go. If we look at perversion in art, the artists (also in TV and movies) are pushing the envelope of what is tolerable and forcing society to dwell on, or meditate on the things they do not currently embrace. The arts usher in whole theories and morals that are not acceptable in culture, and slowly make them tolerable. By doing this, they are prophesying them into existence. The devil has this system in place that works to advance his kingdom, bringing the world further into darkness. We have the privilege of bringing God's revelation to people through our creativity. The prophetic word is a sure word from the Lord and will encourage, direct, predict, and sometimes bring reproof. We need to release this in every media.

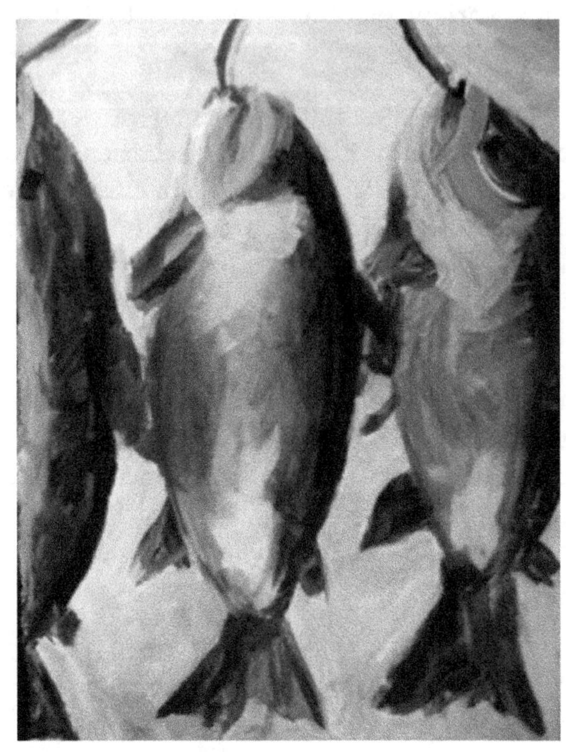

"The Catch" by Nichole A. Ryder

God is now using prophetic artists to paint a prophetic word, and then write a summary of the interpretation and post both on Facebook and on blogs. This is a great ministry using both visual and written media. Our God knows the end from the beginning, and He will use us as we make ourselves available. There are plenty of Christians who are not operating in the prophetic. These prophetic words can encourage them, and show them things He has revealed to us.

As Christians, we can prophesy things into being through our art. There is power in prophesying with our words, but also with our actions and art when directed by God. Elisha told king Jehoash to strike arrows on the ground and shoot them out a window. He struck the arrows to the ground three times. Elisha was angry, "You should have struck five or six times." Because he had only struck three times, he would not completely defeat his enemy. This prophetic action was meant to be established something in the spiritual realm.

God may have us do prophetic actions in our art that will take creative effect in the spiritual realm. We need to clearly listen and obey His voice as His prophets and release it through our creativity and actions. Just as Ezekiel did public actions that were prophetically linked with Israel, so we can do prophetic actions that release the kingdom in our generation.

Sometimes God wants to release prophetic revelation in segments, or in a series. The purpose is to make us ponder the first statement, before moving on to the next. The Lord once showed this to my daughter, Nichole, in a dream. The art was a scroll that gradually was unrolled and over time revealed more. One way this might be accomplished is with a series of paintings, but revealing only one at a time. In the dream, someone took a large stone and placed it near the scroll. This is a prophetic action, much like putting a memorial stone in place. God will show us actions to do, and as we follow His lead we will release His will.

#25 MEDITATION ART

God loves when we dwell on, picture or meditate on Him, His deeds, His creation and His power. David demonstrated this meditation in the Psalms:

> *"I remember the days of old; I meditate on all Your doings; I muse on the work of Your hands." Ps. 143:5.*

David meditated on the days of old, the battles and victories of God, the things the Lord had done in the past. He pondered His mighty deeds. David also remembered the work of the Lord's hands. He spent time enjoying and thinking about God's creation and His creativity. David remembered all the things in His life that the Lord's hand helped produce. He didn't take the Lord for granted. Our art can do these same things and bring glory to the Lord as we meditate on the incredible deeds and creation of the Lord. You can use your art to magnify God, just as David meditated on God's character:

> *"On the glorious splendor of Your majesty and on Your wonderful works, I will meditate." Ps. 145:5.*

Our art, writings and songs can be a point of meditation, a place for people to ponder the awesomeness of our mighty God. David touched the Lord with his love and devotion because he wanted more of the Lord and the great things He had done. The longer he meditated on the Lord, the more the Lord revealed to him of His nature, and His love.

> *"One thing I have asked from the Lord, that I shall seek; that I may dwell in the house of the Lord in all the days of my life, to behold the beauty of the Lord and to meditate in His temple." Ps. 27:4.*

Here, David longed to dwell in the house of the Lord, behold the incredible beauty of God, and to meditate on Him. His son, Solomon, under his father's instruction, built the temple. When it was completed, as people came to bow in worship, they were surrounded with the majestic, magnificence of the temple as

David had envisioned it. Light from the brilliant lamp stand reflected off the golden table of showbread. Even the gold floors shone with radiance. The walls were covered with intricately carved cherubim, palm trees and open flowers. The people would face the ornate fabric of the curtain, interwoven with blue, purple and crimson yarn, with cherubim embroidered onto it. This beauty gave glory to the Lord, and created a wonderful place to meditate and worship. Would you rather meditate in a room like that, than in a sterile environment?

Beauty is a gift from God and it lifts us up. Imagine sitting beside a quiet stream with wild flowers swaying in a soft summer breeze. You actually breathe differently in this place. This is where the Lord leads us to meditate, "He leads me beside quiet waters, He restores my soul." Beauty calms us and helps us connect with Him, the Creator of all beauty.

Art can create a beautiful place to meditate on the Lord, just as the sanctuary of the Lord's temple was. Creating beautiful things can bring His peace. God loves our creativity when it adds to worshipping Him, and meditating on Him and His works.

#26 A WORD OF KNOWLEDGE

I have heard of a man who receives a prophetic picture of a face from the Lord and he paints a portrait of that person, and then brings it to a psychic fair. The person in the portrait walks into the fair and sees his own portrait displayed there (I imagine he is quite shocked). The artist or team then ministers the Lord's love for him. The world is use to seeking psychics and fortunetellers for guidance. They are very open to the prophetic gifts and receive them easier than someone from a traditional religious church. My husband and I have experienced this personally, when teaching on the prophetic in a Bible Study at the shelter. Several people who were from a religious church were offended and sought to lead others away from the Biblical teaching of the prophetic. There are many, however, who are hungry for guidance from God and are open to the prophetic.

We have done art that is created out of a prophetic word from the Lord as a gift to someone. One artist I know does dozens of them for conferences. People sign up, and she ministers a quick painting, or prophetic portrait for each individual. Chapter 13 has prophetic art assignments for more ideas on practicing this.

The Lord showed me a vision for myself and I painted it. Once glance of it is a reminder of His call on my life. I know people who have the gift of singing prophetically over others. What a wonderful way to minister God's love, and bless them with specific words of knowledge and a prophetic message.

#27 ESTABLISH THE VISION

The Lord uses prophetic revelation to establish vision and revelation;

> *"Write down the revelation and make it plain on tablets so that a herald may run with it. For the revelation awaits an appointed time; it speaks of the end and will not prove false. Though it linger, wait for it; it will certainly come and will not delay." Habakkuk 2:2-3*

God instructed Habakkuk to write the revelation down on a tablet so that a herald may run with it. We can draw or paint the revelation, and it gives a message to the people. Here in this verse, we see that it may linger. Paintings can hold a prophetic message that can linger for another time. It may be a painting for another generation. People have a chance to reflect upon the message, and dwell on it. Certain pieces of prophetic art can be placed in ministry buildings to reflect their vision, or prophetic words spoken over ministry. This can be used to keep them focused on the vision. It is a constant point of contact with the heartbeat of God's plan for them and their organization.

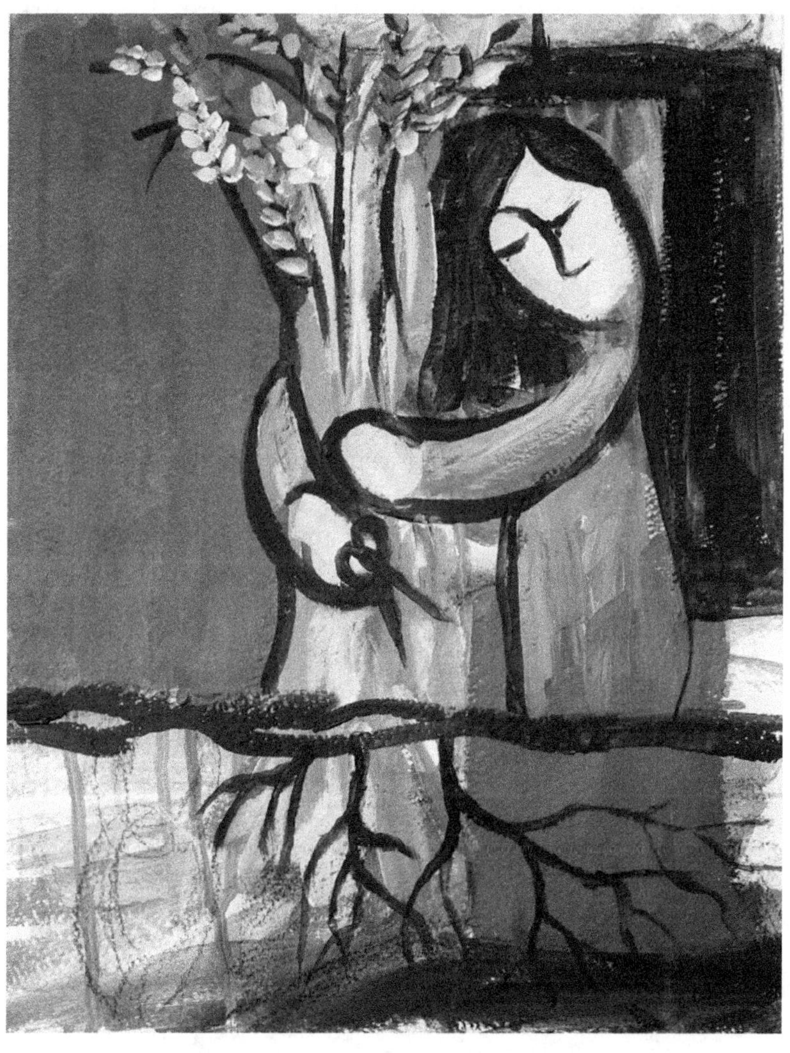

"Harvest" by Laurie A. Stasi This was a prophetic word for myself while leading a Bible Study. God was showing me the Harvest that we get from small groups. We tenderly plant, water and tend our groups, and the joy comes with the harvest.

#28 WARFARE AND BANNER

Another purpose of prophetic art is warfare. This is first done through a rallying and gathering of the troops.

"He will raise a banner [a type of visual art] for the nations and gather the exiles of Israel; he will assemble the scattered people of Judah." Isaiah 11:12.

Some of our artwork can bring people together into a unified vision. This can be done through graphic arts, banners, and paintings. It is a visual reminder or message that brings unity. In Numbers, the banner was used to draw families together in their assigned formation.

Each family had its own standard, or pole, designed with an end cap that represented their family. The specific flags used would represent action that related to movement, mobility, or war. Art can bring together church families and help their identity in Christ. It can direct them in a movement and focus them on the Holy Spirit's lead. The banner is a also weapon during intense warfare:

> *"But for those who fear you, you have raised a banner to be unfurled against the bow. Selah." Ps. 60:4.*

The banner was opened up and used against the enemy. It was a visual sign to the enemy, look out, we are coming to get you. In church, banners can proclaim to the dark forces in the spiritual realm, we are coming to destroy you. Don't underestimate the power of the people who use flags in church. They are waging war in the spiritual realm. Paintings, banners, flags and any other visual media can be a mighty weapon of war.

In Song of Solomon, Jesus himself puts a banner, or visual artwork over us. What it proclaims to the world, and to our hearts is His love. He also declares that his beloved is beautiful, "majestic as troops with banners." Jesus loves the beauty of the banners (prophetic visual art) and the troops who fight in the realm of the spirit using their visual art. They are warriors marching in splendor. The bride of Christ is complete and powerful in His eyes with these gifts. I have been to meetings where groups marched in with flags and banners. Each time it was quite a splendid sight, and was very moving and commanding. These were troops of the Lord's beloved.

Jesus is a banner, a visual sign that draws people to Him. "In that day the Root of Jesse will stand as a banner for the peoples; the nations will rally to Him," Is. 11:10. They will see His beauty, creative pattern, and design, and be moved to join Him. The blueprint of all history flows through His assignment here on earth. The splendor of His sacrifice is more beautiful than any masterpiece ever created. Artwork reflects His life, mission, sacrifice and resurrection. It can draw people to know Jesus, and draw the nations to His side.

In Numbers 2:2 it says, "The sons of Israel shall camp, each by his own standard, with the banners of their fathers' households." The word banner, in Hebrew, "Owth," has many meanings and was also used for the rainbow, circumcision, signs and wonders. From the Hebrew it can mean; sign, signal, a distinguishing mark, banner, remembrance, miraculous sign, omen, warning, token, ensign, standard, miracle, and proof. All of these apply to the visual arts. Art is obviously a 'distinguishing mark,' but it also can be a miracle. It can bring people to remembrance of the things of the Lord, or be a visual warning. And just as the rainbow was a visual sign to remember the miracle of deliverance for Noah, it also symbolized covenant, and how God hates sin enough to destroy and bring judgment. Prophetic art can speak these same principles.

In Psalm 60:4 we see that banners can display truth.:

> *"You have given a banner to those who fear you, that it may be displayed because of the truth. That your beloved may be delivered."*

If prophetic art displays truth, it is a battle cry for that truth to be manifested. In the spiritual realm, the creation of prophetic art releases the truth and then brings deliverance.

People can be set free when they gaze and meditate on the truth. Ultimately, Jesus is The Truth, and they will encounter Him.

God uses the prophetic arts to call to the nations. "He lifts up a banner to the distant nations, He whistles for those at the ends of the earth. Here they come swiftly and speedily!" Is. 5:26 NIV. God uses the banners, to call for judgment. They stimulate the Lord's army to come to bring His justice. The banners were part of His call for activation.

Banners were used in the Bible to gather the banished ones (Is. 11:12), to signal God's people (Is. 11:10), it can terrify your enemies (Is. 31). It can make proclamations to the world (Is. 18), as a warning (Jer. 4), to mark the fall of your enemy (Jer. 50), it proclaims victory (Ps. 20:5), and was used to ambush the enemies (Jer. 51). As we paint and create art, in the spiritual realm we can accomplish these war maneuvers. There is great power with prophetic art in the spiritual realm waging war against our enemy.

Flags or banners were during battle as a means of communication. They would raise certain flags to signal advance, retreat, or interruption of the battle. The specific positions or instructions were told to the captains immediately before the battle, so that the enemy would not be able to know the signals and act accordingly, much like football players running their plays. God gives prophetic artists current information so that we keep our enemy from knowing the spiritual action plan ahead of time. We may be giving battle instructions through the art, for the troops to follow. Banners also marked territory gained during battle. We are taking territory and declaring it belongs to the Lord through our art.

In the spiritual realm, we are warring, and the prophetic throws the demons off track because they do not know what God is up to. Prophetic worship and art confuses the enemy and frustrates his efforts.

In the battle for this generation, the artwork and banners are part of the assignment and are used to accomplish our prophetic assignment:

> *"Pass through, pass through the gates! Prepare the way for the people. Build up, build up the highway! Remove the stones. Raise a banner for the nations." Is. 62:10.*

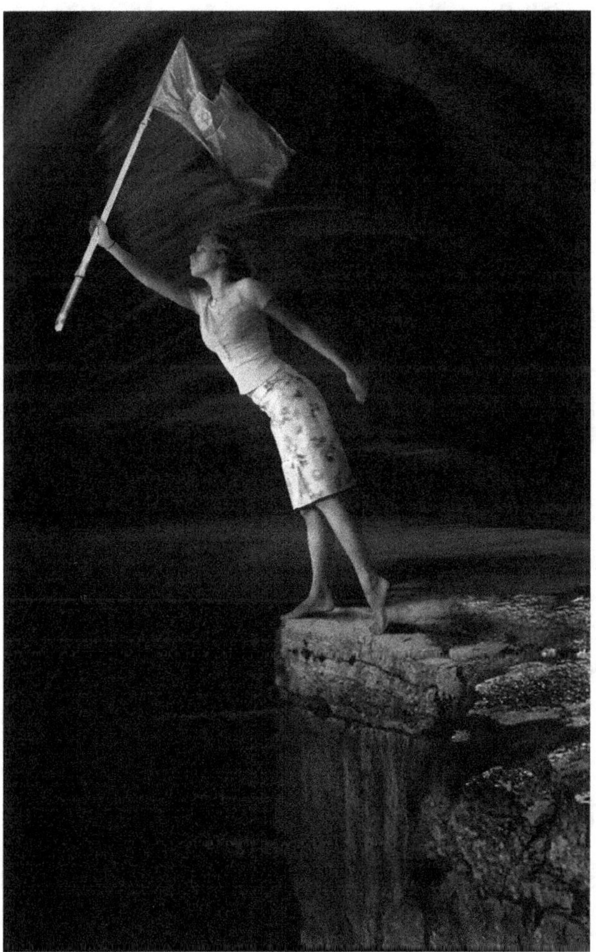

"Flag" By Amanda A. Flowers

As we pass through the gates, which are opportunities to advance the kingdom, one generation has to prepare the way. They need to build up the highway and remove the stones. They are the ones who labor to clear the road for all to follow. Some need to raise the banner, the prophetic arts with current instructions from the Lord. It will draw those following onward in the mission and vision. Without vision, people perish. With vision, we know our assignment and are able to accomplish it. Churches and Christian organizations may want to make up banners, logos or signs with their vision or mission statement to keep it before the eyes of the people. It will help keep focus and passion for the mission.

Another fascinating story of warfare using prophetic art, is in Zechariah 1. Zechariah saw four craftsmen (artists). He asked God what they were for, and the Lord told him they have come to terrify those who scattered Judah,

"But the craftsmen have come to terrify them and throw down these horns of the nations who lifted up their horns against the land of Judah to scatter its people."

It is interesting that craftsmen were used to come against the forces of their enemies, and to "throw down," their power. What power does an artist, or craftsmen have over an enemy? I believe that we create things that wage war in the spiritual realm. I believe this verse indicates that we can come against nations when we war with prophetic art. It may even be propaganda and information that is spread and comes powerfully against the enemies of Israel. We have learned in our generation how powerful propaganda is. Advertising has the ability to sell millions of products. Newspapers and well-written articles can change the mindset of nations. One billboard can stop someone from having an abortion and save countless lives. We can use art to war against demonic forces and change our society.

As we prophetically get information from the Lord, and paint it, it has power in the spiritual realm. Ezekiel, at the Valley of dry bones was told to speak and prophesy. Art can be a proclamation or a prophecy and has power from the Holy Spirit. It is activating the will of God. Prophetic art stirs the people to release the kingdom of God and is a tremendous weapon of battle as we reclaim lost territory for the Lord.

#29 INSTALLATION ART

God cares about the placement of objects as was demonstrated when He gave very detailed instructions for the tabernacle furniture positions. The temple is mentioned 625 times in the Bible, the tabernacle 125. "Make this tabernacle and all its furnishings exactly like the pattern I will show you." Ex. 25:9. God was very specific. Listen to some of the detail that seems very unimportant to be listed in the Bible;

> *"Make twenty frames for the south side of the tabernacle and make forty silver bases to go under them—two bases for each frame, one under each projection. For the other side, the north side of the tabernacle, make twenty frames and forty silver bases—two under each frame. Make six frames for the far end, that is, the west end of the tabernacle, and make two frames for the corners at the far end. At these two corners they must be double from the bottom all the way to the top and fitted into a single ring; both shall be like that. So there will be eight frames and sixteen silver bases—two under each frame." Ex. 26:18-25.*

Every detail of placement matters in God's eyes. He loves detail, form, structure, and order. Many things have symbolism in their placement. The court of the tabernacle represents corporate worship, and the Holy Place represents personal intimacy, but we can go even deeper in the Holy of Holies. There are many books you can find that teach on the details of the symbolism of the temple. You may be called to research this further and incorporate it into your artwork.

The devil uses Feng Shui, an Eastern form of placement of objects in a room to create "balance" or harmony. It is an ancient Chinese system of aesthetics believed to use the laws of both Heaven (astronomy) and Earth (geography) to help one improve life by receiving positive qi. We need to take back all the art forms the devil has stolen. God wants to use interior design and object placement and order to give glory to Him and bring His purposes.

There are gifted people at my church who occasionally set up a temporary prayer room with instructions from the Lord about the look of the room, the lighting, objects, pillows, and where to place them in the room. The Lord spent a lot of time in the Bible describing the temple, the placement of the implements, the colors, fabric, architecture, and symbolic images. This is very near and dear to His heart. Architects, artists, sculptors and designers can have anointing for prophetic installation art.

The art world uses installation art as a similar form of creativity. Secular artists, Christo and Jeanne-Claude hung orange fabric on poles in Central Park in an exhibit called "The Gates" (Jeanne-Claude). It was stunning. They hung 7,503 fabric gates that blew with the New York breeze and this spectacular display drew many tourists. Christian artists should be doing more of this dramatic type of art and opening spiritual gates for people to enter with thanksgiving into the Father's realm.

One church in Baltimore did another type of installation art. They asked people to write out prayers on little pieces of colorful papers. They sculpted the papers into origami birds and hung them from a ceiling in an upward stream of exquisiteness and color. It represented our prayers rising up to the Father. It was a beautiful piece of symbolic art.

#30 COOPERATION WITH A PASTOR'S MESSAGE

A pastor may get revelation and need the artisans to execute it. Moses demonstrated this:

> *"They serve at a sanctuary that is a copy and shadow of what is in heaven. This is why Moses was warned when he was about to build the tabernacle: "See to it that you make everything according to the pattern shown you on the mountain." Heb. 8.*

Moses saw the pattern for the tabernacle and then Bezelel, Oholiab, and the other craftsmen executed it under the anointing of the Holy Spirit. Pastors may get revelation from heaven with ideas for a sermon series, and their artists can use PowerPoint, paintings, banners or other graphics to illustrate the sermon.

There may be a writer who could do a skit or prophetic action based on the topic. There could be a team of artists who work together to make the sermons come visually alive.

Many pastors are accustomed to presenting sermons in purely auditory format. Studies show that the learning style of people has changed over the last few decades. Some say that 65% are visual learners and only 30% auditory (the rest are kinesthetic). This means that when the pastor presents and uses PowerPoint, visual aids or dramas to support his ideas, people will remember God's messages much longer.

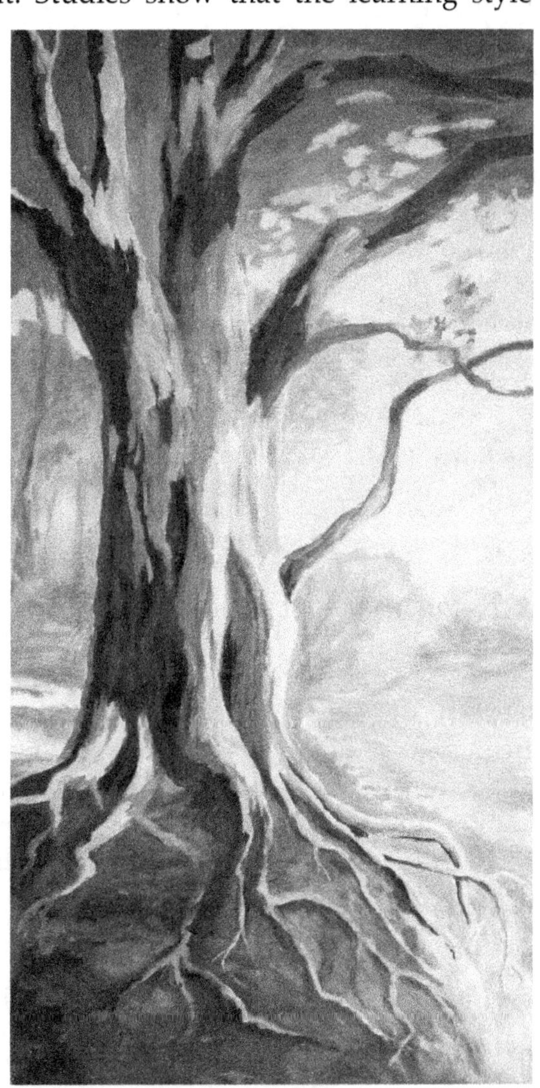

"Psalm 1" By Laurie A. Stasi

Years ago, I was on the drama team and we did six-minute skits that coordinated with the pastor's message. There were people who could remember our skits months (or years) later. The message was visually presented through a skit, and it stuck. Visual memory is extremely strong. Many mission teams use dramas or short skits to present the gospel, and people are deeply moved and come to know Jesus through the message.

What the modern art world calls "performance art" is just one step further away from a drama. Churches in the future may have prophetic actions performed much the same way as Ezekiel or other Old Testament prophets did prophetic events before the people.

A prophetic action does more than give a visual lesson; it activates something in the spiritual realm. God initiates it to release a message and a purpose, much like the prophets in the Bible who were told to proclaim or prophecy. Pastors who are open may be given instructions like Moses was, to have artists create supporting artwork for the church that will have a lasting prophetic impact.

Moses' efforts created the tabernacle, a place of habitation of the Lord. Every church should seek to be a place of habitation.

#31 COOPERATION WITH WORSHIP MUSIC LYRICS

Art or videography can be created to go along with particular worship songs. As God directs artists with visual language to present the song, it will draw people into the greater revelation and deeper worship of our Lord. There needs to be more unity in the arts, musicians and artists working together, along with other arts areas.

In our generation music videos are the standard for the music industry. People are accustomed to the use of visual images linked together with music. Churches who keep creativity flowing will draw more people compared to churches who stay away from creativity altogether. It is another form of anointed worship. Prophetic artists need to be able to be "in the Spirit," and hear what the Lord is speaking through music. Several year ago, I was in line with my family waiting to get into a revival in Lakeland, Florida. We were outside the Ignited Church with several hundred spiritually hungry Christians. A group of young people came from Morningstar School of Ministry, and some formed a drum circle outside. The rhythm of their worship flowed powerfully. I felt the Spirit was speaking through the beats and I heard the word "breakthrough." I asked Nichole, my daughter, to hear what the Spirit was saying through the drums. She paused and listened to the powerful rhythms and without hesitation said, "breakthrough." This group of people returned to Morningstar after the weekend, and revival broke out in their classes. It expanded and lasted for months.

I believe that we can hear in the Spirit and interpret what God is saying through music, and also represent it in art. Artists need to be trained in the prophetic, and consecrated to the Lord so they can start exercising prophetic skills and visually showing the heartbeat of the Father.

Another form of prophetic art done with music and is frequently used on the mission field. One example is artist David Garibaldi; you can watch the video on YouTube (Garibaldi). In the video he worked on a large canvas with music. For a while, the image appeared senseless. Then, with great drama, the face of Jesus appeared on the canvas. This type of performance art combined with music is very emotional and stirs people with the revelation of Jesus.

A new form of art is the creation of images using sand as a performance with music. Castillo is a leading Sand Story artist (Castillo). He forms pictures in sand on a clear Plexiglas with a camera below it. The audience watches as images grow and evolve into many scenes. He has many different performances videos; one is of the story of the cross, another about Jesus birth. It is powerfully executed with spirit-filled music. It is a unique art form that more people are venturing into. There are many opportunities to enhance music and lyrics with prophetic visual images.

#32 RESTORE THE TEMPLE/TABERNACLE

Another purpose of prophetic art is to symbolically restore the tabernacle. It was the first spirit-led art project, a spectacular piece of workmanship for God's glory. It was a prophetic statement of Jesus the Messiah as our sacrificial lamb, as our bread, the one who washes us (the bronze laver), the light of the world (the candlesticks) and the ark of His presence in us. The temple demonstrated our sin through the requirements of the law.

Deep symbolism and significance was imbedded in the tabernacle, temple, and in their utensils and fabrics. There are hidden treasures that speak to us even thousands of years after it was created. It was the earthly representation of the spectacular heavenly tabernacle. Our Father wanted us to have a "picture" of what He sees, and His plan of salvation. It is the script that runs through all time.

We should capture the facets of Jesus in our art, and present the message of salvation, the heavenly temple, and kingdom and represent it here on earth. Let's look at this further:

> *"In that day I will restore David's fallen tent. I will repair its broken places, restore its ruins, and build it as it used to be," Amos 9:11.*

God loved the temple that David built for worship and He wants it restored. Prophetic art is one piece of the puzzle that symbolically restores the Tabernacle and establishes the Kingdom. Other parts are the restoration of poems, writings, the prayer movement and worship music. The first tabernacle was set up as an art project commissioned by the Lord. David made plans to build the temple and the Lord spoke to him,

> *"He shall build a house for My name, and I will establish the throne of his kingdom forever," II Samuel 7:13.*

God told David that his son Solomon would build a house "for My name," for the Glory of God. In His name we find His attributes and His character. Our artwork and creativity can display His name, His glory and character. The promise continues in the verse, "I will establish the throne of his kingdom forever."

When Solomon made an earthly representation of the heavenly tabernacle, it was followed up with the promise that God will establish the throne of his kingdom. We know that Jesus came to usher in the kingdom and He constantly preached that the kingdom was at hand. He told the disciples to preach the kingdom. He instructed them to pray, "Thy kingdom come, Thy will be done on earth as it is in heaven." He wanted us to pray and usher the kingdom to earth.

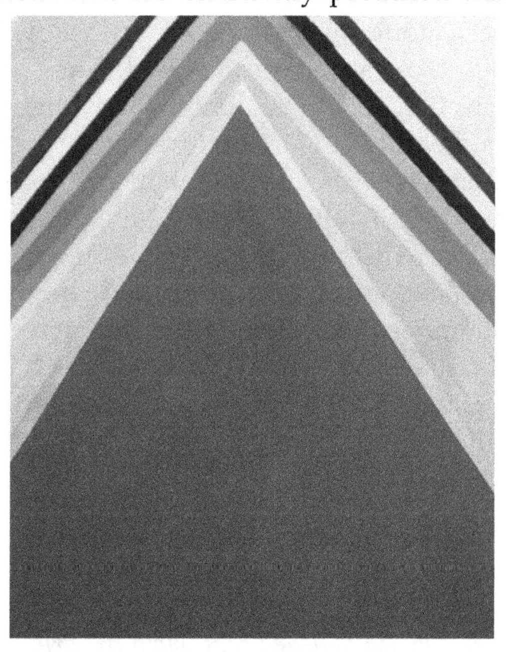

"Halal Praise" By Amanda A. Flowers

Jesus is seated in the heavenly kingdom, which is under His authority, and we see the type of it on earth. For example, in the heavenly kingdom there is no sickness, so the reflection of that in the earth is the release of healing and divine health because Jesus sits on the throne. God wants to release more of the kingdom through us, through the arts, and the church. What exists in heaven we release on the earth.

The tabernacle shows that the purpose of art is to glorify God. The earthly temple was a "type" of the heavenly temple. We can get a prophetic picture of the real kingdom and temple from heaven, and paint, or create a type or example of it. Our art can display His splendor just as the earthly tabernacle and temple reflected His glory. The temple was also decorated for our enjoyment. When people went into the temple they felt the majesty of the Lord through the visual display. They treated Him with reverence in the place of His glory and magnificence. The arts usher in the Lord's glory and bring heavenly beauty to the earth.

The devil counterfeits the principles of God. He set up Free Masonry to have the belief system to copy the heavens. One of their mottos is, "As above so below," indicating their desire to reflect certain stars in the sky that they worship, and create a reflection of those deities on the earth. It sounds like the counterfeit to "On earth as it is in Heaven." They also create buildings with great symbolism and art so that those who know their beliefs will understand the hidden meaning. Every one of the major Washington D.C. buildings was laid with a Mason cornerstone and has their symbols and beliefs etched as monuments to their false religion (Pinto and Monteith). As Christians we must reflect the true heavenly tabernacle that God wants revealed. We can even make monuments that bring beauty and glory to Him.

After Solomon and the artisans completed the building and meticulously and magnificently decorated the temple and furnishings:

> *"It happened that when the priests came from the holy place, the cloud filled the house of the LORD, so that the priests could not stand to minister because of the cloud, for the glory of the LORD filled the house of the LORD." I Kings 8:10.*

When everything is in place in the temple, God comes with incredible glory! I believe God wants to release this glory through the arts in demonstration of His perfect will, the reality in heaven. This also happened when the tabernacle was complete,

> *"Moses could not even enter, because the cloud had settled upon it and the glory of the Lord filled the tabernacle." Ex. 40:33.*

The tabernacle was for God's habitation, because it was a place of praise. God dwells in glory, beauty, and worship. The Bible says He inhabits the praise of His people. He also rested on the Ark of the Covenant made of human hands, in a dwelling made by human frailty. Our hearts are like the ark, we are filled with human weakness, yet God comes and dwells in us. He covers us with gold, the glory. The New Testament tells us we are the temple of the Holy Spirit, and God now inhabits us, (1 Cor. 6:19). We are created as beings of praise, crafted as artists for His glory.

The temple was also a "shadow of things to come." This shadow is a picture of the future kingdom of God. We can use the arts to prophecy the future kingdom of our Almighty God in all His splendor and majesty. We can see events and objects that are coming, which are the will of God, and paint the "shadow" of them for all to see. John revealed shadows of things to come when he wrote the book of Revelation. He wrote and described images of the future, and the coming New Jerusalem. What a great prophetic assignment!

Looking further at the concept of "shadow," Peter's shadow would pass on people, and they were healed. There can be power within a passing, intangible, anointed shadow. Our art is a shadow of what we see in the heavens, and can be as powerful. Colossians 2:16-18 says that the feasts were a shadow of things to come, but Christ is the reality. This is because all the Old Testament shadows prophesied and predicted the future manifestation that would come in Christ Jesus.

Are you a shadow carrier? Have you seen into the heavenly realms and are able to cast a picture or shadow to manifest here on the earth? Are you ready to release His glory? There is an open window into the heavenly realm. Look through it! We can show others what is actually there. As artists, we can see to the other side, but also reach through the window, and grab it, and bring spiritual manifestation here. We can usher in healing, miracles, signs and wonders. We can reflect the glory of His heavenly kingdom!

Let's look at more of Amos 9:

> *"In that day I will restore David's fallen tent. I will repair its broken places, restore its ruins, and build it as it used to be, so that they may possess the remnant of Edom and all the nations that bear my name," declares the LORD, who will do these things. "The days are coming," declares the LORD, "when the reaper will be overtaken by the plowman and the planter by the one treading grapes. New wine will drip from the mountains and flow from all the hills. I will bring back my exiled people Israel; they will rebuild the ruined cities and live in them. They will plant vineyards and drink their wine; they will make gardens and eat their fruit. I will plant Israel in their own land never again to be uprooted from the land I have given them," says the LORD your God." – AMOS 9:11-15*

Could it be that when we restore David's fallen tent (the spiritual tabernacle), then we will possess the land, and see fulfillment of this prophecy, the final harvest? We know that in Israel they are anxious to rebuild the next temple. When God allowed the previous one to be destroyed, it was because he had a much bigger idea in mind. He wanted His church to be the temple. As Christian artists, we are also the temple and demonstrate beauty and glory through the arts and release the creativity of David's tent, including visual, poetic, and musical worship to honor the Lord.

God wants to bring us back to the Holy Mountain, to Zion. It is a place of His holy habitation. At that place we find our dreams again. We also have our fortunes, (spiritual gifts) restored. As we see here in Psalm 126, when we get back to Zion, we will also find our joy, and harvest.

> *"When the Lord brought back the captive ones of Zion, We were like those who dream. Then our mouth was filled with laughter And our tongue with joyful shouting; Then they said among the nations, "The Lord has done great things for them."*
>
> *The Lord has done great things for us; We are glad. Restore our captivity, O Lord, As the streams in the South. Those who sow in tears shall reap with joyful shouting. He who goes to and fro*

weeping, carrying his bag of seed, Shall indeed come again with a shout of joy, bringing his sheaves with him," Psalm 126:1-6 .

As we return to the mountain of the Lord with our art and creativity, God will restore our dreams, our fortunes, and our joy. We will sow seed through our art and creativity, and bring in spiritual harvest.

David spoke to the Israelites in 1 Chronicles 29, and asked what they were willing to consecrate for the temple. The Israelites volunteered their precious stones, gold and silver. It tells us in verse 9:

"Then the people rejoiced, for that they offered willingly, because with perfect heart they offered willingly to the LORD: and David the king also rejoiced with great joy."

David was deeply moved at their offering of precious material and gems to build the temple. He was glad they had a giving heart to bring gifts for the beauty and adornment of the house of Almighty God. In Revelation, John describes the stones that glow are the emeralds in a rainbow surrounding the One we love. This picture expands in Revelation 21, as the heavenly tabernacle becomes the New Jerusalem. It is the splendid place of the eternal throne:

"I saw the Holy City, the new Jerusalem, coming down out of heaven from God, prepared as a bride beautifully dressed for her husband.......The wall was made of jasper, and the city of pure gold, as pure as glass. The foundations of the city walls were decorated with every kind of precious stone. The first foundation was jasper, the second sapphire, the third agate, the fourth emerald, the fifth onyx, the sixth ruby, the seventh chrysolite, the eighth beryl, the ninth topaz, the tenth turquoise, the eleventh jacinth, and the twelfth amethyst. The twelve gates were twelve pearls, each gate made of a single pearl. The great street of the city was of gold, as pure as transparent glass." Rev. 21:2 and18-21.

Is it any wonder that David was pleased when the Israelites brought precious stones and gold for the building of the temple? The earthly reflected the spiritual reality. God wants us to have our hearts seeing His kingdom, and to create based on the heavenly reality.

The coming church is a shadow of the temple in the spiritual realm. She is the Glorified Church; the church in all it's splendor, beauty, working in the fullness of faith, and the creative gifts of the spirit reflecting heaven. This church will be willing to die for her Lord, and live in radical obedience. She will be dressed in white, living in righteousness, and adorned in the gemstones of the priesthood. She will step into apostleship, bringing the kingdom of God to all areas of earthly government and to the mountains of culture. God will reveal the picture of His bride to artists to display her character, her authority, and His love for her. The prophets will receive downloads from heaven of assignments for His bride. Creativity will flow freely from the Lord through His beloved.

#33 GO INTO THE WORLD

God wants prophetic art to go beyond the church, and infiltrate culture. This is the goal of the Seven Mountains teachings. I heard about this teaching at a Morningstar conference. The speaker was Lance Wallnau. He explained that there are seven earthly spheres that Christians should aspire to wage war and take back for the Lord.

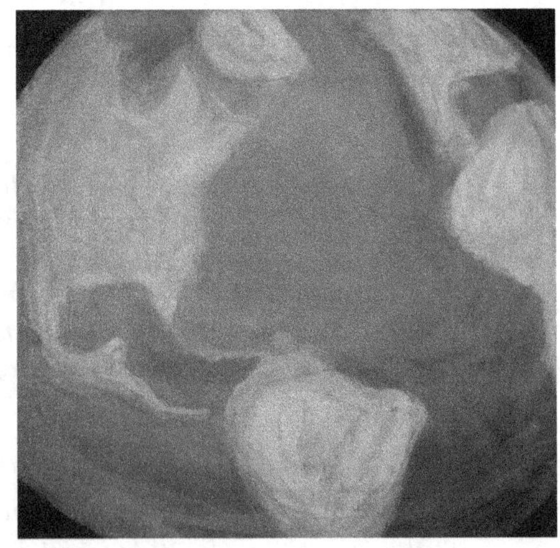

By Nichole A. Ryder

They mountains are: government, art and entertainment, education, business and finance, religion, media, and family. Whoever occupies the top of the mountains can shape nations. Jesus wants us to advance His kingdom and reclaim this lost territory. We can do this by infiltrating each of these areas in culture. Creating a Biblical base in each of the mountains establishes the kingdom, (Wallnau).

As artists, we need to join together and restore the arts for the Lord's glory. Prophetically, we can get assignments to do this. We get strategies from heaven as we surrender our gifts to Him. He will give us creativity and cutting edge ideas that will shock the world. It reveals God as Creator. We can restore the base of truth, purity, and Biblical standards that were stolen from the arts. God will then bring His purposes back to the arts for His glory.

If you are a graphic designer, illustrator, cartoonist, movie set designer, actor, screenwriter, or in any arts field, you are put there for such a time as this. You are an Esther who God will use, if you are surrendered to hearing from Him and being obedient to His voice. He may use you for subtle messages that bring Him honor through holiness and beauty. Or He may require you to be bold and make a stand for the kingdom and the spread of the gospel. You will receive revelation from the Lord that will make you prosper.

God's revelation can give us back the mountain of arts and entertainment. When we do any art for Him, the glory is due to Him. Thus, satan cannot have the glory. This is the first way we take back territory from the kingdom of darkness. Next, by unifying with other Christian artists, we build the army that will be able to stand the attacks of evil. On our own, we are weak. United, we can stand against the demonic realm by praying for the arts together. Building networks higher in the infrastructure of the art business will gain footholds for Christians. The gradual goal is to establish Christian morals and values, reflecting the character of the Father. The artwork will then bring more glory to God. Eventually, we infiltrate the highest levels, as owners, producers, editors, directors, and top-level artists. We then will have toppled the domain of darkness.

GO FORWARD WITH PROPHETIC ART

The previous section was a list of forms and examples of prophetic art. God is very creative, and He keeps releasing more inspiration to each generation. As you review these types and areas of prophetic visual art, I hope it stirs more creativity in you. God may be calling you to one of these or another form of prophetic art not listed here.

When we ask what prophetic art is, we need to remember to seek God for guidance. Jesus, as our example, only did what He heard or saw the Father do:

> *"Very truly I tell you, the Son can do nothing by himself; he can do only what he sees his Father doing, because whatever the Father does the Son also does." John 5:19.*

God wants to show us creativity and revelation and let us release it. We are the middlemen, the prophets, and the painters who have receive a message from the Lord and are sent to deliver it.

CHAPTER 5
THE TRUTH ABOUT IMAGINATION & REVELATION

How do we use imagination to support our creativity? What does God allow? Ephesians 3:20,21 says,

> *"Now to him who is able to do immeasurably more than all we ask or imagine, according to his power that is at work within us, to him be glory in the church and in Christ Jesus throughout all generations, for ever and ever! Amen."*

This is a powerful scripture that gives us some insight to one of the great blessings and powers that we can have through Christ. But there is a catch. Before we understand the wonderful working of God-led imagination, let me explain that the Lord spoke to me many times and warned me about the dangers of imagination. I feel you must understand the gravity of using imagination over God's revelation.

"Imagination, is from your own thought process and human insight," says my pastor, Paul Zink. He continues, "God gives revelation. You can see things in the spiritual level that you would never see in your mind." It is very important that we understand the difference.

In the Ephesians 3 verse, 'imagine' comes from the word Noeo; (to understand with the mind, have understanding, to think upon, heed ponder consider; to see, understand, perceive think.) It translates better in NASB, "more than all we ask or think." It does not necessarily mean we are supposed to 'imagine', as we know it. If we 'see' what God is revealing and showing us prophetically, it is different from visualization techniques that the world now teaches, and even some Christian leaders.

There is a powerful type of imagination that opens a door to the flesh. This imagination has a dark side. I believe the devil has access to our imagination. It is a creative realm where our soul is more open. Imagination is letting ourselves play a "what if" game. This lets our guard down, and the boundaries and limitations God has set in place are easily neglected.

The Lord spoke to me and reminded me that the world uses guided visualization, and there are measured results from their ungodly "imagination." Remember, it is God's will for us to pray and allow The Spirit to give us visions and creativity, and not to muster up a false imagination. There is a very fine line, and many do not have discernment to know the difference.

The Bible warns about those who prophesy out of their own imagination, and the same applies to those who do prophetic art out of their own imaginations:

> *"Son of man, prophesy against the prophets of Israel who are now prophesying. Say to those who prophesy out of their own imagination: 'Hear the word of the LORD! This is what the Sovereign LORD says: Woe to the foolish prophets who follow their own spirit and have seen nothing!" Ezekiel 13:2,3*

They were prophesying from their own imagination, from the Hebrew word 'leb' (meaning inner man, mind, will, heart, understanding, inner part, midst, soul.) This imagination can come from the inner will and soul of a man. It is not the same as receiving from the mind of God. They were following, "their own spirit" and "have seen nothing!" They were not getting vision and revelation from the Lord.

We will be condemned if we use guided imagery or suggestive thought. In this method, people use their imagination to attain their mates, houses, and can activate things to materialize in their life. They might put a picture of the kind of mate they want to attract on their refrigerator and "imagine" this is their wife. Many times, it is successful through power that comes from the devil. They use their own wishes and desires, and then create a mental image of it. They imagine these things coming to them. They meditate on it and let the imagination flow from the soul and inner man. The Bible tells us:

> *"The god of this age has blinded the minds of unbelievers, so that they cannot see the light of the gospel that displays the glory of Christ, who is the image of God." 2 Cor. 2:4.*

Their eyes are blinded to truth and they do not receive the real thing, the revelation and light from God. Many Biblical principles are mimicked by the devil and repackaged, but contain a slight twist to the truth, making them corrupted.

David E. Bresler, PhD, (a secular mental health practice), on his web site defines his guided imagery practice this way,

> "The term "guided imagery" refers to a wide variety of techniques, including simple visualization and direct suggestion, using imagery, metaphor and story-telling, fantasy exploration, and game playing, dream interpretation, drawing, and active imagination where elements of the unconscious are invited to appear as images that can communicate with the conscious mind," (Bresler).

Dr. Bresler uses guided imagery to heal physical and emotional problems. Others in the world are using it to create a life of success through the power of their imagination. There are many best selling self-help books based on imagining your success. There is a principle in the spiritual realm that unleashes power, but if it is not linked with God's will, it is demonic. It is actually a form of witchcraft!

There are church leaders teaching this same method as a guide to prosperity. They teach that you just need to 'visualize' what you want, imagine it, and it will come. But imagination without God's revelation or Biblical support is a dangerous game. It must be taught that revelation from God and guidance from His Word are the keys to holy imagination.

IMAGINATION WITH REVELATION

What we really need is revelation, a pearl of great price. There is great sacrifice for it, but it is well worth it. The cost is intimacy, time with the Father, prayer, soaking, and studying the Bible. It is waiting on the Holy Spirit for guidance and direction.

We can study the word and join our vision to the promises from the Lord. Using revelation and linking it with faith activates a type of imagination based on God's truth. It is how we can have spiritual eyes of faith. With faith-eyes, we see what God's will looks like, and we attach our faith and prayers to it. Then we can access the promises in the verse:

> *"Now to him who is able to do immeasurably more than all we ask or imagine, according to his power that is at work within us" Ephesians 3:20.*

Our God-guided imagination can do immeasurably more because of God's power in us and is led by His revelation, far superior to what we are able to imagine. Our imagination is submitted to God's will and authority in our lives. Abram is a great example of God initiating imagination. God made a promise to Abram:

> *"He took him outside and said, "Look up at the sky and count the stars—if indeed you can count them." Then he said to him, "So shall your offspring be." Gen. 15:5.*

God prophesied to Abram that he would be the father of many nations. When God showed Abram the stars in the heavens, the stars became a vision of his future, it was revelation and truth from God. Abram's faith linked with it, and every time he looked up at those stars, in his imagination, he saw his destiny in God and this created faith that was credited to him as righteousness. The Lord brought it to pass in the Jewish people and the nation of Israel. If we get our faith-eyes attached to God's revelation, we will see God activate what God wants to happen. If God calls you to start a church, and you keep the vision before you, profess it, pray it, act on it and link your faith with the vision, you will see it manifest.

If we get a vision from the Lord and paint it, pray it and prophecy it into being, it will happen because God initiated it. We received it as revelation. We attach our faith to it and it becomes substance in the spiritual realm. It becomes building materials for it to exist in the natural.

If God prophesied a healing ministry in your life, you should attach your faith-eyes to it. Use your spiritual eyes and Godly-imagination to see yourself praying for people, and God releasing His healing on them. Your faith-imagination sees what is possible with God. It sees what God has prophesied into being. This is totally different from soul-imagination where the author is our flesh. If our soul-nature is the initiator of the image, we are unsound in our vision.

There is a man, Mel Bond, who visualized himself in the stories of the Bible with Jesus doing miracles. Then, miracles started to happen in Mel's life (Bond, Mel. Interview by Sid Roth). Jesus said, "Greater things than these you will do." We can stand on that scripture to "imagine" ourselves doing greater things. I have heard of faith-healers who would "see" and imagine themselves doing miracles before they were common in their ministry. This is not of the flesh because we have scripture to back it up. Jesus told us all to heal the sick, raise the dead, and cast out demons. Meditate on that a while and watch heaven invade your life.

Visualize or imagine what the Lord has revealed in prophecy or in His Word. Dwell on the things He instigates. I saw another interview on the T.V. program "It's Supernatural," about a preacher, Sandra Kennedy, who was bit by her dog and part of her lip was missing (Kennedy, Sandra. Interview by Sid Roth). They sewed it together, but doctors told her she would never smile again and would need multiple surgeries to make it a little better, but it would be deformed. She rejected the report of the doctors. She refused to look at photos of cleft lips that they wanted to show her to discuss her problem. She knew if she got those images stuck in her mind, it would influence her faith. It would be part of negative imagination and limit her healing. She was a preacher with the gift of healing, and knew God wanted to heal her.

Sandra hung old photos of her old, beautiful smile around her house, and commanded her lips to re-form in Jesus' name. She said we must speak to our mountains, and she did. Life and death are in the power of the tongue. When she doubted, she spoke to Satan and told him he was the father of lies. Within weeks, her face reformed, without additional surgeries. She has the most radiant smile. You would never know there had been anything wrong with her mouth.

Sandra used images to be a focus for her prayers and spiritual warfare. They helped her keep vision and imagination on wholeness and healing from the Lord. She knew that the Bible tells us it is always God's will to heal. We can use art to be a focus of the vision God has put before us. It gives us eyes of faith to 'see' the correct picture or situation, and not believe the devil's picture. Our art can help others meditate on God's truth. Our logical mind is the biggest obstacle to accessing what God is releasing. My pastor, Paul Zink says, "Faith is not logical. Logic can block God and barricade God's progress. Vision comes to the spirit and must convince the mind. You can limit your progress by reason. Our real creative edge comes from the Father" (Zink). Don't let your mind block and limit your faith in what God wants to accomplish.

I fully believe we can draw a picture of what God wants to release, meditate and pray, speak to the mountain and use the picture as a reminder to support our faith. God will release the miracle. Conversely, if you dwell on the negative and look at images that will decrease your faith, you will loose the battle. The devil will even use it as an open door to give you the spirit of fear. Art and pictures can be used by the devil to bring demonic presence into someone's life. Some people watch the news and they take in the spirit of fear. They become afraid to walk their dog at night because they have dwelt on murders and the crime rate and they imagine the worst. Do not dwell on the darkness of the enemy.

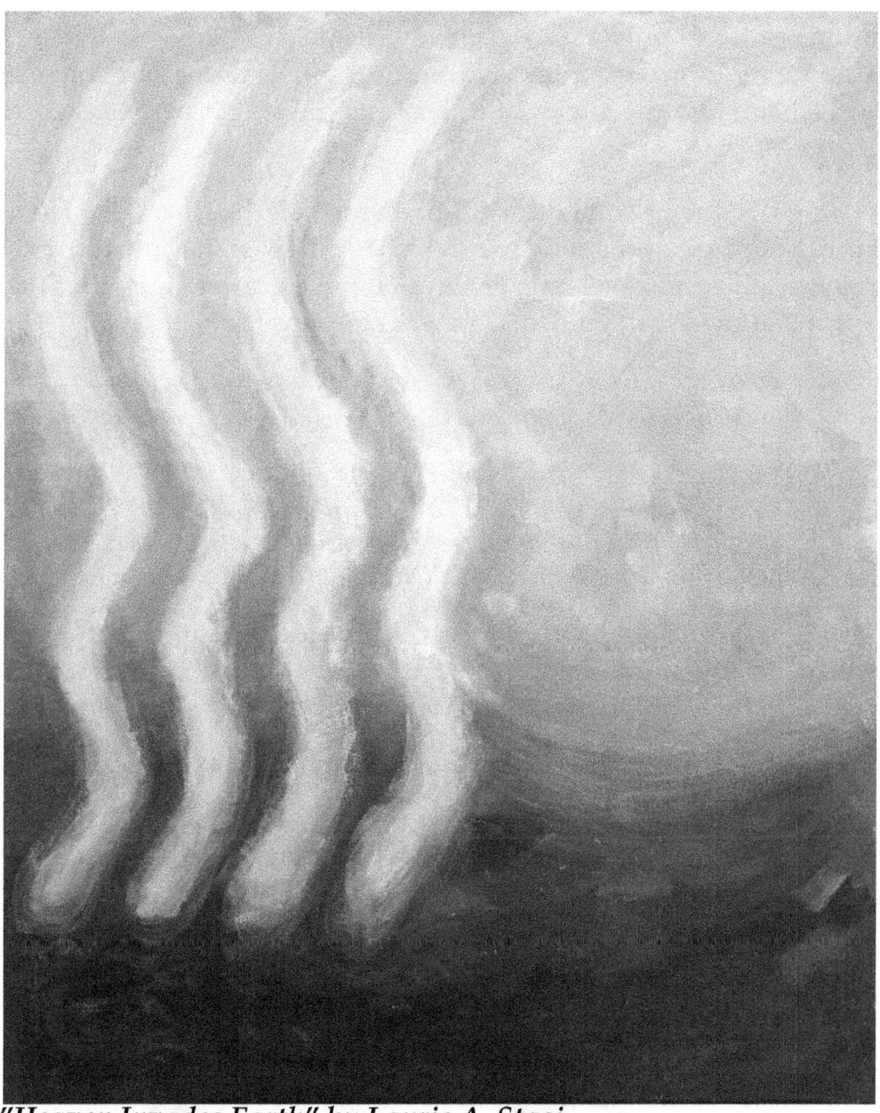

"Heaven Invades Earth" by Laurie A. Stasi

In Gen. 30, Jacob peeled the bark off of some sticks, and put them before his sheep in order to have them bear young with stripes, speckles and spots. There is a spiritual principle at work; what you put before you, you will produce. This principal applies to the power of visual art. Pastor Paul Zink likes to say, "What you behold, you become." If you watch raunchy movies, you will be filled with filth. If you take in and dwell on the things of God, you will become more like Him. Prophetic art has that same influence and power. We can dwell on the miraculous and authoritative images from God and let our imagination connect with them, and the supernatural can manifest and be released in our lives.

We do not want our soul-nature to call the shots. The Holy Spirit must guide us, and we will have power in God through prayer, faith and revelation. This is how we activate miracles; the Spirit and the Word guides us in what to pray.

> *"We do not know what we ought to pray for, but the Spirit himself intercedes for us through wordless groans." Romans 8:26.*

> *"For prophecy never had its origin in the human will, but prophets, though human, spoke from God as they were carried along by the Holy Spirit." 2 Peter 1:21*

The Holy Spirit guides us and gives us prophetic information as we spend time with Him. Christians need to learn how to be "in the Spirit" and not in their imaginations, and flesh.

> *"For those who are led by the Spirit of God are the children of God." Romans 8:14.*

God has plenty of revelation for us, if we are willing to pursue Him. The Holy Spirit takes directly from the Father and releases to us. We are "carried along by the Holy Spirit."

> *"But when He, the Spirit of truth, comes, He will guide you into all the truth; for He will not speak on His own initiative, but whatever He hears, He will speak; and He will disclose to you what is to come." John 16:13*

This is one of my favorite Holy Spirit verses. He gives us so much. We have a guide who leads us into truth. Holy Spirit hears from the Father and reveals revelation to us, including things in the future, "He will disclose to you what is to come!" I love the prophetic! God is so filled with love for us, He gives amazing gifts!

In Revelation, John was "In the Spirit on the Lord's Day." He knew the secret to revelation. First, of course, we need to be filled with the Holy Spirit. Second, we need to take time to meditate, worship, and pray in tongues. To get "In the Spirit," as John was, is to spend deliberate time with the Lord. Through this he received revelation. Jesus took time to be alone with The Father. He said He only did what He heard or saw His Father doing or saying. This is our example as artists, to see and hear the Father, like Jesus did. Jesus did not run off on His own imagination, He received from The Father.

The people at the tower of Babel found the keys to demonic imagination. They discovered that unity, combined with a unified vision, or imagination, is powerful. The problem, of course, was that they did not have God's vision, but their own. God knew there was power in their "imagination," especially when they were in unity, so He destroyed their unity to break their power.

The modern world has found unity and vision. They create many forms of the Tower of Babel, to make a name for themselves. You see it in the arts, Hollywood, media, the music industry, business, etc. They have cartels and monopolies to rule their mountains. It is not God's will for their creativity to be used in this way. Our abilities, talents and productive works were meant to glorify the Lord. Our unity with other believers is powerful when our gifts and imagination are used for Him.

Once God gives us revelation, we should act on it. He may have us do prophetic action to release His kingdom. My daughter, Nichole, and I knew a couple that was talking about getting a divorce. The husband had given up on the relationship and was

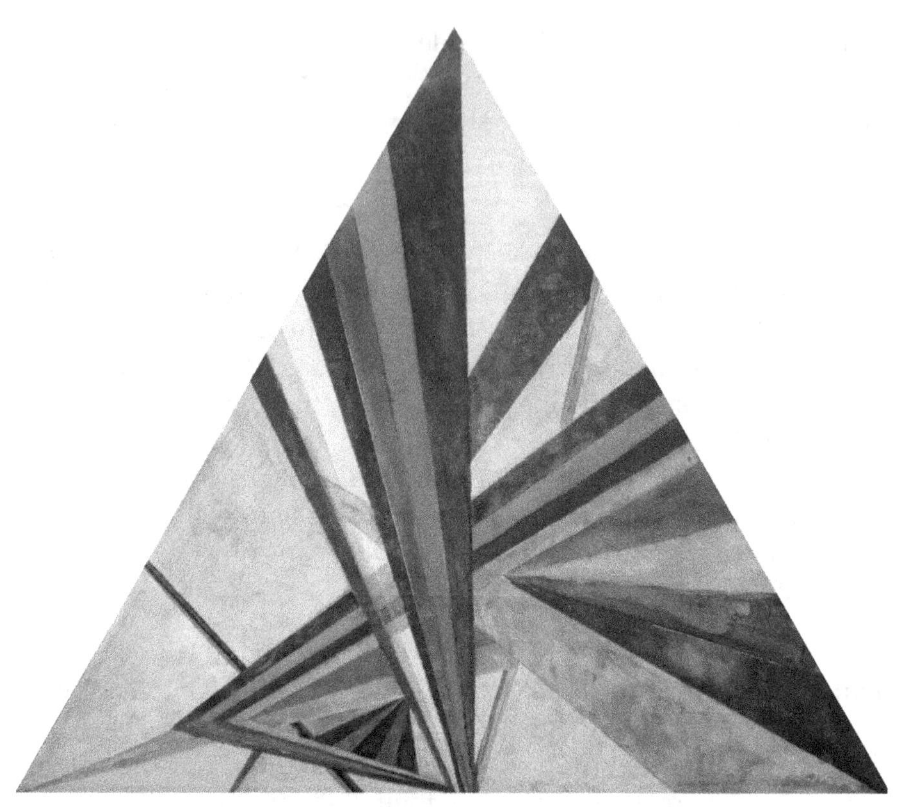

"Trinity" By Amanda A. Flowers

seeing a younger woman. In the natural, all hope was gone. Nichole and I got together to pray on a night when a Christian Was sent to counsel the couple. We knew the scriptures say that God hates divorce, so we stood on His word. Nichole and I were linked with His will in asking for restoration in their marriage. We determined that we just needed a miracle. In our family room we had three huge iron keys hanging on the wall, and the Spirit was leading us to do a prophetic action. I took the keys down and I said, "We need access to the kingdom of heaven for a miracle." Next to the keys on the wall was an abstract prophetic painting. At that moment the Holy Spirit made me think the painting looked like keyholes, so I turned the biggest key in the imagined "keyhole" and asked God to release a big miracle from heaven.

In the Spirit, we felt the miracle had been released and we waved our arms and sent the miracle North, in the direction of the couple that needed the miracle. By being led by the Spirit and through prayer, we were accessing heaven. We were states away from the couple. That night the couple stayed up and talked until five in the morning and determined to make their marriage work. That year he got a new job and the next year they had another baby. It was a big miracle because God led our imagination and intercession. Jesus said to pray, "On earth as it is in heaven." We can release heaven on earth through prophetic prayer. Psalm 23 says, "He guides me in the paths of righteousness." He wants to guide our intercession in good times and in the "valley of the shadow of death."

God's revelation is the key. We do not need to play games with imagination, but we need to be willing to play with God, His games, His way. We need to come with faith like a little child. We need to dance with Him, and prophetically act out things He leads us to.

> *"I keep asking that the God of our Lord Jesus Christ, the glorious Father, may give you the Spirit of wisdom and revelation, so that you may know him better. I pray that the eyes of your heart may be enlightened in order that you may know the hope to which he has called you, the riches of his glorious inheritance in his holy people," Eph. 1:17-18*

As creative prophetic artists, we need "the eyes of our hearts enlightened." "Enlightened" is such a rich word. It means "to furnish knowledge or give spiritual insight; or to shed light upon." This can only happen with the Spirit of Wisdom and Revelation through Holy Spirit. It was also translated in Greek, "photizo," where we get the word photo. The spiritual insight we receive is often in the form of a spiritual photo or vision. The "eyes of our heart" can see, or imagine, what the hope of our calling and inheritance is. The word photizo also means; to bring to light, render evident, or cause something to exist and thus become clear to all. We, as prophetic artists, create or develop a rendering of revelation that brings to light and reveals something from the spiritual realm. We cause it to exist in the natural, exposing the spiritual message.

Our Lord will guide us in prophetic actions, and in what to create or paint. Ask for the Spirit of Wisdom and Revelation and He will give spiritual insight about the things He wants to manifest in the earth. Allow yourself to come like a child, and imagine His will. He will tell us prophetic actions to accompany our prayers. He will show us things to come, and we can partner with Him in faith, and intercede for it to manifest.

Todd Bentley wrote a prophetic word for a Grand Rapids conference, in which he talked about a vision in a realm of creativity. Todd "visionates," by dreaming of things to do for the Kingdom. He does this in the realm of the Spirit:

> "And I saw a whole lot of created things 'calling forth the things that be not as though they were.' And things that existed in the eternal realm that weren't visible. . .we build the visible realm by the invisible realm and just like the Heavens themselves were framed by the Word of God…I saw a building, a framework in the spirit framing things out by the declared Word, by the spoken Word, calling and decreeing. . .There are a lot of things...that are without form; they're void. They're real, they exist in your heart, they exist in the realm of dreaming with God, they exist in the spirit realm, but the earth was without form, the earth was void." (Bentley)

Todd's imagination is linked with God's heart. This is the birthing place in the spirit where the idea exists without form. We can "visionate" and dream with God and access the framework for creating. Then we need to prophecy it (as God spoke, "Let there be"), and pray for God to release it in the natural realm.

JoAnn McFatter is a prophetic worship leader who wrote about creativity and imagination (McFatter). She explained that we are all born with creativity in our DNA. Children are creative but our Greek-minded schooling squeezed our creative gifting right out of us. This has hindered our ability to grasp the supernatural and have faith for believe. She goes on to say:

> "Sometimes we don't even believe when we see...we've lost our ability to even receive a thought from God in our mind's eye-our imagination. Imagination does not have to be a bad thing."

> "Our imagination is engaged in faith for the supernatural. Are we going to believe for that thing we cannot see? . . . Our faith causes an image to form in our imagination. We come into agreement with God and He causes our imagination to see what He says is real. It is something yet to be, at least in the physical realm, though in God's mind it already is. To be or not to be, truly is the question being proposed to us by faith, itself! We can agree with what God is telling/showing us, and thereby co-labor with Him to bring it to pass."

Our faith must be actively involved when God shows us His will; it is how we co-labor with him. We cannot please Him without believing:

> *"Now faith is the substance of things hoped for, the evidence of things not seen. But without faith it is impossible to please Him, for He who comes to God must believe that He is, and is a rewarder of those who diligently seek Him." Heb. 11:1,6*

"Faith is the substance of things hoped for." Faith is the active ingredient that makes things materialize from the supernatural realm into the physical realm. It is a tangible "substance." Our whole relationship with God is based on the faith we have in Him in believing and "seeing" with our mind's eye, that our God, and Jesus exist. We don't see Him physically in the room with us, but our faith believes in what we do not see. Without faith, it is impossible to please God. Faith is a requirement and we can actively develop more faith in God's heavenly kingdom and the spiritual realm. When God shows us a vision of what He wants to release, we must have faith that God is going to do it. Our imagination can rest in the assurance that if

God initiated the vision, it will be accomplished. Abraham had this kind of faith, and it was credited to him as righteousness.

Pastor Paul Zink says, "When you pursue," your vision, "it is evidence of your faith. Tenaciously go after it without wavering, without doubt, pursue it with your whole heart and being. God will give you the desires of your heart. Vision is the guidance system of your faith." When are led by revelation and vision, we are following God's lead. "If God is guiding, you are taking the limitations off your entire life" (Zink). God can do so much more than we can imagine.

Creativity is different from imagination; it is the Holy Spirit whispering in our ear, directing the creative process. In the next chapter we will look into this great gift.

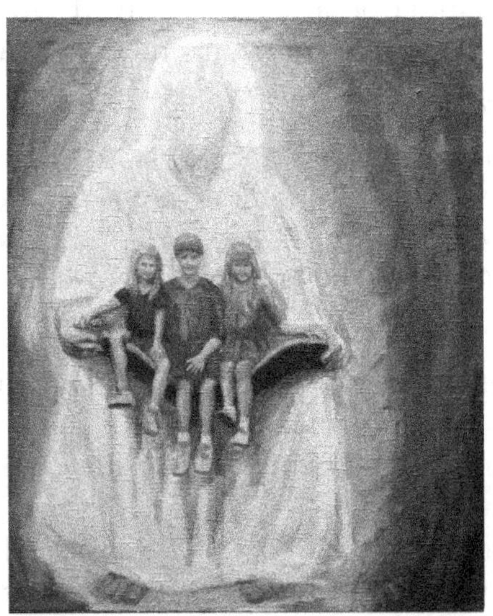

"The Book of Life" Laurie A. Stasi

CHAPTER 6
THE TENDER HEART OF CREATIVTY

In a previous chapter I discussed Bezalel and Oholiab, who were the artists and craftsmen chosen to create the implements for the tabernacle through the Holy Spirit. The Bible tells us God put wisdom in these men and the other craftsmen:

> *"And in the hearts of all that are wise hearted I have put wisdom, that they may make all that I have commanded thee;" Ex. 31:6b.*

This little verse is of great significance for artists. It gives us a great clue to creativity. The phrase, "and in the hearts," refers to the inner place God plants wisdom in the "wise hearted." If we understand this place, we tap into the seed of creativity that we possess. Recognizing it within yourself will help you connect to God's wisdom easier.

"Heart" is the Hebrew word Leb, which refers to: *the inner man, will, heart, understanding*. It is the *midst, the soul.* It refers to the *mind and knowledge, thinking, reflection and memory.* It includes *inclination, resolution, determination, conscience, and heart of moral character.* It is *the place of the seat of appetites, emotions passions and courage.*

When you think of your creativity, and reflect on these words listed in the previous paragraph, there are places within us that resonate when the Spirit stirs us with creativity. We can reflect on some things, and find inspiration from the Spirit for a painting. A memory can trigger a poem. Our conscience can bring an awareness of emotions that inspires a worship song. We can have an inclination, which sparks a thought process of creativity for our next art project. This "Leb" location of creativity within us is the seat of our emotions and passions in our spirit.

When we feel an emotional tug in our spirit, there may be a creative flow that God wants to come out of that place. This is what I call the "Poetic Breeze." We might feel a stirring in our emotions and passions in a situation, or even the environment we are in. Something within starts to feel the poetry of the moment. This breeze is the Holy Spirit leading us into creativity. These are all workings of the Holy Spirit from the "Leb," or heart of God within us. When we are in tune with this place and feelings within us through the flow of the Spirit, we learn to recognize Him speaking in these areas.

We need to train ourselves to be sensitive to these clues from our creative God who is speaking and guiding us. I believe David knew the Poetic Breeze, and wrote the Psalms through the Holy Spirit's guidance in his heart (Leb). David felt the stirrings through the *passions, courage, reflection, conscience, and emotions* within him and responded in verse as worship to the Lord. Look at the verse again about the craftsmen:

> *"And in the hearts of all that are wise hearted I have put wisdom, that they may make all that I have commanded thee;" Ex. 31:6b.*

God put the wisdom in the hearts of, "all that are wise hearted." These are people endowed with wisdom in their "Leb," or heart. These are selected ingenious people; artists, composers, craftsmen, writers, dancers, etc, who were chosen to receive creative wisdom within their soul. I have been with many artists, and some possess a great intuition and sensitivity. They seem in tune with their own passionate soul as it is connected to God.

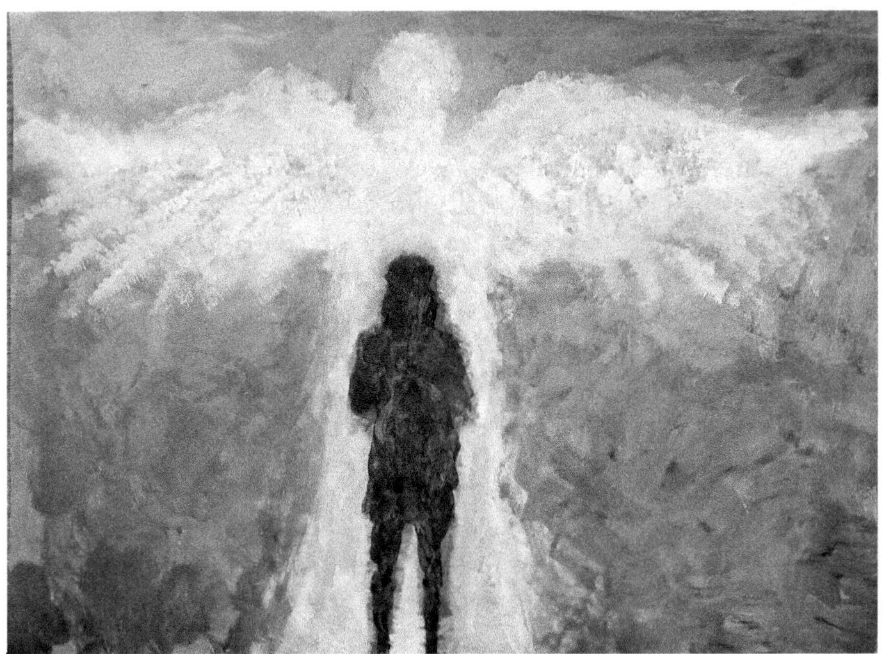
"Vision" by Laurie A. Stasi

This is another plane of spirituality that allows for the flow of inspiration to come from heaven through the prophetic; but also connects with the creativity from the heart and soul.

CREATIVITY APPLIES TO OTHER ABILITIES

You would be amazed at the world of creativity we have around us. I have compiled a short list of some of the professions that rely on creativity. Just imagine what the world would be like without these gifts:

THE CREATIVE FIELDS LIST:

Accompanying, Acting, Advertising, Animation, Architecture, Art history, Arts management, Art restoration, Art theory, Baking/Cooking and Food presentation, Banner and flag design, Ceramics, Children's products/ toys and games, Choreography, Circus arts, Clothing, Commercial illustration,

Computer-aided arts and design, Conducting, Conservation of cultural materials, Community arts, Costume design, Crafts, Dance, Design, Digital composition, Drama, Drawing, Fashion, Fine arts, Furniture design and craftsmen, Glass arts, Graphic Design, Illustration, Improvisation, Indigenous art, Industries, Inventions, Instrumental Music, Interior design, Jazz studies, Jewelry making, Magazines, Medical research, Metal works, Movies, Multimedia, Musical theatre, Musicology, Opera, Painting, Performing arts, Photography, Printmaking, Product design and implementation, Publishing, Puppetry, Radio, Scientific photography, Sculpture, Set design, Sewing, Silversmith, Software, Sound production, Stage lighting, Textiles, Theatre, TV production, Videos, Video games, Vocal studies, Web design, Weaving, Writing (Plays, Books, Screen Plays etc.).

Creativity can also affect business solutions, problem solving, program planning and development, structural systems and organization. We apply creativity to inventions, investing and every aspect of our world. John C. Maxwell states:

> "God is the great Creator. It doesn't make sense not to bring God-the Creator of the universe-into the creative process. No matter how much natural talent God has given us, He can always make it greater, better, bigger. That's why I pray for creativity. And when I pray for creativity, I ask for two things: I ask God to give me an idea or give me an example. In our fast-paced, competitive marketplace, few resources are more valuable to organizations than creativity." (Joyce Meyer quoting Maxwell)

Our God can give messages and creativity to scientists, inventors, or soccer coaches, as much as to artists. There is edge when we live in God's creativity that will make what ever we do, more successful, to His glory. He can give us a prize winning brownie recipe, a quilt design, a new perfume, or a solution to cancer. A friend of mine was given a dream of a natural cleaning product. She works in a bank, and cleaning products are not her field of study, so she had to do research. She recently developed this green product and is selling it to a major natural food chain. God stirred the creativity in her and she will be blessed. John

Maxwell understood that it was very simple. We can pray, and ask. God is faithful to release His kingdom and creative flow to us because He loves us.

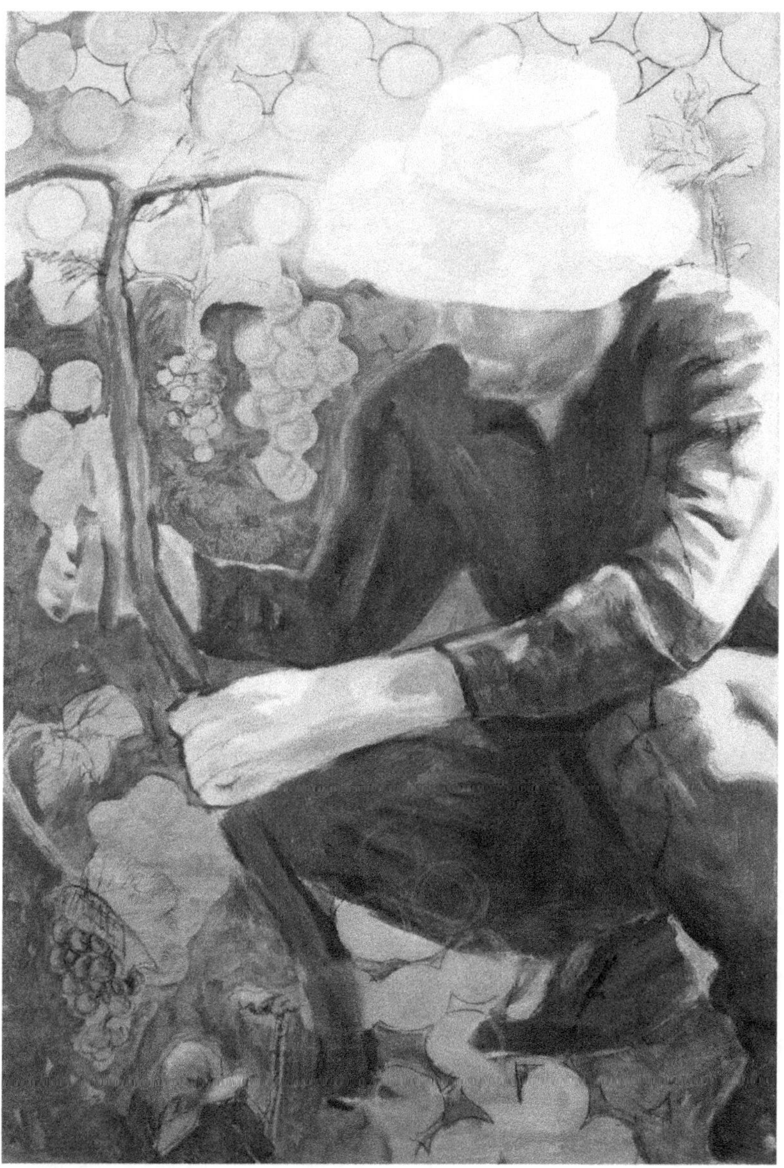

"The Gardener" By Laurie A. Stasi

CHAPTER 7

GOD SPEAKS; ARE YOU LISTENING?

There are many ways we receive revelation from God. Years ago when I started painting, I would have a strong desire to paint something, and I knew it was the Lord. When I read about the potter and the clay, I felt so drawn to it that I studied everywhere in the Bible that mentioned potter or clay. The message God gave was about rebellion, and repentance and I just had to paint it. When that painting was nearly completed, God gave me another one that I just "felt" I needed to paint. Now, I hear from Him in more ways as He guides me in my creativity.

This next section will highlight ways God speaks to us as we listen in our hunger for Him:

THE WORD

> *"All Scripture is God-breathed and is useful for teaching, rebuking, correcting and training in righteousness, so that the man of God may be thoroughly equipped for every good work," II Timothy 3:16-17.*

David would meditate on the word day and night. He was probably one of the most creative people in the Bible. As we meditate on the Word, God speaks to us. He gives us messages, revelation, and instruction. The Holy Spirit speaks to our hearts and gives us images and messages for our art. If you feel God speaking through a passage, take notes and draw sketches. Maybe you need to release what He is speaking into poetry, art, or music.

> *"For the word of God is living and active. Sharper than any double-edged sword, it penetrates even to dividing soul and spirit, joints and marrow; it judges the thoughts and attitudes of the heart." Hebrews 4:12.*

The Word is so powerful. It penetrates into us, judging us, and our attitudes. It is the living breath of God and probably the easiest form of revelation from God. You can't argue with the Word. If you don't feel like you hear from the Lord, or you are in a period when He is very quiet, start by getting more into the scriptures. He is speaking. I cannot tell you how many times I just open my Bible, and there is a word from God, directly for me, jumping off the page as if God had written it five minutes ago and highlighted it for me. He is speaking, and we can hear Him clearly in His Word.

THE SPIRIT

We hear God through the still, small voice of the Holy Spirit. In 1 Kings 19, Elijah didn't hear God in the wind, earthquake or fire, but in the still small voice of the Holy Spirit. Many people confuse this voice with their own thoughts. It is so subtle and quiet, you have to try and hear Him. "Be still and know that I am God," Ps. 46:10. Sometimes we need to "be still." Take some time to ask Him something, then just sit and wait. Listen.

Imagine for a minute, that one day you randomly thought of your Aunt Tammy, and urgently felt like you should give her a call. When you called her, she said, "Oh, I really needed someone to talk to, I was so depressed." You were hearing from God, He wanted you to call and encourage her. That is how we hear from God through the still, small voice of the Holy Spirit. Most Christians hear without realizing it. Others learn to develop and grow in their listening skills. The Lord is always speaking to us; the problem is we are not taking the time to listen. Spend some time quietly before the Lord and write down what you think He is saying to you. When you have "random thoughts" of someone, God may be speaking about them. You may develop this gift and can hear God very clearly!

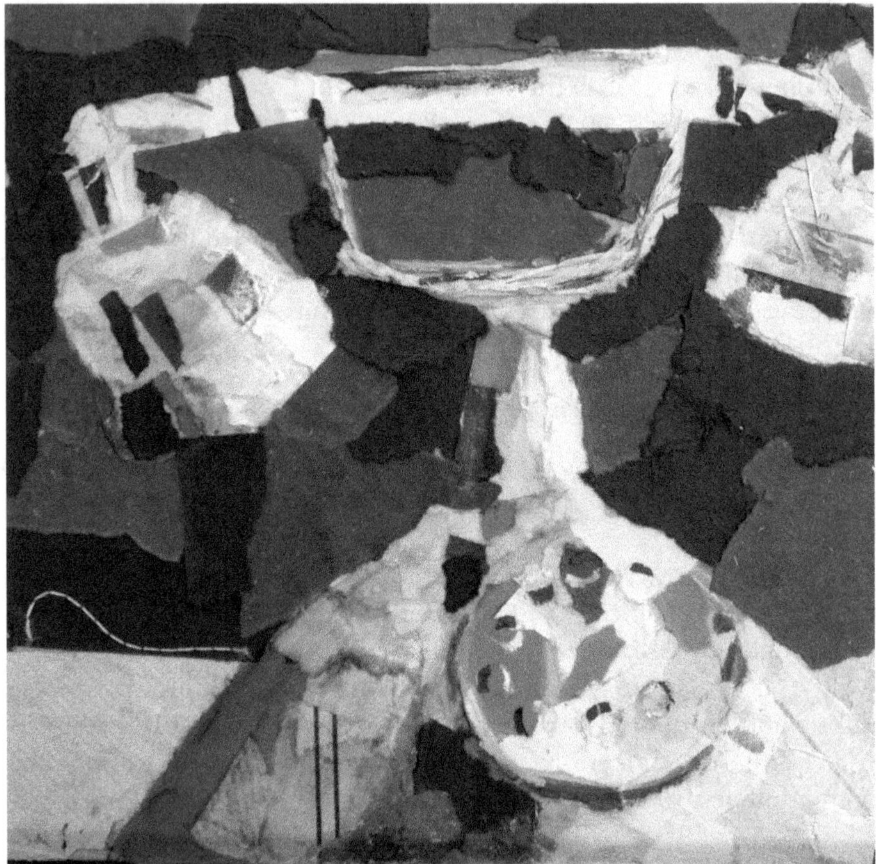

"Waiting for the Call" by Nichole A. Ryder

Sometimes we may have a "knowing," about something we did not know before. I ran into a rest stop along the interstate and saw a man. I immediately "knew" he was a politician. I asked him, and he confirmed it. I was able to encourage him because the Lord gave me a word of knowledge about him. The Bible says,

"We have the mind of Christ." That means, we can know things we would not know in the natural mind. We can ask to think His thoughts, feel His desires, know whom He wants us to minister to, what He wants us to pray, and what He wants us to paint or create.

> *"When he, the Spirit of truth, comes, he will guide you into all truth. He will not speak on his own; he will speak only what he hears, and he will tell you what is yet to come. He will bring glory to me by taking from what is mine and making it known to you." John 16:13-14.*

In this verse, God promises that, through the Holy Spirit, "He will tell us what is yet to come." This means getting revelation from God about the future. The verse says that it brings glory to Jesus. If God wants, He can have you paint, (write, sculpt, etc.) about something that has not yet happened.

Jesus said in John 10, that His sheep know His voice. If you are one of His sheep, you should learn to recognize His voice. In Jer. 33:3 it says,

> *"Call to me and I will answer you and tell you great and unsearchable things you do not know."*

When we call, God promises to answer us and tell us great things, things we could not possibly know in the natural. I have asked God things, and softly heard an answer. This is dialogue, an interaction with God. It is important that we have relationship with Him, and talk with Him regularly. In my marriage, if my husband didn't talk to me for a week, he would be in big trouble. God wants relationship. He wants us to:

> *"Ask and it will be given to you; seek and you will find; knock and the door will be opened to you," Matt. 7:7.*

He wants us to open the dialogue and in turn, He will speak to us. If this is difficult for you, there are books you can find on hearing God more clearly, some are referenced at the end of this book. Dialoguing with God is the best way to learn His voice. He loves us longs to have relationship with us.

GOD SPEAKS THROUGH HIS PEOPLE

My pastor can preach a sermon, and I feel God wrote it just for me. God speaks through godly people in our lives. In the book of Proverbs God tells us to listen to our parents and to wise counsel. Some people have the gift of prophecy and we can hear a more focused word from the Lord through their gift. God wants to remind us that we are the body of Christ and that we need each other, so He uses other people in the Church to speak a word to us. In Proverbs. 24:6 it says,

> *"For by wise guidance you will wage war, And in abundance of counselors there is victory."*

We need the guidance and instruction of people in our life who hear from the Lord.

DREAMS AND VISIONS

When I was in fourth grade the Lord showed me this dream: I was small, and the Lord was huge. I was about the size of His thumb. On His lap was the Book of Life and He was paging through it searching for my name. I was trying to jump into the book because I knew I was not in there, but kept sliding off the pages. Finally, He closed the book and I woke. I realized that I had not made a commitment to the Lord. I got up out of my bed, went into the dark living room and gave my life to Him. That was the day He wrote my name in the book of life. Dreams are a very important method to receiving instructions from the Lord. In the book of Job it says,

> *"For God does speak—now one way, now another— though man may not perceive it. In a dream, in a vision of the night, when deep sleep falls on men as they slumber in their beds, he may speak in their ears and terrify them with warnings, to turn man from wrongdoing and keep him from pride, to preserve his soul from the pit, his life from perishing by the sword." Job 33:14-18.*

God speaks to us in our dreams to give warnings to keep us from making the wrong decisions, to turn us from bad behavior, to keep us from being pompous, prideful, and preserve us when the devil is out to kill us. God gives us instructions that help us in life. It is a great gift! In Joel 2 it says,

> *"I will pour out my Spirit on all people. Your sons and daughters will prophesy, your old men will dream dreams, your young men will see visions. Even on my servants, both men and women, I will pour out my Spirit in those days."*

In this prophetic verse, God promises to send His Spirit and we will all prophesy and have dreams and visions. Throughout the Bible, God gave directions to His people through dreams. Joseph was given prophetic dreams and interpretation that saved people from famine. God warned Joseph and Mary to go to Egypt to protect Jesus. He warned the wise men not to go back to Herod. From the beginning of the Bible to end, God spoke through dreams and He can speak to you through them too.

Let God speak to you, write down what you dream and ask God to give you revelation to interpret. There are useful Christian books on dream interpretation that help tremendously and they provide Biblical meanings to the symbolism found in dreams.

Jesus himself saw dreams or visions from the Father in order to accomplish the Father's will. He was fully man and was limited by the same limitations we have. He used the prophetic just like we do, to hear from God. The Father "showed" Him things:

> *"I tell you the truth, the Son can do nothing by himself; he can do only what he sees his Father doing, because whatever the Father does the Son also does. For the Father loves the Son and shows him all he does. Yes, to your amazement he will show him even greater things than these." John 5:19-20.*

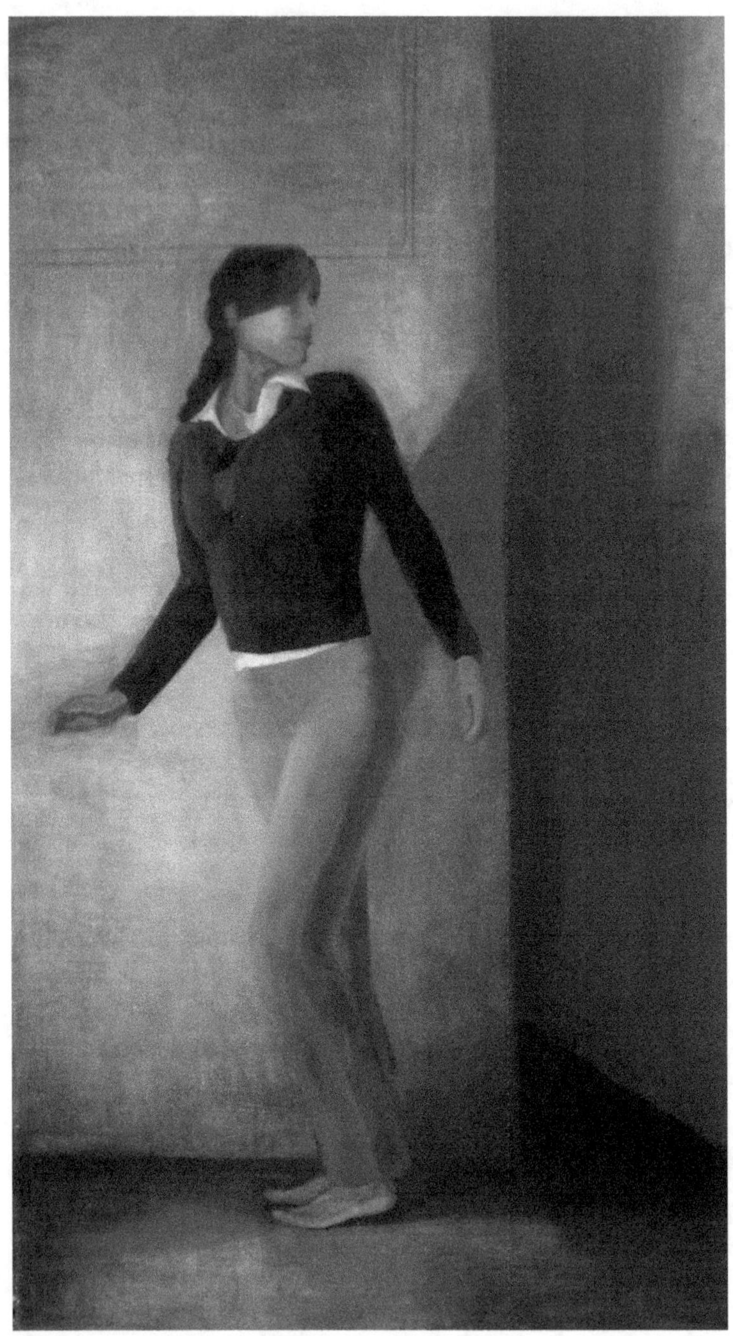

"The Voice of the Lord Behind Me" by Amanda A. Flowers

The simple truth is that God tells or shows us what to do for the advancement of the kingdom. Generals give orders to those under them so they can take new territory. We need to get our orders from the King of Kings. God wants to give prophetic revelation for our art and creativity. He wants to use it to minister His love to others.

ANGELS

Throughout the Bible God spoke through angels, and He still uses His servants today. Many people now testify of having an encounter with an angel. They are sent with messages from the Lord. I have not seen one with my natural eyes, but have seen them in visions. In Hebrews 1:14 it says,

> *"Are not all angels ministering spirits sent to serve those who will inherit salvation?"*

They are assigned to minister to us and serve. They are sent by God and are used by Him and some even help with our art. I have heard that there are angels of creativity, or angels for writing ability. In one dream, God sent an angel to help me get organized in my writing (I really needed it). I had piles of random information with no clear order to any of it. At an arts conference, someone saw a colorful angel behind me, they said was sent for my creativity. God still speaks and uses angels today.

PROPHECY

The gift of prophecy is still used by God to speak to the body of Christ. In the Old Testament prophets were also called seers. 1 Sam. 9:9 tells us,

> *"Formerly in Israel, if a man went to inquire of God, he would say, 'Come, let us go to the seer,' because the prophet of today used to be called a seer."*

The prophets would "see," or have visions from God and this is still a way God speaks to us today. There are people hungry to understand and hear God. Many attend conferences and schools that now teach "The Prophetic." Our three children attended Morningstar School of Ministry, a school which taught them how to hear from God more clearly. We can all press in and ask for more prophetic gifting. In 1 Cor. 14:1 it says,

> *"Follow the way of love and eagerly desire spiritual gifts, especially the gift of prophecy."*

1 Corinthians 13, tells us to seek love above everything. We are supposed to "eagerly desire" the gift of prophecy. Dig in and study some books on the prophetic, attend conferences, press in for this gift. Ask, and it will be given to you. We minister prophecy out of love to others. Love is the framework that supports all the gifts and ministry, without it, our efforts are a clanging cymbal or quite useless and even annoying.

God can use prophetic revelation to speak to us to guide our art and show us what to paint or create. Press in and ask for more, He really wants to give good gifts to His children.

MIRACULOUS SIGNS

God also speaks through unusual events or signs. The Bible is filled with miraculous signs like the dove that Noah sent out and came back with the branch of green leaves. God used a burning bush, He proved Himself through Elijah calling down fire from heaven, and the manna testified of God's provision for His people. Jesus demonstrated His authority through the miracles and signs He performed. Signs speak to us and they also declare the glory of God.

When my husband, Paul, and I were members of a very traditional church, we were hungry to know the Holy Spirit. We were talking in our kitchen one night questioning who the Holy Spirit really was. We had the kitchen blinds open, and a white dove landed on a phone wire outside. Our yard light lit him up like he was on a stage with a spotlight. It was not a pigeon, it was a pure white dove. It is no coincidence that when we were on a spiritual quest, searching for the Holy Spirit, God sent a sign, the dove, that He lit up like Christmas. He may show people signs all the time, but we pass it off as coincidence. Step out in faith and believe that He is talking to you. Believe in the supernatural, miraculous ways of God.

Just a few years ago, another strange thing happened. My husband is a director of a drug and alcohol program and the women in the program were looking at a sunset from their window. The clouds formed into the shape of three angels, then one of the angels turned toward them. They saw his wings lift and drop. All of the women were moved by God, and immediately feel to their knees in prayer, knowing it was a sign in the heavens sent from the Lord. Daniels tells us:

> *"He rescues and He saves; He performs signs and wonders in the heavens and on the earth." Dan. 6:27.*

Throughout the Bible, God demonstrated His power through miracles, revealing His nature and His great love for us. God can still speak to us through miraculous signs; He has not changed.

OUR SENSES

God can also speak to us through our senses. He can speak to us through our smell, taste, feelings, touch, hearing, and seeing. God wants us to listen with all of our senses. One time during a closing on a house, I got this overwhelming feeling. My spiritual senses were screaming at me and I wanted to run out of the room. I did not know it, but my husband felt the same way. We both ignored it and signed the papers. Shortly after we purchased the property that we intended to fix and flip, the market flopped. We lost thousands of dollars and wasted our time. Had we listened to

God speaking to us through our "feelings" in that meeting, we would have been much better off.

Another time, while I was driving, I had an overwhelming sense that cars were driving recklessly and someone was going to hit me. I prayed for protection. Several miles down the road, I stopped at a light turning red, and I was rear-ended. If I had not prayed, I could have been injured or worse. The car could have pushed me into the oncoming traffic.

God also speaks through the gift of discernment, which can operate similarly to "feeling" something. Have you ever met someone and had a bad feeling immediately about him? Paul, my husband, works with street people and addicts. He can "read" people and know things about them. It is the gift of discernment. He has also tasted alcohol in his mouth when he met certain people. God revealed to him that they were alcoholics.

Some people have smelled fragrance during worship; it was God speaking to them through their sense of smell. God can use smell to demonstrate who He is to us. In any of our senses, we should be "listening" to Him. Don't ever doubt that He wants to speak to you, and He will do it any way He wishes! Ask Him what the smell signifies. Dialogue with Him.

Sometimes, we can be fully in the Spirit with our senses locked into "receive mode" from the Lord. We may not be "hearing" with our ears, but all our senses are on high alert. In this state, we might paint, or do other prophetic actions. We may just have a "knowing" of what action to take, and our senses are guiding the direction. This can even get deeper, into a trance state. This is when the Holy Spirit takes over and there is less of you and your flesh and more of Him. We allow ourselves to be overcome by His presence. Surrender to feeling Him and do not be afraid of what He wants to do. There is so much more revelation as we let ourselves go to this place in Him.

CIRCUMSTANCES

God uses circumstances, or situations that some would say was chance, to get our attention and speak to us. Some may think it is coincidence when they accidently drop a jar of oil on the floor. It is probably God telling you that if you are not careful, the anointing (oil) will slip from your fingers. God is speaking all the time. Do not ignore these odd occurrences. If your mind suddenly thinks, "boy, that was very random," at some odd event, question the Lord immediately and ask if He was saying something to you. The Holy Spirit will bring things to your attention and teach you through these random events.

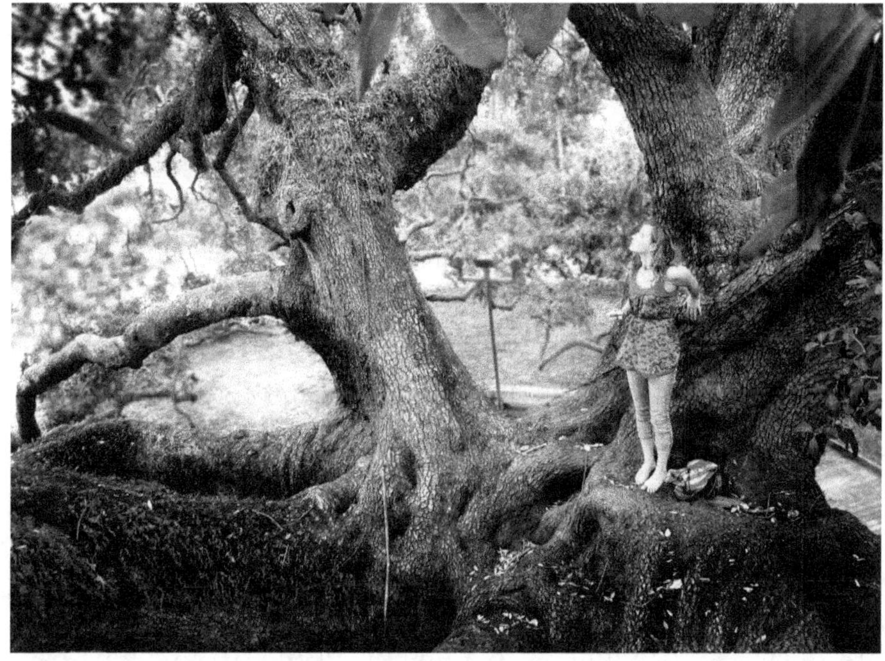

"Secret Place" By Nichole A. Ryder

HOW TO HEAR FROM GOD

The most logical way to hear from God is to sit in the throne room. What that means practically, is going after the heart and presence of God with all your heart, soul, mind and strength. It means worshipping, and loving the Father, getting to know Him personally. Pursue Him. He promises you will find Him.

> *"I love those who love me, and those who seek me find me." Proverbs 8:17*

We are in a love pursuit of God. We get revelation based on intimacy and relationship with the Father. Another verse that gives exact direction on how the process works is in Habakkuk:

> *"I will stand at my watch and station myself on the ramparts; I will look to see what he will say to me, and what answer I am to give to this complaint. . .*
>
> *Then the LORD replied: "Write down the revelation and make it plain on tablets so that a herald may run with it. For the revelation awaits an appointed time; it speaks of the end and will not prove false. Though it linger, wait for it; it will certainly come and will not delay." Hab. 2:1-3*

First, Habakkuk was standing his watch as an intercessor. He was in the place of his assignment, "At my watch and station." We need to be where God has assigned us to be. This means you must be in the exact city, and neighborhood that is your station. You can also be an intercessor for a distant country, but be on your spiritual station praying for them. Habakkuk was looking for a word or vision from the Lord, "I will look to see what He will say to me." He was seeking understanding regarding the rise of the evil in the world around him (see Hab. 1). Habakkuk was grieved at wrongdoing, idolatry and the prosperity of the wicked. He was pursuing revelation for the people of the Lord. The Lord responded by giving revelation, or chazown, the Hebrew word meaning a vision.

The Lord told him to write the vision down and herald it, proclaiming the message. As artists, we write down what we see in the form of drawings or paintings. We are the Visual Prophets of the Lord. Some people record the word of the Lord in writings, or poetry. The Prophet Kim Clement releases his revelation in song.

Next, the Lord said to Habakkuk, "The revelation awaits an appointed time." Our job is to release the revelation. Fulfillment may be in another time period because God's timeline is not the same as ours, it will happen in His time. This is the clearest outline for God's revelation. Pray for the people, situation and countries that the Lord puts on your heart. Then dialogue with God and ask for revelation! "You may ask me for anything in my name, and I will do it," John 14:14. Revelation builds on revelation. It gets deeper as we ponder what He as given us, and then He gives us more.

Dig for more from Him; cry out for insight. Go in hot pursuit as if you were looking for hidden treasure:

> *"My son, if you accept my words and store up my commands within you, turning your ear to wisdom and applying your heart to understanding—indeed, if you call out for insight and cry aloud for understanding, and if you look for it as for silver and search for it as for hidden treasure, then you will understand the fear of the LORD and find the knowledge of God. For the LORD gives wisdom; from his mouth come knowledge and understanding." Prov. 2:1-6.*

On one occasion, I misplaced a special ring my husband gave me. It is a beautiful sapphire ring, with six diamonds. What do you think I did? I searched every pocket, every drawer, and every purse until I found it. I could not sleep well until I recovered my "treasure." It was a priority. I have to admit I got a little frantic in pursuit of recovering it. God wants us to have urgency in our pursuit of His treasures of wisdom, revelation, knowledge and understanding. Seek it! Cry aloud for it!

If you are baptized in the Holy Spirit, revelation will come easier. Talk to Him and ask Him questions. If you are going to paint something for Him, ask what He wants you to paint. He may show you a vision. I believe praying in tongues stirs up our spirit, and draws us "In the Spirit" like John in the Book of Revelation. We are reminded in Ephesians:

> *"And pray in the Spirit on all occasions with all kinds of prayers and requests," Eph. 6:18.*

Some of my richest revelations from the Lord are just from sitting, praying in tongues, and rocking. It looks like the bobbing the Jewish men do. We met Sid Roth at a meeting years ago, and he told my husband and I to pray in tongues everyday. I pray with my mind or worship, while I pray in tongues. If you pray in tongues everyday, it stirs up the gift of the Holy Spirit within and opens you up to the spiritual things of God, the prophetic, visions, and hearing God clearer.

Worship Him! He loves to reveal things to us during worship. Take a sketch journal with you and record what the Lord is saying. Spend time in a prayer room and wait on the Lord. You will also hear Him when you read the Bible, as you listen to His voice. Dialogue with the Lord. A picture may come to mind as you read, and you just "know" you are supposed to paint it. A theme from the Bible may hang on you, and you feel compelled (led by the Holy Spirit) to paint it or write a poem or song about it.

As I mentioned before, always be ready to receive revelation in dreams. Keep a dream journal by your bed. Write down everything. Some people do not write down anything in the night that seems confusing, or is a piece of a dream (they forgot most of the dream). Trust me, write down what you remember and look at the information you wrote down in the daytime. The Holy Spirit can reveal information even from little faint memories of dreams. I have gotten revelation that have changed my life from one or two sentences of prophetic instructions that were remnants of dreams. Ask the Lord to reveal things for your art, He will be faithful. He longs to find willing servants who are ready to listen to Him.

Listen all day, every day. He is speaking. While you are making dinner, or driving, He is speaking! He wants to share things with you. He loves you and enjoys relationship with you. Maybe you are going to do a still life painting and certain objects may jump out at you, trust that the Lord is speaking. Experiment and play with Him. Learn to hear Him. Ask Him what colors to use, and then wait, and get revelation. Feel the Holy Spirit guide your motions, your words, your music.

I pray that the Lord would enlighten the eyes of your heart with the Spirit of wisdom and revelation and you would know your calling and inheritance:

> *"I keep asking that the God of our Lord Jesus Christ, the glorious Father, may give you the Spirit of wisdom and revelation, so that you may know him better. I pray that the eyes of your heart may be enlightened in order that you may know the hope to which he has called you, the riches of his glorious inheritance in his holy people, and his incomparably great power for us who believe."* *Eph. 1:17-19.*

Follow my blogs or Facebook page for more information and videos related to prophetic art.

My web page: www.shadowpainter.org
Facebook page: The Shadow Painter.
My poetry and creative writings:
EverydaySonnets.wordpress.com

CHAPTER 8

GOD'S UNIQUE VISUAL LANGUAGE

When I first started having visions, I was in shock. I had no idea what they meant. I sketched them in my journal and wondered what I was going to do with these random images. Soon, I found a good Biblical dream interpretation book and it helped tremendously (The book is listed in the resource section). That year, our whole family started having dreams and visions regularly and we sought God's help in interpreting them.

I remember the day we first successfully figured out one of the complicated dreams. The light bulb came on, Wow! God is really speaking to us! Nichole had a very visual, confusing dream. In the dream a schoolmate was putting on red lipstick while sitting on a picnic bench. We asked the Lord what the red-lipstick meant. The Holy Spirit told us it was a warning about gossip at the lunch table. God was warning Nichole and she was listening. The very next day, the same girl in the dream randomly sat with Nichole at her lunch table and began gossiping and Nichole was ready to shut it off immediately. She did not take the bait. She would not make any comments and avoided the conversation. It was amazing! God cared about what was happening in her everyday life! He was leading her to be holy. He was guiding her in how to avoid problems and the wave of gossip that was sweeping through the school. We cracked the code on our first dream, and we were hooked. God dazzled us with His love, and His concern for the details of our lives and we fell more in love with Him.

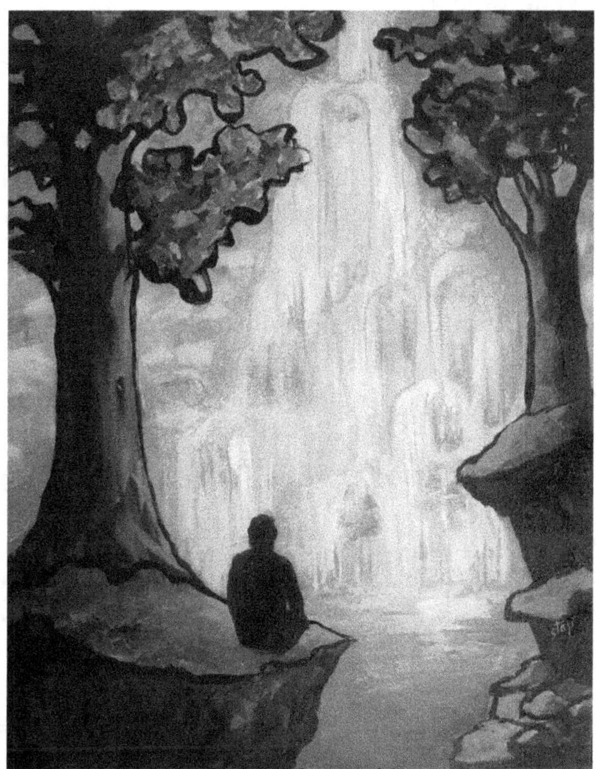

"Time to Get off the Edge and Jump In"
By Laurie A. Stasi

During the summer, Nichole and I spent time every day interpreting dreams. God was teaching us His language. He wants to engage us, and for us to pursue Him. He said, "It is the glory of God to conceal a matter, and the glory of kings to seek it out," Prov. 25:2. He conceals, and He calls us kings when we seek out an interpretation for what He is saying. All throughout the Bible God spoke in dreams, visions, and parables. Daniel and Joseph were noted for their gift in understanding dreams. We can have that same gift as the Holy Spirit guides us to understand God's prophetic language.

When we want to understand the interpretation of what He has given us, the first place to look for understanding is the Bible. Many things you have seen in dreams or visions may be explained in scripture. For example, an olive tree represents Israel. But you will find that there are things from your dreams that you will not locate in the Bible. Buy a good Biblical dream interpretation book. It will be very helpful. You may still question the exact meaning of particular objects or scenes; ask the Holy Spirit to determine what it represents. He guides us and we receive confirmation from Him when we are interpreting revelation correctly.

Some objects or events in dreams represent something personal to you in your life. In some of my dreams the setting is in Chicago because what it represents to me personally having been raised in the suburbs there. Ask yourself, what does this objects (situation) mean to me? Some people like cats, and it represents companionship, or something positive in their dreams. Others dislike felines, and the meaning for their dreams is quite different and may even represent witchcraft. One orange cat in our neighborhood reminds me of an old TV show cat on a program "Early Edition." In the show, the main character "Gary" would open the door in the morning and find the cat sitting on a newspaper, with news that was one day early. So, to me, that cat represents the prophetic. The Lord has a dream and communication language that is specific to each one of us. It is based on relationship. He knows everything about you, intimately. Every little detail of your life matters to the Lord. He uses elements from your life to speak to you.

Be diligent in seeking out interpretation. He who is faithful, much more will be given. God will continue to give you guidance, instruction and rebuke in your dreams and visions. If you are faithful to seek them out, much more will be given! Understanding the language and images of dreams directly affects our work as prophetic artists.

When we ask for a vision for a painting, you may not know the interpretation. Go ahead and paint it. There may be someone else who will interpret it. The Bible says that there are some who speak in tongues, and others who have the gift of interpretation of tongues. The same applies to prophetic art. Sometimes when I paint something, someone else comes along and tells me what it means. Others may be given a deep understanding of what God is trying to say and have a message to give. The body of Christ is in unity when we all take part in it.

There are times when you understand perfectly what God is saying and as you paint it, you 'feel' the interpretation in your spirit. You become like a mother who understands her child better than anyone else. That painting was birthed through you and you understand perfectly the deep message that God is trying to say. You may have opportunity to share this revelation with others.

Jesus said, "How shall we picture the kingdom of God or by what parable shall we present it?" Mark 4:30. Jesus knew He was presenting parables as 'pictures,' much the way we as visual artists present pictures that can be like the parables. Several other arts areas that are presented like parables are writing, drama or videos. There are wonderful movies that are powerful parables for our day.

Jesus explained the purpose of speaking in parables to His disciples. It was so the people would be "ever seeing and never perceiving." He intentionally spoke in parables and riddles, with the intent that some would not understand the hidden meaning. God loves interacting with us as we dig deep and seek to know His truth. The treasure is for those who are hungry enough to pursue it.

When we use symbolism in our art, we present ideas as a riddle, as something that people have to think about and it challenges them. If you watch people walk through an art museum, the paintings that are clearly presented and easy to comprehend they walk right by. They glance at it for about one second, literally. But when there is a painting that is not straight forward, with layers of hidden meanings, or a combination of images that makes the viewer question, "what is going on here?" then they stop and really look. Their mind has been challenged. That is God's approach to giving revelation. He loves to make us stop and contemplate.

Jesus used parables in a day when storytelling was probably an art form. They did not have TV or videos. He was creating word pictures in their minds. He used settings they could relate to; a farm and sowing seed, a house and lost coins. God wants us to relate to His revelation. He wants us to connect to what He is saying. He gives images in our dreams that we can relate to. As artists, we want people to connect with what we are illustrating. Be creative and present picture parables relevant to our culture. For instance, in a drama you can write a script about someone craving Starbucks to represent craving more of the Lord. Another example would be to use situations that are culturally relevant to our audience, like being confused and misunderstood like characters in "The Office."

Christians with a "religious spirit" are often afraid to be relevant to our culture. A few years ago, I had a "religious spirit" and disliked Christmas trees because of their ancient pagan roots. Then the Lord gave me a dream, using a Christmas tree in the "storyline" to show Him blessing someone. I questioned the Lord, "How can you use a pagan symbol to represent your goodness?" Well, He straightened me out. He told me He was not as condemning as I was. The Pharisees made extra laws and rules, which were only bondage. I had made a judgment on which Christmas symbols were correct. I had to get rid of my personal rules and realize the Lord was not as uptight as me. Of course, we don't want to cave in to filth from our world, remember that holiness is our guide and we don't want to lead others into sin. Find the middle of the road, where the ditch on the right is the self-righteous Pharisee thinking, and the left is the worldly, sinful ditch. The middle is the path of holiness. Be relevant and righteous in your art. Use dialogue that relates to your audience.

God's language is so incredibly, visually rich. The Bible has many stories that could be acted out, illustrated or painted. Have you read the Bible and 'pictured' the story? The Father loves to let us "see" the Bible in visions and in creativity.

Seek to know God and His language. Spend time with Him. He will reveal His heart to you and you may 'feel' what He feels. If you are a visual artist, you must press for more revelation and understanding. As we press, sometimes He even speaks clearly! There is one verse I love, it says,

> *"Though I have been speaking figuratively, a time is coming when I will no longer use this kind of language but will tell you plainly about my Father," John 16:25. (italics added)*

When this happens, it is so beautiful and intimate. How amazing to have a conversation with Him, the God of the Universe! I believe as we near the end times, more of our conversations will be plain and our understanding clear. Moses spoke with God this way;

> *"With him I speak face to face, clearly and not in riddles; he sees the form of the LORD," Numbers 12:8.*

This should be our prayer, to hear God clearly and not in riddles, and even see the form of the Lord. Keep pressing, and ask. Seek Him for guidance in all your creative endeavors and let Him speak and flow through you.

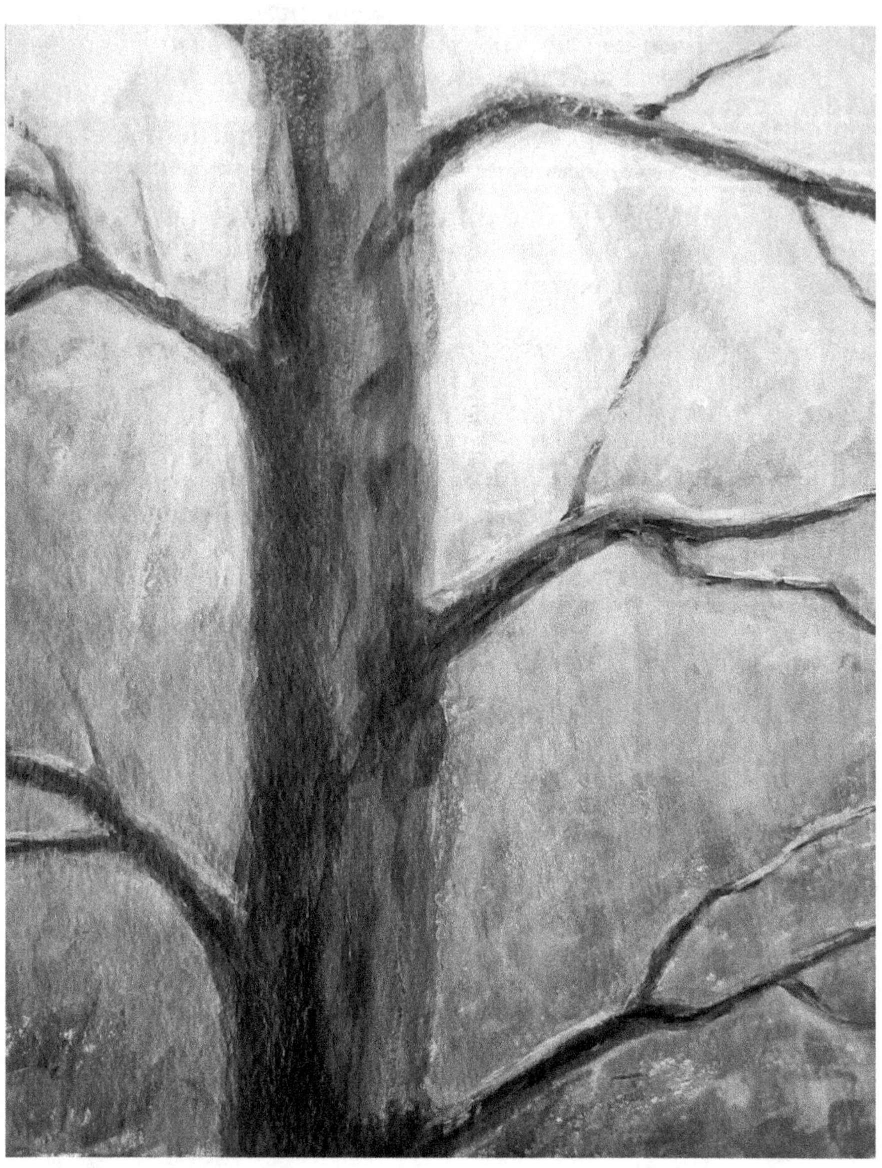

LADDER #1 by Laurie A. Stasi. This was my first vision of a ladder. I have seen over 100 different types of Jacob's ladders or stairways in visions. They represent accessing the heavenly realm. There are many ways to go up. Sometimes it is like climbing a tree as you did when you were a child. It can be playful! You must come like a child. This one would be very easy to climb; the branches lead you right up!

CHAPTER 9 TRANSFORMING SPIRITUAL PRINCIPLES

We have to be spiritually minded and seek to understand the spiritual realm. The principles of that realm are different from the flesh realm. We must comprehend the activity of angels and demons and understand the wars that go on and the spiritual battles and plans of the enemy. Learn spiritual principals and the way things are in heaven. We are operating as sons and daughters seated in heavenly places. There are both a physical realm and a spiritual realm that we are living in. We need the Spirit to guide us in the things of the spirit. Understanding these principles will affect our art and creativity. The following section includes examples of some spiritual principles that apply to our creativity:

ACTING IN FAITH

> *"And without faith it is impossible to please God, because anyone who comes to him must believe that he exists and that he rewards those who earnestly seek him," Hebrews 11:6.*

We need faith to live prophetically and receive from Him. This takes childlike faith and playing in the Spirit. Since we have the power of the Holy Spirit within us, we must go with what He is doing, and not override it with our rational thought. His power can manifest in us, and give us physical sensations. We have to think and act on them. Some of these things might be messages for our art, our writing, dance, music, etc.

We must believe that our prophetic actions, which are led from the Lord, have an effect in the spiritual realm. Elisha told Jehoash to take some arrows and strike them to the ground. This was not just a prophetic message. How many times he struck them to the ground had an effect in the spiritual realm. But he only struck them three times, so he would only defeat his enemy three times, and not totally destroy them. Our actions, as led by the Lord, instigate actions and effect in the spiritual realm; they dispense angels and they break strongholds. They can release the Lord's will. This is a spiritual principle that prophetic artists should be willing to pursue. It takes faith to follow through on God's direction.

SHADOWS

Hebrews 8:5 it says that the sanctuary on earth was a shadow or copy of what is in heaven. It says that the pattern for the tabernacle was given to Moses. That is the spiritual principle prophetic artists act upon. We are given a vision, which can be like a pattern, and we create a copy here on earth. The earthly copy has many purposes, as discussed in earlier chapters. It takes spiritual wisdom to believe and create this kind of prophetic art.

HEAVENLY REALITY

The actions and visitations we have, in a trance or vision from the Lord, are more real than our world or what we call "reality." This is a prophetic principle that we need to get deep in our gut, so that we learn to live more in God's spiritual realm than our own fleshly realm. Interacting in a trance can release God's message and purpose. Ezekiel and John both were given a scroll to eat, which tasted as sweet as honey, but turned their stomach sour. This was the taste of the prophetic message they were to give to the people. They ate and carried the message. They interacted with all mankind when they followed the Lord's directions in the heavenly realm from the visions and God manifested it upon the earth.

IF YOU SEE IT, YOU CAN ACCESS IT

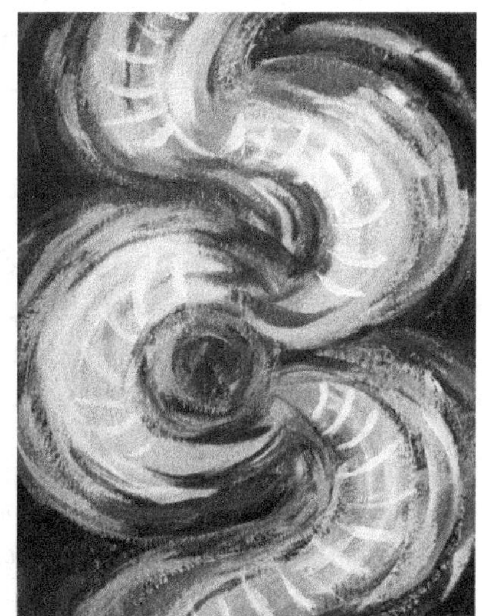

The Lord has taken different individuals to the body parts room in heaven. This is a place where the parts, like arms, or eyes are stored until they are released for people who need miraculous replacements. This room demonstrates that God wants to heal and deliver new body parts for people's healing. Once you accept and have faith for the heavenly reality, you can access it here on earth. This is a spiritual principle. When Jesus shows you something, He is giving you access to it. If I see something that God wants others to access, and I paint that thing, it helps them receive it. For example, if I am in a meeting and I see a vision of keys that Jesus is giving out. I paint the keys for other to see. They view them and can receive them in faith. What we see in a vision, we can access.

PRAYER ACTIVATES

God wants us to pray to release His will. Using the previous example of the vision of the keys, we should pray, "Jesus, please release the keys and open doors!" Prayer activates the Lord's will. We can speak to dry bones and prophecy life to them and our art can do the same. You can use art to prophecy over a person. You can speak by faith and also paint by faith and release with prayer.

GOD IS THE ARCHITECT

Pastor Ron Carpenter once said, "God is an Architect, not a Builder...He gives you the PATTERN, then YOU take action and build it." This puts the responsibility for construction into our hands. We are assigned to fulfill the mission on the earth. Creation is groaning and waiting for us to take action.

CREATIVITY FLOWS THROUGH US

We are to be Jesus' hands and feet as His disciples. We are to minister to others with the power of Jesus flowing through us. We release His healing, love and forgiveness. This same principle applies to His creativity. As we read in Colossians, all things have been created through Him:

> *"For in him all things were created: things in heaven and on earth, visible and invisible, whether thrones or powers or rulers or authorities; all things have been created through him and for him. He is before all things, and in him all things hold together." Col. 1:16-17.*

I believe there is a creative flow, from Jesus, that is released through us. People can have creative miracles because we have, "Christ in me, the hope of Glory," Col. 1:27. And, "the Spirit of him who raised Jesus from the dead is living in you," Rom. 8:11. The God of the universe lives in us. Picture it as a limitless power and creativity. If God prophetically guides us, we can create just like He did. I am almost afraid to think of the possibilities. I do not want to overstep my bounds, but Jesus said to us,

> *"Believe me when I say that I am in the Father and the Father is in me; or at least believe on the evidence of the works themselves. Very truly I tell you, whoever believes in me will do the works I*

have been doing, and they will do even greater things than these, because I am going to the Father. And I will do whatever you ask in my name, so that the Father may be glorified in the Son. You may ask me for anything in my name, and I will do it." John 14:11-14.

Jesus knew that the Father was in Him, and He was in the Father. We are also in Jesus and He is in us. Understanding this concept is crucial to attaining "greater things than these" that Jesus promised and "Christ in us, the hope of Glory." It is when we spiritually accept the truth and revelation of Christ in us, we access His glory. Jesus said that He only did what His Father showed Him. We must only do what the Father shows us. This is obedience and sacrifice. In that place, if He reveals something He wants to create, or a creative healing, we will see it manifest in the natural. He is Elohim, which means "Creator." He can flow creatively through us. All things are possible.

THE SOUND OF PRAISE

Our sounds, and voices echo and continue to testify endlessly, because sound continues to travel continuously into creation. Our praise continues. It makes an eternal testimony. In the study of Physics, they have found sound waves recorded in rocks. Jesus said that the rocks would cry out if man did not worship Him. There is praise contained in inanimate objects, and all of creation contains praise. Our art can contain praise. Our art can contain anointing. Our art is created and also is displayed in heaven. Our movements are recorded forever. Our art can prophesy and bring things into existence.

We know that the tabernacle in heaven is more real than the earthly one was. The paintings in heaven are more real than the earthly ones. They testify of God's greatness and bring glory to the Father.

GLOBAL RELEASE

Sometimes there are prophetic words that are for the body of Christ in many locations, possibly even globally. God may be speaking the same thing to you in your prayer closet as He is speaking to people in Chicago or Tokyo. These are Global Messages from the Lord. For example, I saw a prophetic artist post on Facebook of her painting of a horse. It was quite beautiful, and many people were drawn to it. The Lord started showing me horses in my dreams the next day. Then another artist posted a prophetic word from Chuck Pierce released two days prior and posted on Facebook:

> "I have a new way for you to leap over that which has been in front of you, a new way for you to go over and into that next phase that I have called you into. I have a new way. I have a new horse for you to ride. It is not the horse of the flesh but the ruling white horse of My Spirit. Get ready to mount up, for I have an army that is not confused. I have an army that I am mobilizing. I have a team of warriors that will now win the war! I am releasing royal horses of war, royal horses that have been prepared for the day of battle. They are made of My invisible, invincible power which is holiness. If you will mount up on My royal war horses you will move with power and distinction. You will be audacious in the victories you will win as I blow My wind over you." Prophetic Word by Chuck Pierce on Monday, February 6, 2012 at 7:57am.

Many times God wants to get His bride in unity and have them thinking about what is on His heart. He desires for us to more forward with Him. He whispers these same thoughts to different people for them to share and proclaim to those around them. Once, in my church in Florida, I heard a message that was clearly a "now" word of the Lord. I traveled to Chicago and visited a different, non-spirit filled denomination, and the pastor was preaching the same message. The Lord speaks to His children globally with some prophetic words and we can play a part in releasing it through our creativity, songs, and social media.

PROPHETIC TIMING

The prophetic is a wonderful gift, and many artists (and most Christians), don't understand the mystery of its timing. There are some who believe they must receive a vision the day they are painting at a church meeting, otherwise it is not a "now" word for the church. It seems many Spirit-filled pastors believe this also. When I began in the prophetic, I wondered about this timing issue and asked the Lord about it. I had been giving short words of knowledge to women in my weekly Bible Study. I wrote about two sentences on a piece of paper that was a little bigger than a fortune cookie message for each of the women. I found that it gave them a very personal note from the Lord who loves them. The women treasured these little statements, and even kept them in their Bibles.

One week, I knew I would be very busy, so I asked the Lord to give me words for the women a week ahead of time. I asked Him again about timing, "Is this okay, is it going to be accurate a week ahead of time?" The first vision He showed me was for Doris. She was pouring coffee for others. I recorded what I saw added wrote that Doris poured herself out for others, giving love to them. I continued to ask for words for each of the women and wrote them down. I arrived the next week and the women very anxious and immediately asked for their prophetic words. I opened the first one for Doris, and said, "Doris was pouring coffee out for others..." As I said this, everyone looked at Doris, who was standing, quite shocked, holding a coffee pot pouring coffee into little Styrofoam cups for the women in the group. (Normally we would just pass the coffee pot.) I wish you could have seen their faces and heard their reactions. We all marveled at God's perfect timing!! They could hardly believe it, and I was amazed that God answered my question through a beautiful demonstration about His timing of prophetic revelation.

God can speak to us and it will be a now moment in His timing. As we grow and operate in the prophetic, we have to remember His timelessness and keep it in mind when we minister His revelation. I recently opened up a five year old journal I used to record what the Lord was showing me, and found current revelation tucked on the page for the day I re-found it. I had been questioning weather I should take time to blog on a particular matter, and there was a prophetic word given to me years ago, saying I would share with others on that particular subject. God's timing is amazing!

Our minds are so linked to clocks and calendars; we have to change our time perception and think the way He thinks. We see time on a linear plane, one day at a time. God sees the whole plane at the same time. The very nature of prophecy emphasizes the fact that God knows the future. Words of knowledge prove He knows people's present and past. If we are going to be His prophets, we have to understand these principles and have the flexibility to use the prophetic this way.

Getting training in the prophetic will help you grow in your understanding and in the gift of the prophetic. Find books that will help you grow your gift (there are some listed in the appendix). "Eagerly desire the spiritual gifts, especially the gift of prophecy," 1 Cor. 14:1. Hunger and pursue this anointing and God is faithful and will generously give it.

In 2007, Rick Joyner prophesied regarding art, "There is a power in art that the Church has not generally recognized for many centuries now. It must be recovered because the Lord is going to give the artists in His house unprecedented power to prophesy through their art....the highest art of mankind will come from a love for God" (Joyner). God wants to release this power! Our love for God is key and should be placed at the highest priority in our lives.

CHAPTER 10 RECLAIMING THE ARTS

Many years ago my husband, Paul and I were at a Christian, social work conference. All the attendees were given free passes to a play. We did not go to plays often and I was excited. I put on a dress in anticipation of evening of elegant entertainment. We arrived and settled in plush seats. Dramatically, the velvet curtain rolled aside and we were drawn into the make believe world displayed before us.

Within minutes, the enjoyment turned sour as the story unfolded. The plot was about witches who were required to kill someone. In a cloak of lighthearted comedy, a sinister evil was forming before us as the characters plotted murder. The storyline was about the inner workings of a coven, evil at its worst, but presented in a way to have people receive it. The audience laughed at the dark jokes, and my stomach flopped. I desperately wanted to run. I have low spiritual tolerance for anything to do with witches, the demonic, anything perverted or gory.

I whispered to Paul, "Let's get out of here!" He was in full agreement and we left. I felt the devil had tricked us with the offer of something "free," alluring us with the trimmings of an elegant theater and he had the intent to corrupt our soul. Sadly, we did not see any of the other Christians leave.

This is the plot of the enemy. He entices us with the desire to be "entertained." But this is no new seduction. When my husband and I were in Memphis, Egypt, our guide pointed out a stone idol that was an image of a dwarf. He said this was the god of entertainment. The root of this demon goes all the way back to Egypt! The pharaohs would call the clown-like dwarfs into their court to make them laugh. The Egyptians then created a stone idol to worship the god of entertainment. In our day, the enemy uses all arts; T.V., movies, music, dance, visual art, drama, (all kinds of "American Idols"), to pull us into his demonic, perverted world. Sometimes it is very subtle. Gradually, he expands his kingdom as we become more accepting of his thoughts and his ways and we abandon holiness.

When I was a college art student on a field trip in Chicago, we went to a contemporary art museum. I walked into a gallery by artist, Cindy Sherman. I was instantly gasping in horror. The exhibit was larger than life realistic images of vandalized personal body parts, vomit, and blood. It took me about 2 seconds to realize the evil in the room and I froze my eyes to the floor as I headed straight for the exit. It is hard to believe that a room filled with demonically perverted sadism is allowed in the name of "art."

In the next gallery of the museum, I found a very tranquil landscape. It was the size of an entire large wall. In the picture a beautiful woman floated in the air with her crossed legs like a Hindu idol, in meditation. Other smaller floating Hindu-type idol women dangled in the air with her. It was very dream-like and calming. This artwork made their religion feel and look very attractive. The devil was using art to deceive people. Our enemy, Satan, very carefully uses the arts to his plans and purposes, to expand his kingdom. He is the father of lies, always taking people away from the Lord. He always steals or mimics God's gifts for his purposes.

The Church has underestimated the power of the arts. Our whole culture has been redefined through them. In the 1950's the family was seen as wholesome. It was the "Father Knows Best," generation. As T.V. and movies in the following decades attacked the family, portraying mothers and fathers negatively, the plot of

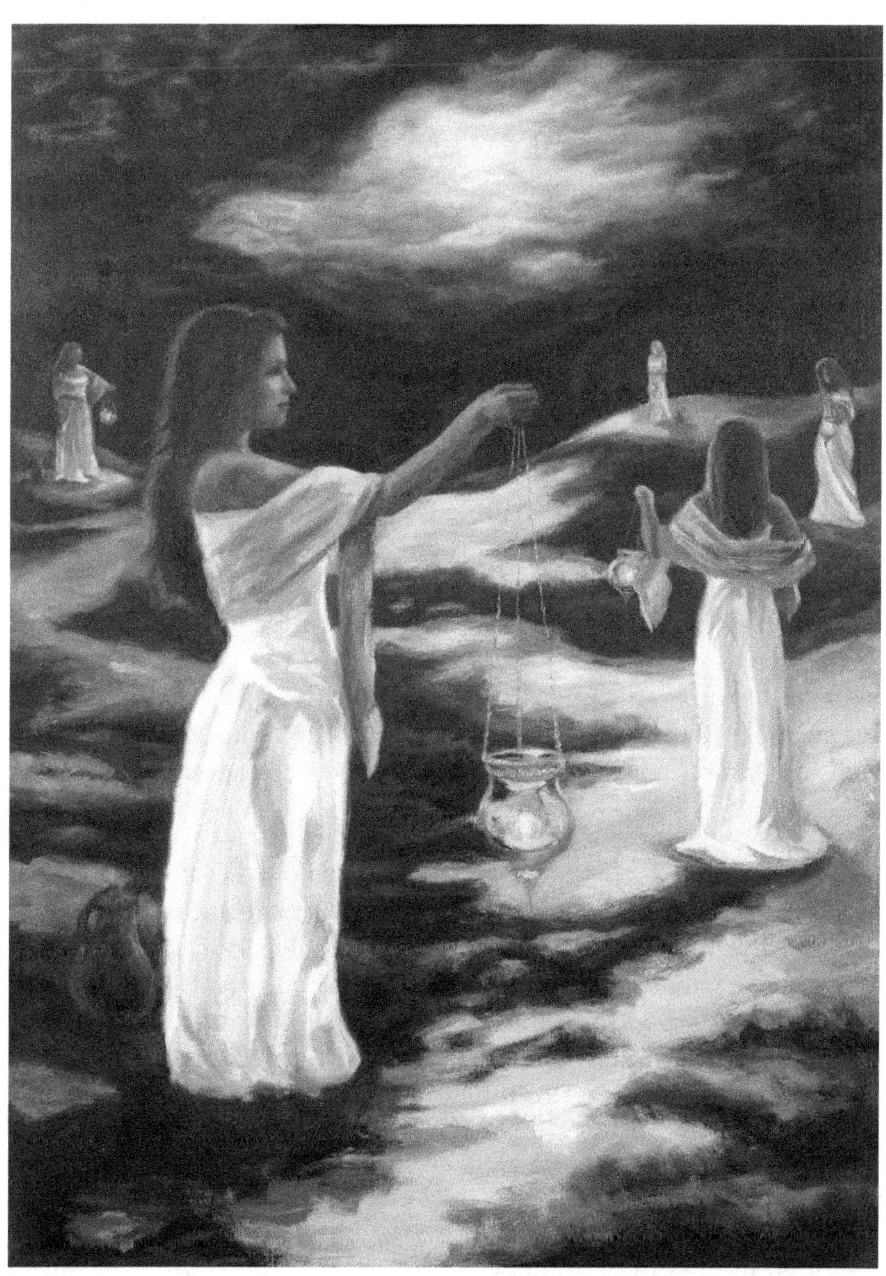

"The Five Wise Virgins" by Laurie A. Stasi

the enemy was successful. The divorce rate soared and his scheme won. Now even marriage itself is being questioned. Sex has been turned into a product to sell, even something you do on your first date, or worse. All this has been achieved through the arts and media. There was an actual homosexual manifesto drawn up that was to promote the homosexual lifestyle. One of the steps in the manifesto was to use T.V. and present gays in a light-hearted, accepting way. A number of gay comedians gradually appeared in various shows. They succeeded and America is now accepting and protecting their way of life.

The devil decided that the arts were a powerful tool. I believe Christians should counter his strategy. The arts originated from the Lord and the devil stole them. It is time for the arts to be a powerful tool for the Kingdom of God! It is time that we restore creativity to glorify God. Right now, most of the arts glorify Satan. How dare we let the enemy receive glory and not fight to take it back! We must, for the honor of our Father. As David said about Goliath, "Who is this uncircumcised Philistine that he should defy the armies of the living God?" I Sam. 17. We need to have the same attitude towards the devil and his perversion of the arts.

The visual arts have just begun to emerge, as God desires them to be. God wants Christians in the marketplace arts and entertainment arts. We need to take the arts through the crucible and cleanse them so they can truly honor the Lord. If you are an artist, I pray that God will use you and your creativity to bring glory to the Father and take back lost territory. Pray daily for the visual arts mountain to be infiltrated and taken to display creativity and messages for the Lord.

We need to discuss several other important areas in order to answer the question "Why reclaim the arts?" We will look at what the devil has stolen in the arts in order to reclaim it and restore it to the kingdom of God.

RECLAIM WHAT THE DEVIL HAS STOLLEN

In the past, when movies and T.V. first came out, the church pronounced it as evil and ran from it. In some denominations they pronounced it a sin to go to the movies. Of course, there were some legitimate reasons for them to object to what was being presented to them. What if they had formed groups of creative people and filmed their own movies? There would have been competition to the evil that was beginning to emerge in our society. Instead, they ran and hid.

Our absence in art gave the world full ownership and authority over it. Now they make the rules. They decide what's "in" or acceptable. We stayed out of making plays, painting public forms of art, creating sculpture, writing musicals, and writing the scripts for T.V. Christians gave rights away when they quit objecting to obscenity that was slowly increasing year by year. Our absence of voice gave us the programming we see today in the culture of the arts and movies.

The opportunity still exists for us to stand up and have a voice. Sherwood Baptist Church, Albany, Georgia, decided to make movies that reflect God's position and standards. They have done a great job with their movie, Fireproof. They used it to launch resources to help marriages. They also released, Facing the Giants, and, Courageous, showing that one church can infiltrate the movie and arts mountain, and bring the presence of the Lord and communicate His message (Sherwood Pictures). I recently showed Fireproof to about 60 clients at the Salvation Army, including many homeless people. They laughed, they cried and they heard a clear gospel presentation through this great movie. It was amazing. For them, it was much better than another stiff sermon. God poured His love on me as I drove home that night. He was very pleased.

Churches need to actively promote their writers, musicians, visual artists, dancers and give them opportunities within their church communities to develop those talents. They need to put money and resources behind it. Churches could promote creative worship nights. It is sad to see gifts lying dormant within the church. There are writers, photographers, artists and dancers whose talents are untapped, or are used for secular, worldly purposes. Promoting their talent is an investment in God's creativity and expanding His kingdom that will impact others. Many people have a dream that never gets realized. The church can encourage and support talent so that fruit may grow.

Churches should have visual images during the service and promote live prophetic art, exhibit nights, and art for sale in their stores. They can financially support the artists through art sales. All forms of art should be encouraged through small groups focused on the arts. They can have a coffeehouse night with stand up poetry, Christian comedy, video, photography and other arts. God loves when the church embraces the arts and when they glorify Him.

Martin Luther once said, "Why should the devil have all the best music?" The founder of The Salvation Army, William Booth said the same thing, and then used the world's bar tunes, changed the lyrics and evangelized the streets. The Salvation Army came out with the very first full feature film. It is too bad they did not push through and continue in the movie business. It seems the Christian musicians have found their place in our Christian culture, refining their talents and using them for God. Most churches support musicians and use their talents to the fullest. We need to pray that churches start to activate the other creative gifts in their congregations.

When I was young, in the 1970's, Contemporary Christian music was not anything to brag about. Over time, the standards were raised, the quality improved and musicians became as good, or better than the world's musicians. A Christian dance troupe should be as talented as the world's dance groups. The visual art quality needs to improve and educating artists needs to become a priority.

At first, there might be low quality art and creativity that breaks the ground to make way for creativity to come into the church. The next step is to raise the standard. There is not one church that would allow someone to come in and bang on a guitar who never took a lesson and barely knew how to play. There is a standard that is expected. For the sake of allowing art to start in the churches, we have let people paint, dance, do drama, who are not trained in any way. Frequently the lack of quality shows, and it does not reflect the Kingdom of Heaven in a good way. If we are to advance the arts, art education should be promoted. Training should be developed including workshops and seminars. We should not stop the arts from happening in this infancy form, but keep challenging and directing it.

THE BATTLEGROUND

The devil is always trying to steal creativity and artists. The prophet Jeremiah wrote that Nebuchadnezzar specifically took craftsmen and smiths as captives from Judah. He wanted them to be used for his purposes. They had a value in his eyes. They were pulled into a world of darkness and bondage. The Lord made a promise regarding these captives:

> *"My eyes will watch over them for their good, and I will bring them back to this land. I will build them up and not tear them down; I will plant them and not uproot them. I will give them a heart to know me, that I am the LORD. They will be my people, and I will be their God, for they will return to me with all their heart." Jeremiah 24:6-7.*

I believe this is encouraging for artists. God has a promise over us. He wants to bless us and place us in the good land. He will bring us back, and He will build us up. "I will give them a heart to know Me."

The Bible indicates that there is always an intense battle between establishing the arts for God, and the idolatry of the arts. We discussed earlier, Bezalel, the first Spirit-filled craftsman. God wanted the arts to be used for His glory. Bezalel's commission to create the tabernacle and the implements was given in Exodus 31 and the very next chapter was the story of the golden calf. The

Israelites used the arts for idolatry immediately after God selected the arts to be used for His glory. The devil did not waste any time. The devil used the arts to corrupt the people and draw them away from God. While Moses was up the mountain the devil drew them into idolatry.

God hates every form of idolatry and commanded the people to destroy idols when they entered other territories. There is always an intense spiritual battle between Satan having control of the arts, and the arts being used for God's glory. We need to aggressively advance God's purposes in the arts and tear down and destroy the works of the enemy.

THE PARABLE OF THE TALENTS

We all need to keep in mind the parable of the talents in Matthew 25:14-30. God distributed talents in varying amounts to different people.

> *"The one who had received the five talents came up and brought five more talents, saying, 'Master, you entrusted five talents to me. See, I have gained five more talents.' His master said to him, 'Well done, good and faithful slave. You were faithful with a few things, I will put you in charge of many things; enter into the joy of your master.'*

The servant who was afraid of the Master buried his talent in the grown. The Master was not happy with him!

> *"For to everyone who has, more shall be given, and he will have an abundance; but from the one who does not have, even what he does have shall be taken away. Throw out the worthless slave into the outer darkness; in that place there will be weeping and gnashing of teeth."*

Even though this originally applied to money, it also is symbolic of our gifts from the Lord. We will stand before Him one day, and He will ask what we did with our talents. We are encouraged not to bury talent, but to develop it. When someone is productive in a work environment, they may notice that their boss gives them more responsibility. Our daughter, Amanda, was working so hard in the office at the Jacksonville Symphony; they kept giving her more responsibilities. She was doing as much as a full time worker, even though she was part time. When she left the position and moved to Baltimore to go to art school, they replaced her with a full time employee and they even found a job for Amanda at the Symphony in Baltimore. She easily received a new job because of her diligent work.

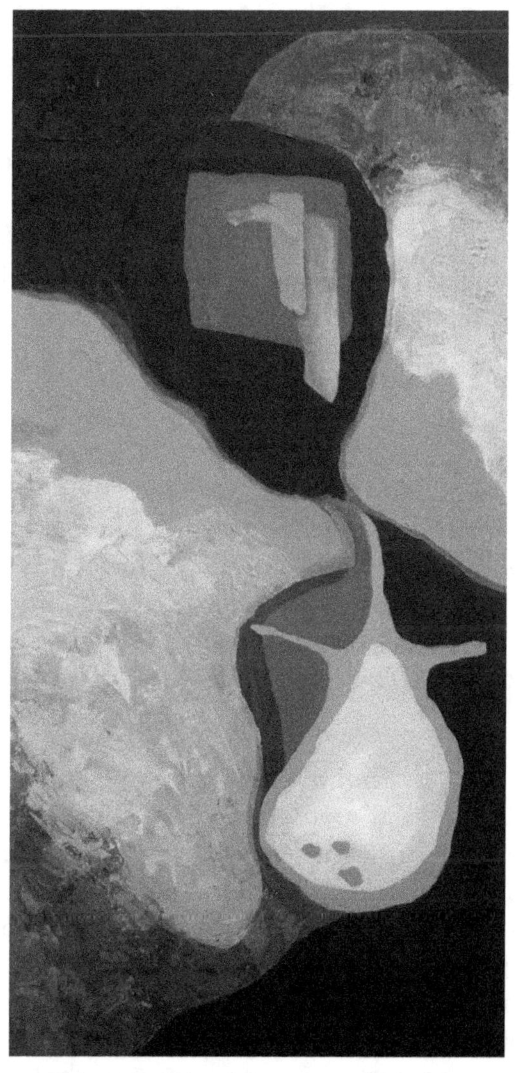

Abstract By Amanda A. Flowers

In this parable, the Lord did the same thing. He took away from those who were not doing their job and gave more to those who were responsible. God does shifting of assignments and gifts based on our obedience. If someone does not follow through on his or her creative assignment, He finds someone who will get the job done. They will discover that their creativity and anointing increases as

God blesses them in their work. God will release more opportunities for the artist, and more finances when we are truly faithful.

Too many gifted individuals find themselves wasting away as they neglect their gifts. Or they were not able to become "famous" so they gave away the talents entirely because they did not make it big. Some people think they should become known for their talent, but they do not want to practice. They are not willing to invest in themselves. There is a price to pay for quality, we have to work hard and grow our gift.

I believe the parable of the talents also applies to churches, as mentioned earlier. Do they even know the talent that lies dormant in their church? I think it is a tremendous tragedy, much like burying many dozens or hundreds of talents in the ground. Sometimes, there are select favorite individuals in the church that are used for ministry, and other talented individuals feel "unused." They feel rejected and unworthy and do not try and find a place for their gift.

We need to embrace the talents of our Young people, who love different media than the older generations. A message from the Lord can come in the form of a poem or stand-up skit just as easy as a sermon! In God's eyes, one form is not greater than another. He used David's songs and poems, which were an art form carrying the Lord's messages. All creativity is talent that should not be buried. The ego of some pastors may lead them to believe that the only form of revelation from God comes through them, the pastor. I hope and pray that God releases revelation to the masses of creative Christians who are willing to run with it. I also pray that the Churches will be willing to open up and be creative! Use your talents and don't bury them. Help your church promote the talents in your congregation.

IDOLOTRY

Ancient civilizations used art to create "gods" which helped establish demonic strongholds in those cultures. Some of those "gods" and sculptures became objects for demons to inhabit. The demons could easily transfer to people, as the people were willing to receive the spirits of the "gods." What if, for example, a spirit of lust can be on an object (a car, jewelry, etc.), and as people get drawn into it's lure, they receive a spirit of lust. I have heard that in some cultures they put a chant on objects so that people will buy them.

There can be demonic powers in objects, and in art. It can imbed in a culture and effect a whole civilization. India is totally infiltrated with idols and demons. America has a spirit of lust for things exhibited through materialism; this is activated through the objects themselves, and through advertising. People view ads, which create desire. The people making the ads do not know it, but they are in cooperation with the spirit of lust to tempt people. Be honest with yourself, have you ever seen an ad and felt desire for that object? You could not stop thinking about that thing. Weather it be the new car, or computer, or jewelry, or I-phone, it is all the same. The spirit of lust brings us to idolatry. America is one of the most idolatrous nations of the world.

According to the Bible, the intent or the use of an object matters. When the Israelites came into the Promised Land, there was one tabernacle that they carried into Israel to worship the Lord. The tribes of Reuben, Gad and Manasseh decided to stay on the other side of the Jordan, but they were required to fight the battles with their Israelite brothers to gain the land. When they had finished, they went on their way back to their land. They stopped near the Jordan and build an altar. Their brothers in Israel heard they set up an altar and were angry. They knew there is only one Tabernacle where they were commanded to worship the Lord, and only one altar to burn sacrifice. How dare they set up a false altar to worship? They planned on attacking their brothers in defense of the Lord to break down this idolatry. They felt it was rebellion against the God of the Israelites.

The tribes of Reuben, Gad and Manasseh responded about the altar:

> *"On the contrary, it is to be a witness between us and you and the generations that follow, that we will worship the Lord at His sanctuary with our burnt offerings, sacrifices and fellowship offerings. Then in the future your descendants will not be able to say to ours, "You have no share in the Lord." If they ever say this to us, or to our descendants, we will answer: Look at the replica of the Lord's altar, which our ancestors built, not for burnt offerings and sacrifices, but as a witness between us and you." Joshua 22:28-29*

The intent of the altar they built was to be a witness and a reminder to their descendants. The other Israelites agreed that this was permissible and retreated. The intent of this man made piece of art was at the core of the disagreement. They were willing to kill their brothers over it. They thought, if they are using it for worship, then it is wrong and we will destroy it. But if it is a reminder of the one true altar of the one true God, then it is permissible. In the Old Testament, if there was any object that honored other gods, the Lord commanded it be destroyed. They were merely following the Lord's guidelines.

Intent should have been considered in art in the middle ages, but wasn't. The Catholic Church had begun using art as icons and worshipping the art. The response during the time of the Reformation (particularly under John Calvin and Calvinism) was a holy rage, a war against all iconoclastic and religious art. They felt they were being obedient to the Lord in destroying idolatry. They eventually wanted to burn all large-scale Christian art. They should have looked at the intent of the art and made a decision based upon its purpose. But they ransacked churches and destroyed both idolatrous art, and art that was made for the Glory of the Lord. Much of the art illustrated the One True God and His eternal altar, the sacrifice of Jesus on the cross. Most of the art during that period was a visual picture of the stories of Jesus to help people who were illiterate learn about the Lord. Unfortunately, a great deal of it was destroyed, along with the idolatrous art.

In some countries, there are spiritual manifestations on art. One statue of Mary in Akita, Japan had tears flowing from her eyes. Another example is a painting in Romania that started weeping tears in 1694. Although, some people cry out to God and pray to Him at these occurrences, others flock to see these manifestations and worship them, instead of worshipping God himself. This is a case where the author of the art may have had pure intentions for his art, but beyond his control a supernatural event has occurred and the art has become an idol. God does not want a manifestation to lead people into idolatry. Our God is very jealous:

> *"Break down their altars, smash their sacred stones and cut down their Asherah poles. Do not worship any other god, for the Lord, whose name is jealous, is a jealous God." Ex. 34:13-14.*

God desires our full affection. He is the bridegroom who wants the Bride to gaze only on Him. His jealousy is like fire.

Some in the Church still insist that God does not want any graven image. I knew a pastor's wife that insisted that the church should not use a baby doll in the Christmas play because it was idolatry. The truth is, God did not want people worshipping any graven image. The Lord Himself told the people to make objects, like the altar, memorial stones, tabernacle pieces, and the snake on the pole. When it was an object used for God's glory it was permissible. When it became an object of worship, it had to be destroyed. This is the principle for all art. Intent matters.

Every church generation needs to make sure the art is not worshiped. Art can be a tool, a picture to lead people to Christ. It should never be prayed to, or worshipped as an idol. This is difficult, because art can be a connecting point, a place where people visualize a truth about God, and it brings them closer to Him. Thus, it becomes a place of worship. They may stand before that art, in a holy, pure position of worship of Him. A person right next to them may be entranced in the piece itself, and have wrong intentions. In some cases, the Bible says if something is a stumbling block to your brother, you should remove it. Education about idolatry may help keep people from it and we all should be speaking the truth in this matter.

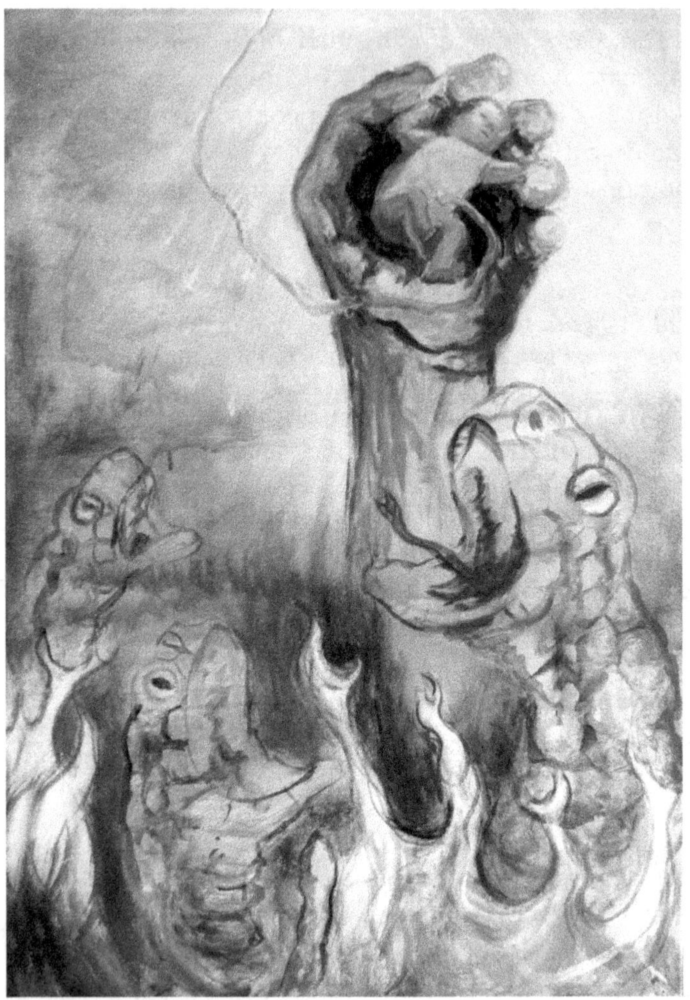

"Saving the Babies" by Laurie A. Stasi

CHAPTER 11
WEARING THE MANTLE

What are the keys to living the life of a prophetic artist and being productive? We need to have focus on several main areas to be used by God to our fullest:

BE FILLED WITH HOLY SPIRIT

We cannot fully receive from the Lord if we do not have the Holy Spirit. He opens us up to dreams, visions, trances and revelation. If you are a Christian and feel dry, and are not getting any of these gifts, just ask!

> *"If you then, though you are evil, know how to give good gifts to your children, how much more will your Father in heaven give the Holy Spirit to those who ask him!" Luke 11:13.*

This verse is a promise that our loving Father will give us the Holy Spirit if we are hungry and ask! The Holy Spirit gives the gift of tongues when He comes on us in power. Some people desire to speak in tongues, but have not felt the breakthrough. Keep pressing in to the Lord. When I spend more time praying in tongues, it opens up revelation for me, and more of the Holy Spirit and His power. When we are hungry for Him, He comes.

Pray and ask, "Lord, I want more of you!" He responds to our desire. Long for His love and relationship and for Christ to dwell in you.

"...the mystery that has been kept hidden for ages and generations, but is now disclosed to the Lord's people. To them God has chosen to make known among the Gentiles the glorious riches of this mystery, which is Christ in you, the hope of glory." Col. 1:25.

What is the great mystery? We have Christ in us, the hope of glory. How amazing to think that the God of the universe can dwell in us. He brings His glory into us. But, there's more!

"And if the Spirit of him who raised Jesus from the dead is living in you, he who raised Christ from the dead will also give life to your mortal bodies because of his Spirit who lives in you." Rom. 8:11.

The Holy Spirit fills us with resurrection power! We have so much to give as artist, when we operate under the power of God. There is limitless potential with the God of the universe residing in us! He even gives life (healing and divine health) to our mortal bodies through His Spirit in us. Meditate on that a while and start receiving the supernatural body God wants you to have! What creative power flows out of us is based on the power within us.

We cannot be prophetic artists without The Holy Spirit who gives us power from on high. The Holy Spirit came at Pentecost and gave Peter the boldness he needed to preach to thousands of people, and 3000 men got saved in a day. Many people are afraid in their art, afraid to take risks, or afraid of doing public prophetic art. Fear is the opposite of faith. If you are afraid, remember the boldness of Peter. Pray, and ask for Holy Spirit to fill you with boldness. Pray as they did in the book of Acts:

"Now, Lord, consider their threats and enable your servants to speak [paint, create, write, sing, prophecy] your word with great boldness. Stretch out your hand to heal and perform signs and wonders through the name of your holy servant Jesus," Acts 4:29-30.

Have you wondered about the process of designing Solomon's temple? How did the creative ideas come? The Bible says that David told Solomon how he received detailed plans for the temple:

> *David gave Solomon, "the plans of all that the Spirit had put in his mind for the courts of the temple of the Lord..." 1 Chron. 28:12.*

The Holy Spirit put on David's mind all the intricate details of the temple. God revealed the specific instructions of His building project. This is how we may receive directions for our prophetic art. God can download the information just like David received it.

> *"All this," David said, "I have in writing as a result of the Lord's hand on me, and He enabled me to understand all the details of the plan." 1 Chron. 28:19.*

God, through the Holy Spirit, will give us understanding to execute His ordained projects. If God has called you, He will fill you, anoint you through the Holy Spirit and give you plans and ideas of how to execute the creativity. He will then give you the boldness to bring your art and your message where He wants it. But it is based on relationship. David worshipped and loved the Lord and was given the Spirit, who then gave inspiration freely.

SPEND TIME IN MEDITATION AND PRAYER

Prophetic artists should also be intercessors. Our quiet time births the prophetic and as we seek His face, He responds. We need to be at the feet of Jesus and anoint Him with our love and like John leaning on Jesus' chest, and hearing the heartbeat of the Savior through intimate relationship. Jesus reveals mysteries and His plans for our lives, for others, and for the world. We are called to pray for the things the Lord shows us in visions, or speaks to our hearts.

We need to be obedient to this call and stand before the courtroom in heaven on behalf of His wishes. In the courtroom, we see Him as judge, and we are part of the judicial system that changes the earth, contending through the blood of Jesus.

Daniel was an obedient Jew who prayed three times a day. He did not contaminate himself with the sins of the secular world. In his obedience, God gave him the gift of dream interpretation. In Daniel 6, when they passed a law against praying to any god but the king, Daniel prayed as usual. He never compromised his relationship with the Lord, and the Lord continued to give him favor, protection, and the ability to interpret dreams. When we are faithful with a little, God gives us so much more. Pursuing a holy, consecrated life in love with God, like Daniel, is the first step to living as a prophetic artist.

In Acts 10, Peter went up on a rooftop to pray, and God put him into a trance. The heavens opened and he received important revelation for the church. Take time to let God speak to you. Prophetic artists must be in tune with the Lord. We need time in our schedule that we designate for prayer, studying the Bible, worship, praying in tongues and soaking. We should keep a dream journal, and sketch journal and be faithful to intercede regarding the things the Lord is showing us. The point of being a 'prophetic artist,' and not just 'an artist,' is the fact that we hear from the Lord. Make time in your life to listen to God.

To dream we need time to rest. Jacob was in a place of rest, Bethel, when he received the vision of the ladder. If you are a dreamer, do not feel guilty about the time you need for sleep. The Lord has reminded me that He desires to speak to me and I should not rush in the morning, but should linger to receive. There is a place where He takes me in the morning, which is after deep sleep, and before awake-alertness. It is a place where I receive a lot of visions. I lay in His loving arms and He shows me things. When He started teaching me how to do this, my flesh wanted to sleep. Mysteriously, I would feel a physical nudge or tap that pulled me out of deep sleep. At that moment I remembered the dream I had been having. I believe an angel was assigned to awaken me and teach me not to sleep so deep.

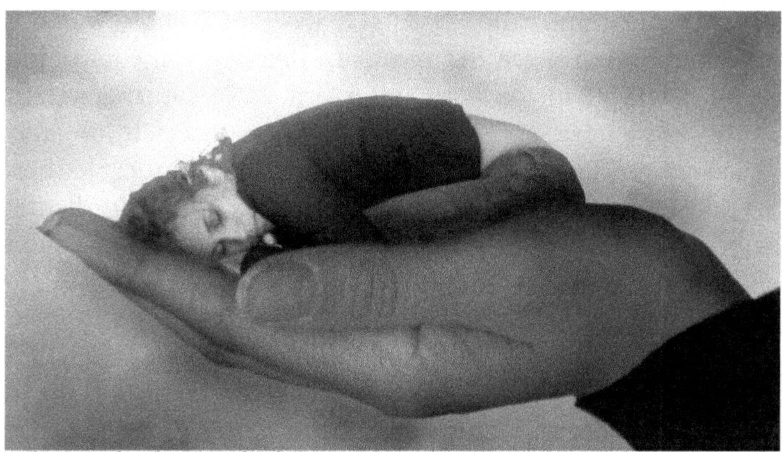

"The Motherly Hand of the Father" by Amanda A. Flowers. God can be tender, compassionate, sensitive, affectionate, loving, and nurturing with the characteristics we feel are "motherly."

Sometimes there would be a sudden noise that woke me. I would hear a door open, or shut, or footsteps, but when I looked, there was no one in the room. I felt a hand on my shoulder to wake me several times. My husband has also experienced this. I am sure the Lord reaches out to people in this way, and many brush it off and miss God. Receiving this way is a very Biblical pattern:

> *"He wakens me morning by morning, wakens my ear to listen like one being instructed." Is. 50:4.*

God loves us and wants relationship. The more you surrender, the more He gives. Our flesh wants to sleep, but it is worth the price to receive a word from the Lord. It is possible to dialogue with Him, ask Him questions, and drift into sleep again and receive revelation and vision. He wants to dialogue back to us. Of course, we can train ourselves to hear like this in the day time also. We need to fine-tune our listening skills and make time for learning how to hear from the Lord. I love that He instructs us on how to hear Him and learn from Him as our tender teacher and good shepherd. How this happens is different for everyone.

We can have the title, "Bethel," over our beds, a place where we meet God and see the things of heaven. Put that name over the chair you sit in for your quiet time. We can meet with Him anytime, anywhere. We send up our praise and petition, and it goes to the Father, like the angels ascending the ladder. He then sends His angels back down to give revelation and fulfill His purposes on the earth. This ladder can connect us with heaven and the God of the universe.

We can climb the ladder and access heaven. We are seated with Him in heavenly places. We go up and enter the kingdom of heaven, get a picture and piece of the glory and the Lord's will, and release it here. The Lord wants us to establish His dominion on the earth. We need to have a lifestyle of living with our head in the clouds of heaven. We can ascend into the heavenly places because Jesus paid the price for our position there. We are seated with Him, having spiritual positions of authority. Prophet Chuck Pierce says,

> "You can go up in heavenly places because you already live in heavenly places. You live in heavenly places and you walk in the earth with the revelation of heaven. When you learn to believe that, you begin to see things differently from what you've seen before. What is produced in you is glory! Glory has the final word of operation in your life in the earth because you have experienced this glory in the heavens. The goal in our life is to experience His glory and walk in this glory until glory covers the earth (see Hab. 2:14, 3:3)" (Pierce) page 19.

There are artists who are fortunate enough to be working alone in their studio or study, and are not forced to share their attention with the world. This is a great gift, because it allows them to keep in step with the Lord. Paul said that we should pray without ceasing. Living in constant communication with the Lord devoid of distraction is a tremendous blessing. We need to learn to abide in the Lord. Jesus is the vine; we are the branches. When we abide in Him, there is the constant flow of Him through us, just as the water and nutrients flow through the branches of a plant and bring life.

Anna, the prophetess, spent all her time in the temple ministering to the Lord and dwelling in His presence. Her heart was connected to Him, and He could use her to prophecy. When the moment of visitation was upon her, she did not miss it because she was in the right place for a prophetic proclamation. We need to be like Anna, ready to release a prophetic word in a painting, poem, song, or creative art of any form from the Lord.

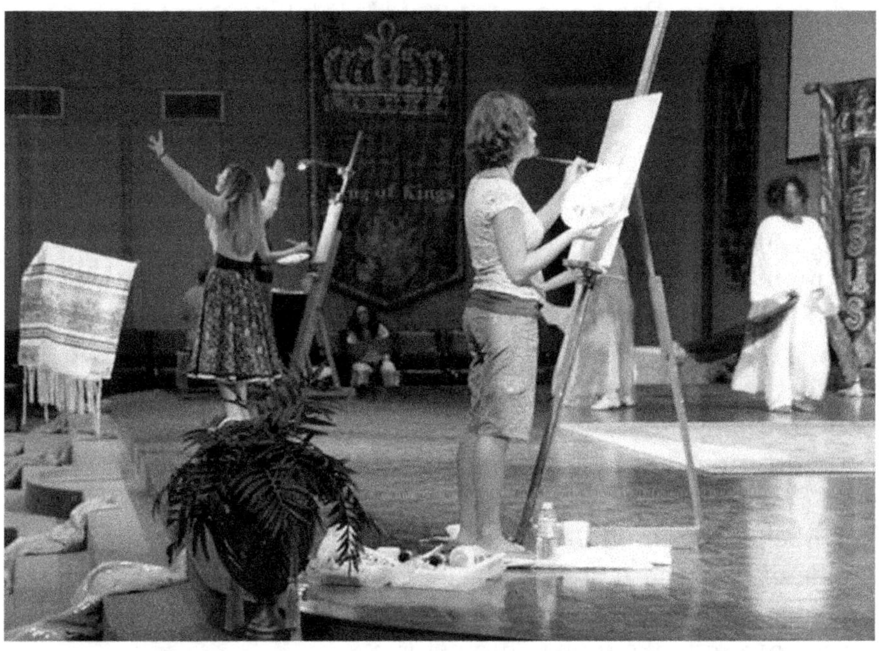

Nichole A. Ryder painting at a prophetic art conference.

She was a woman of prayer and a great model of someone we should emulate. Always ask for revelation and guidance in prayer. Use the dreams He gives you.

When prophetic artists find their flow in the Lord, they listen all the time and take notes or sketches of what He is saying. When they are asked to paint publicly, they always seek the Lord's message for that meeting. Everything they paint, at home, or publicly, is led of the Lord. Their time is too precious to spend painting art that does not connect with His will. Once, someone asked me to paint a picture of their dog as a favor to them. I gently said, "That's not really my specialty and I would not feel comfortable doing it." If people find out you paint (or other media), they come up with all kinds of crazy requests, frequently expecting you to do it for them as a favor. Your time is the Lord's. Learn to say no. Paint or create what He is telling you to.

IMMEDIACY

When the Lord will give you an idea and if you let it slip from your mind, it may be gone forever. You must be obedient in the moment. Learn to stop what you are doing when the Lord gives you a creative thought. One night, you may be inspired to paint a particular piece of art, (or write a song, etc.) and you feel the momentum of it within your belly. If you do not drop what you are doing, that energy will fade, and you will wonder what really inspired you to paint on that subject. This applies to every art form. Many songs have been lost because a songwriter did not feel like jotting down lyrics in the middle of the night. Do not let the devil steal these precious gems from the Lord. Keep a journal, or voice recorder with you to record creative ideas. Just let the ideas flow and take time to brainstorm.

In the parable of the seed, some of the seed was sown on rocky soil and the enemy came to snatch it away. This can happen with our seeds of creativity. They are easily stolen by the devil. We have to make our lives fertile ground for creative ideas.

The Holy Spirit loves obedience, and we prove it to Him when we flow with His agenda, not ours. Other people may think your behavior is strange when you need to drop everything and run for a pen to scribble down an idea in the middle of a dinner date. I have news for you, if you are an artist; they already think you are a little bizarre. But you are in good company, many people considered the Bible prophets crazy. Can you imagine hanging out with John the Baptist a few weeks? If you are not willing to live in obedience, do not count on God to show up when you are ready and He is not. He tests us in our obedience to His timing.

HOLINESS

I believe the life of a prophetic artist should be held in high esteem. We should consecrate ourselves to the Lord. When David was planning to build the Temple he described the work that needed to be done and said to the people;

> *"Who then is willing to consecrate himself this day to the Lord?" 1 Chronicles 29:5.*

We should value consecration and holiness in order to create out of a pure heart. I cannot imagine that God would want to pour a valuable anointing into a dirty jar. We are a vessel for God to use. We want to pour out to others through our art. If we are polluted by the world, and watch unclean movies, and curse with our mouths, then we will pour out uncleanness to others through our art. Carefully guard your eye gate. Anything that enters visually can go into your soul. If you want pure dreams and visions, you do not want to have them tainted with the violent movie you watched last night. Take advise from Job:

> *"I have made a covenant with my eyes; How then could I gaze at a virgin?" Job 31:1.*

Job actually made a covenant with the Lord regarding what he looked at. I believe this is an excellent example for us. He took it seriously and used it as his defense for his purity. A covenant is a serious commitment. If you want to be a seer and God to take you seriously, get serious with Him and covenant. If your eye-gate is a weakness for you now, wrestle and fight for your deliverance. The Holy Spirit can bring us into holiness through the blood of Jesus and the power of the Spirit. As Paul said, "walk by the Spirit, and you will not gratify the desires of the flesh," Gal. 5:16.

David was a man of bloodshed, and the Lord would not let him be the one to construct the temple, the greatest art project ever. The Lord wanted a man of peace to build the temple. We need to be at peace with others, and not an instigator of troubles. We need to have a higher standard than those around us. God did not want to use David because of the murderous filth that had touched him and taken away his purity, because he was a man of war. I cannot watch movies with graphic bloodshed. The Spirit strongly pulls me away from seeing these things. Guard yourselves in every way as the Spirit leads, to be a pleasing sacrifice to the Lord and to be used by Him.

> *"Whatever is true, whatever is noble, whatever is right, whatever is pure, whatever is lovely, whatever is admirable, if anything is excellent or praiseworthy, think about such things." Phil 4:8.*

ACCURACY

Being a prophet is serious business. If you are a prophet for Him, you are called to the lifestyle of a prophet. The prophets in the Bible were all eccentric characters, but very dedicated to what the Lord was telling them. If you are not willing to be obedient to Him, get out of the prophetic art realm. If you prophesy out of your flesh, or withhold a word from the Lord, the Bible says God will hold you accountable.

Ezekiel was told to deliver messages of punishment, and if he would not deliver the messages, their blood would be on his hand, see Ezekiel 3:20. There were prophets in Jeremiah's day that prophesied lies, and the Lord said, "Those same prophets will perish by sword and famine," Jer. 14:15. There is grace while learning the prophetic, but we need to press in for the Lord's word and impart it into our art. This is solemn business and we need to deliver the truth in love. I know we do not always have the whole picture, "For we know in part and prophesy in part," I Cor. 13. We must be faithful to our part.

> *"But one who prophesies speaks to men for edification and exhortation and consolation," 1 Cor. 14:3.*

We bring the prophetic message with this verse as a guide to our delivery. We must bring the message of the Lord with love and encouragement to build up believers, but never with compromise.

PRACTICE

You must study and master your area, constantly growing in your skill. The more you put into it, the more proficient you become and you will have an easier time giving in to the Spirit when He wants to lead. You will not have to spend thought on design, composition, or struggle to develop the form or anguish over what colors work well together, it will all just flow out of you from your training and practice. You may play guitar, but have not mastered it enough to play creatively when the Spirit leads. Then you are limited to the level of skill you have. It will be obvious that you are not versatile enough to flow in the Spirit. The same goes for painting. It is hard enough painting in your studio, but if you want to paint publicly or during a service, you have to work very quickly to produce what God has shown you in a short amount of time. This takes practice. Be faithful with your gift and develop it so that when the prophetic word of the Lord comes, it will easily flow through your art, writing, instrument or your body as you dance for the Lord. Do it with excellence.

All of the arts should be done to God's glory and fine-tuning them gives Him glory. Watching children perform ballet and occasionally tripping may be cute, but adults who want to dance for the Lord should not be on stage tripping over their toes. We need to hone our abilities to represent the Lord well. This applies to every art. Encourage one another. Lift each other up. Share guidance and tips. Grow in your skill.

We also need to practice the prophetic. If you are inexperienced, you may want to find a group that teaches the prophetic. Prophesying to others is another great way to grow in the prophetic. Another way to grow your seer gift is to spend time in a prayer room and sketch what the Lord shows you.

JOURNAL

In my art class when I was in school, we were required to write in our journal/sketchbook everyday. We had to record creative activities that we did each day. We could write about how we decorated a cake, wrote a poem or illustrated a story. We could sketch in our book, paint, make a collage or write notes for ourselves. We had to show our instructor that we had done something creative every day. This is a great discipline to enhance your creativity. The Lord is our instructor, and wants us to continue to develop our gifts for Him. Every day Holy Spirit wants to teach you something, if you are willing to let Him.

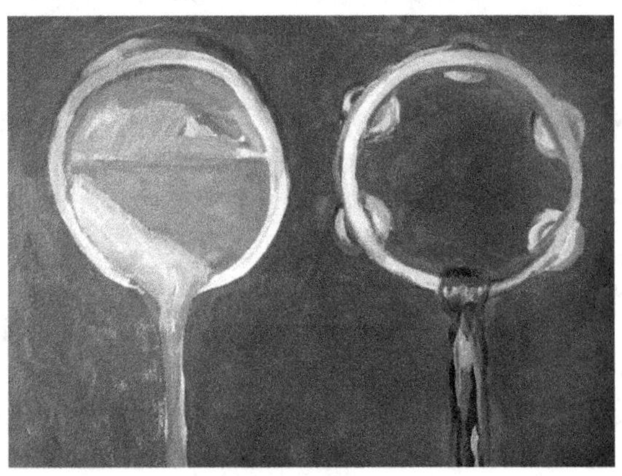

By Laurie A. Stasi

Having a sketchbook is a home base for our ideas that the Holy Spirit gives us throughout the day or night. Those ideas will not get lost because they have a place. I have sketchbooks from 15 years ago, and sometimes go back to remember the profound creative thoughts the Lord was giving me in that season.

A sketchbook (or for a writer or song writer, a journal) is a place to run to when we are bored or have just a little spare time. In those moments, give yourself a short assignment, write for five minutes whatever comes to mind, or sketch your hands, feet or the person in the room with you (always very good practice!), or whatever picture the Lord is showing you. This will make better use of your unproductive time, like waiting in a dentist office, or for the train. I took mine to the airport for a trip, and found that we were delayed seven hours because of snow. There were hundreds of people stranded. For hours, I did gestural sketches of people and studied their posture and body language. It was better than having a figure class. I had so many people to choose from. Use your free time to develop your art skill, or your writing.

As inspiration comes, create a "To Do List" of creative projects on the back page of the sketchbook or journal. Artists may be inspired by the Holy Spirit to do a series for an exhibit. For a writer, it may be a list of possible books or poems to write. You can find your list quickly on the back page when you want to add to your "To Do List," or to get going on one of the projects. Even years later, you can easily find it your old journals.

As visual artists, use your sketchbook to develop your art. Grow in your skills and develop your talent. The more you draw people, the easier it is to quickly render them for the prophetic art God wants you to create. Also, practice drawing animals. The Lord may give you visions to paint of lions, horses, etc., and through your practice they will become accurate depictions, carrying the beauty of the animal with the prophetic message.

If you do not have a sketchbook or journal, get one this week and get started! Your ability will increase and you will be able to do so much more with your art for the Lord.

EDUCATION

The world has great artists, writers, and performers, who are amazing at their talent. The artist who studies and performs for the Lord should attempt to be as good, or even better than the world. It may mean going to the world for education to learn to be the best. I know it is a difficult choice, pray for the Lord to guide you. There are some Christian artists who should learn at the top art schools in the country. Unfortunately, as my daughter, Amanda, found out, it is a very secular place to be and has challenges. It is also extremely costly.

Frequently, believers receive an anointing for the prophetic before their creative talent is developed. They have the opportunity to develop their gifts as an offering for the Lord. Some of these artists should take classes at a local level, and also be taught of the Lord. Find the best teacher in your area or the best program you can afford. Let God guide you and challenge you. He may have you do research on the Internet to learn more. Do not give in and get lazy or discouraged. Your gifts matter to Him. The devil attacks artists with depression and puts spiritual chains on them, keeping them from working in their art form. This struggle can happen for years. Fight for your freedom, and advance yourself in your art. Jesus came to give you life, and life to the full. He gave you those gifts, so be a faithful steward. Always try and create art worthy to behold.

Expose yourself to other prophetic artwork. See what painting styles (poetry styles, music, etc.) they are using. When you practice, spend time with the Lord. Do not forget He is in the room. Enjoy His company. Let Holy Spirit guide your movements and choices. Listen to Him, He is the best teacher of all.

EXPERIMENT

Take some time to experiment with the Lord guiding you. If you normally do not paint abstract, ask Him to teach you. Listen and let Him select your subject matter, your strokes, and your choice of color or key of music. Do not be afraid to be a beginner. Have fun. The Lord loves experimentation. He thoroughly enjoys creativity! He is the Creator! Sometimes we find "happy accidents" when we are free and willing to do something different than was have done it before.

BE A CONNOISSEUR OF GOOD ART

On the practical side of living as an artist, you need to keep viewing art, read art magazines, look at art in galleries, going to exhibits and search online, hearing different poetry, or listening to trends in music so that you stay in tune with culture. Visit art museums, musicians visit music festivals and learn from the masters. When you see great art, you are challenged to work at that level. If you never see images by Renoir, Picasso, Rembrandt, or the other masters, you will not have greatness to strive towards. We all can feel we are good artists if we compare ourselves with the amateur artist painting in our art group.

Remind yourself of what quality looks like and eventually you will be better than the artists in our generation. If artists are sitting alone in their studios and not seeing excellent art, they forget to strive for the level of superior quality.

CONNECT

Get connected with your church and with other prophetic artists or art groups. Have meetings with local artists and have everyone share what they are working on. Share what God is speaking to you. If one doesn't exist, start an arts group. Have coffee dates to discuss art and visit galleries. It is important to support each other and advance the arts for God's glory. We can grow and inspire each other.

READ

I do not know where I would be if I did not have the books I have read. There are wonderful books on the prophetic, being a seer, dream interpretation, intimacy and worship. I have a whole collection of books of my favorite painters. Buy the best books on your art area. If you do graphic art or illustration, purchase books to keep you at the top of your game. Amazon has used books very cheap. Of course, the greatest book to read is the Bible. I feel it is important to get our daily bread, The Word that feeds us. Make time in your schedule to sit with your books, listen to the Lord, and grow. Then buy books on your favorite artists, and on art technique. Study from the best! What you behold, you become!

WHERE TO PAINT

Obviously, where you paint can vary. Prophetic art can be executed in the privacy of home or studio. This can be a very personal and mysterious time with the Lord. I find an overwhelming sense of His presence when I paint alone. The art pieces created from our private time may be put on display for others later, or kept for our own encouragement or for a particular person we know. These art pieces are usually more detailed because there is not the pressure of a short time period.

Conversely, prophetic art may be created in a public place for others to watch as it is created. At our church, we have several artists paint during a particular service called "Burning Heart," once a month. When you paint publicly, try to focus on the Lord and that you are doing it for Him and do not dwell on the audience. Of course, a painting that is painted in two hours is not the same as a painting done over several months. Church paintings have to be quick and loose, with much less detail, unless it is executed over a long conference.

Some people may paint "plein air," (French for 'in the open air'); by going out to paint nature or to paint on the streets as a ministry. The Lord should lead you to the location where you should paint. At first it may feel awkward if you are used to painting in a studio or classroom. Trust the Lord and do not give in to the fear of painting somewhere out of the ordinary. Don't be surprised if people approach you to talk. If this is a problem for you, bring conspicuous headphones to avoid too much distracting conversation. Or, you may be called to minister to those He has sent to you.

BE YOURSELF

Everyone looks to others for inspiration. This is a normal part of the learning and growing process. However, we must get to the point where we are willing to accept who God created us to be, and not look to others to see if we measure up, or have more or less talent than they do. We need to find our unique style. Larry Randolph said, "We are born an original. The sad fact is that most die a copy. It insults God." As an artist, keep looking for yourself; find your unique style and medium. Learn from the masters and from others, but then go on a quest to discover the real you. God will be pleased to take you on this journey.

Understand your preferences by asking, "When I create, what makes me happy?" God lets us take joy in our gifting. I really dislike working on realism and painting ultra-fine details. I prefer being loose and free in my strokes and colors, so I know this is more of my style right now. God wants us to find our niche and He will guide us. Try different styles of art to figure out what you are good at and enjoy doing. God may surprise you with a new assignment. Don't make excuses, however, not to do the little tasks that must be done that are not enjoyable! We all must clean our brushes, fix errors in our work and put the agonizing last details on our projects. Follow through with your projects! (I am preaching to myself as well as you.)

Sometimes God may give you an assignment that might be difficult, or contrary to our nature. If you surrender to His will, you will find joy even in those projects. However, when you are doing the work you were uniquely designed for, it will just flow out of you. You will be led of the Holy Spirit, and when you look back at your work and review it, you will see His hand in the process and hardly recognize it as your own.

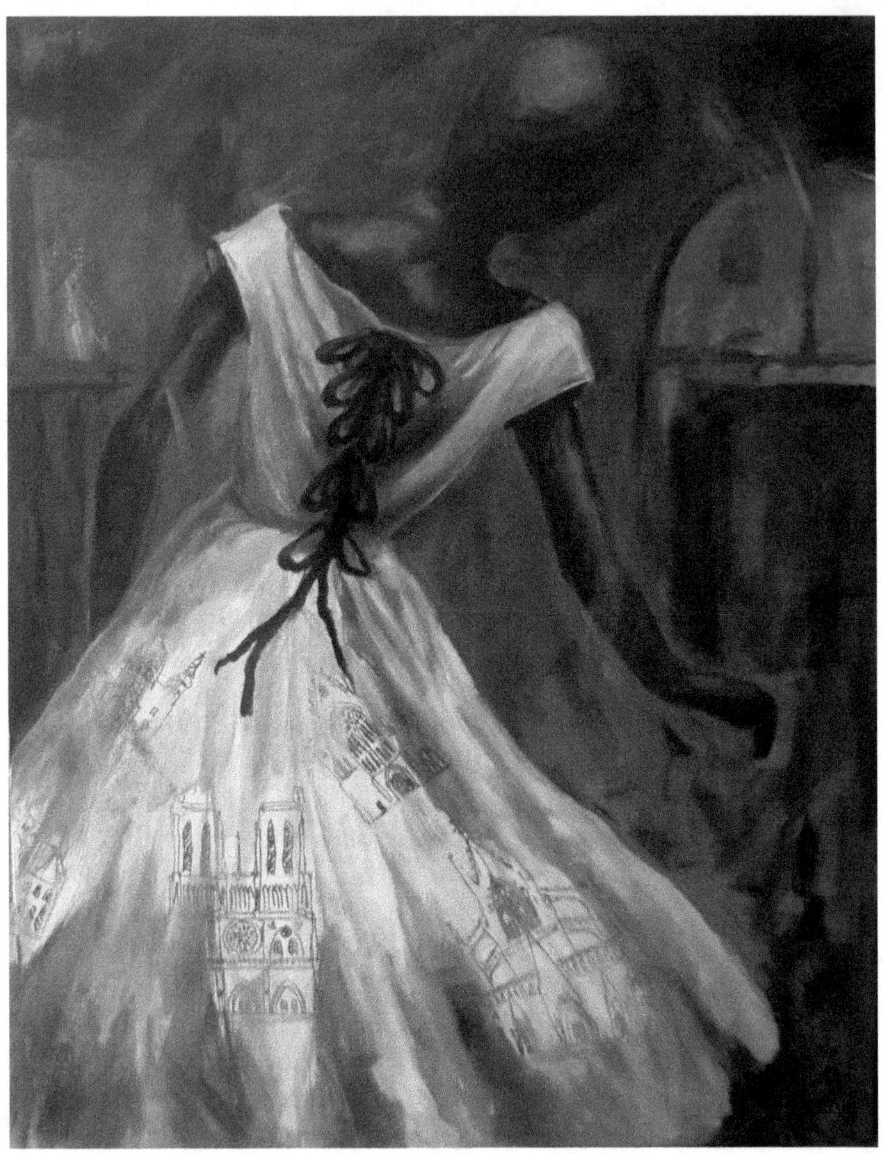

"Trousseau for the Bride" By Laurie A. Stasi. I saw a storefront window when we were in Strasburg, France. There was a dress inside with sketches of dresses pinned to it. To me it looked amazingly striking. I took a photo. I knew the Lord was speaking that He wanted me to paint it with sketches of beautiful churches on it, because we are the church, the body of Christ. At home He spoke about the Trousseau He was preparing for the bride. He will surprise us with many gifts and mantles. I painted it at a women's conference.

Learn to find peace, and create peace in the process. Some people work better with worship music playing while they create. Others need silence. Each preference is based on the way God wired us. Years ago, I read the book, "The Way They Learn," by Cynthia Tobias (Tobias). It explained the different learning styles and opened our family's eyes to each of our differences. God made us so complexly distinctive and our creative flows are unique. If I am not comfortable in the room I am working in, the creative environment, it slows the process for me. My husband, who is very type-A and left-brained, loves to work in silence. Discover the process and location that works for you.

Find yourself and your unique creativity and enjoy the journey, for you are finding your Creator at the same time. He made you and knit you together in your mother's womb.

> *"For you created my inmost being; you knit me together in my mother's womb. I praise you because I am fearfully and wonderfully made; your works are wonderful, I know that full well. My frame was not hidden from you when I was made in the secret place, when I was woven together in the depths of the earth. Your eyes saw my unformed body; all the days ordained for me were written in your book before one of them came to be," Psalm 139:13-16.*

Knitting is a picture of a craftsman making a beautiful garment or piece of artwork. In 2011, my husband and I visited Egypt and watched as children and young people worked on handmade, knotted rugs. There was a strong foundation of threads running, floor to ceiling, on the loom. These were the warps threads. The wefts ran the other direction. A dark-haired Egyptian boy, about 15, chose a particular strand of color, and wound it around two warp threads, and passed it through the center of those two threads, making a knot and slid it down into place in the intricate pattern he was creating. His pace quickened, and we watched him make dozens of knots in a minute, his hands worked like lightening. There can be up to 550 knots per inch along a single line of thread!

God made us that intricate, choosing the colors and fabric that make up who we are. He works like lightening, with His power at work within us. Every Egyptian rug is unique. There is no way, even with the same pattern, that they could come out exactly alike. God made us so unique, even twins with the identical DNA package are different! God loves variety as expressed in the various peoples of the earth, or the assortment of beautiful roses we enjoy. According to everyrose.com, here are over 7500 different types and colors of roses now. Discover your Creator and His love for your uniqueness, and express variety and distinctiveness of creativity in your art and every facet of your life.

DO NOT GET DISCOURAGED!

The devil attacks artists to stop the call of God on their life. I guarantee, anyone who has a call from God will feel this sabotage trying to get him or her off course. Below is a list and response to the enemy's attack against you:

LIES THE DEVIL TELLS ARTISTS:

LIE: "You'll never amount to anything." He attacks your self-worth. The enemy knows if he can stop your creativity, he can stop your calling, purpose and destiny.

THE TRUTH: You are made in God's image, to create. You are a son or daughter, an heir and seated in heavenly places. You are the bride. God gives to you richly and out of His abundance of creativity. You are designed to create and you have His favor.

LIE: "There is no purpose in art." The devil tells you, "What will you do with that art? It will end up in storage or the garbage." He attacks the value of your creativity.

THE TRUTH: There are so many purposes for God to use art (see Chapter four). Your art is praise to Him. God loves when you create. Trust Him to use it to touch others. Your work may have significance on the earth or in heaven.

LIE: "It's a waste of money and time."

THE TRUTH: Everything worth doing for the Lord is worth the investment of your time and money. Our time is God's time. Practice good time management and prioritize, making art higher on your list. See the expense as a love offering to the Lord. Pray for financial blessing. Speak Deut. 28 blessings over your life, that He will bless: your basket and kneading trough (creativity and place to make bread-money), your crops, livestock (your fruitfulness and business), barns (your bank account), "The Lord will open the heavens, the storehouse of his bounty, to send rain on your land in season and to bless all the work of your hands." Deut. 28:12.

LIE: "You have to be the best to be used in as an artist. Your art abilities are not perfect, so you should not do it or show it to others. You are not good enough." He intimidates and pressures you with insecurity. Many people quit because of intimidation.

THE TRUTH: God leaves room for grace and a learning curve. He knows it takes time to develop talent. Even simple pieces of prophetic art touch many people's lives because they accurately carry the message from the Lord. I remember a young friend that was learning his guitar, and practicing worship songs. He was able to prophesy to others by singing to them. I only heard beauty and encouraged him. Others heard his imperfections. After only a few years he was leading worship at an International House of Prayer, glorifying the Father. Do not give up.

LIE: "You need to be involved in the arts full time to be considered an artist." This lie stops many people from doing art in their free time for the Lord.

THE TRUTH: Use what time you have available, and whoever is faithful with little, much more will be given because of your faithfulness. The apostle Paul was a tentmaker to support his ministry. Many artists have to have a "day job" to cover the expense of their calling. You are still an artist, even if it is part time, because God designed you to be an artist and it is part of who you are. Prophecy and speak it out loud, "I am an artist," (musician, writer, etc.). Many people cannot say the words, they are afraid to speak out their identity. Prophecy them!

LIE: "It will be fruitless."

THE TRUTH: God judges fruit. The fruit may be the time you have spent with Him, enjoying creating with Him. You may have limited fruit, through exposure to people on various occasions. Some fruit takes an enormous amount of time. An avocado plant can take up to 5-13 years before it bears fruit. Avocados are one of my favorite fruits, so some farmer's investment of time produces what I consider to be a very valuable fruit. Develop your gifts and trust God for the fruit.

LIE: "Nobody understands you. You are a misfit."

THE TRUTH God delights in your eccentricities because He made you unique. He understands you perfectly. You are His "one of a kind masterpiece." God will find your perfect fit, "wait on the Lord and keep His ways and He will exult you to inherit the land." Your identity is in the Lord; so do not look to people to find fulfillment and understanding.

LIE: "Don't you want to become rich and famous?" The devil wants to lure you into the trappings of the world and change your focus from God to self-centered idolatry.

THE TRUTH: "The American Idol" is an idolatrous fantasy in our culture. Most of the people who get "famous" do not know how to handle their success and are miserable. Fame is not the goal. What we create is for God's glory, to make HIM famous. Keep your heart centered on honoring Jesus. Some people may be called to the world, but don't dwell on, or lust after this. If it is God's will, He will open the doors for you to be out there. Our riches are laid up for us in another place. You are meant to create and you must do it. Van Gogh sold one painting in his lifetime. He never stopped painting because it was his call. His art was ahead of his time, as much prophetic art will be. If God brings you success, give Him the glory and do not get caught up in the trappings.

LIE: "A little compromise will help you sell your art (book, music, etc.)." The devil wants you to use more seduction, or create less "religious" work. He wants to get you off course and out of holiness.

TRUTH: Stick to the pure message that God has given you. Do not give in and sell out. God will take your art where He wants it to go. Be holy and create out of that holiness. Remain faithful until the end.

Many people get discouraged, depressed, and wonder why they should spend time and money to advance in their art. A lot of artists do not know where they are supposed to fit in, especially if they are around people who lack creativity. They agonize and long for the place of a proper fit. The lack of funding and support of art causes many to leave the calling on their lives. Finances limit our projects and drain our bank account. The Christian community does not know how to support and encourage visual artists. The calling of the prophetic artist is misunderstood and not valued in its priestly role. Visual artists get "used' by friends and others easily.

Understand that we do not war against flesh and blood, but against principalities and powers in high places. This is a spiritual battle, and we need to fight it spiritually. Pray for God to release your gifts. Pray for revelation and opportunities. Trust in Him as He guides you. The devil will try to make you believe that you are not a good artist and your work is not worth creating. The enemy also makes you insecure. By attacking self-esteem he cripples many artists. He will put obstacles in your way so that you do not have time to create. You need to value your creative time and not sacrifice it to other things. He uses fear to stop you from advancing. You may have the fear of man. Are you over-sensitive to criticism of your art? Sometimes you let their

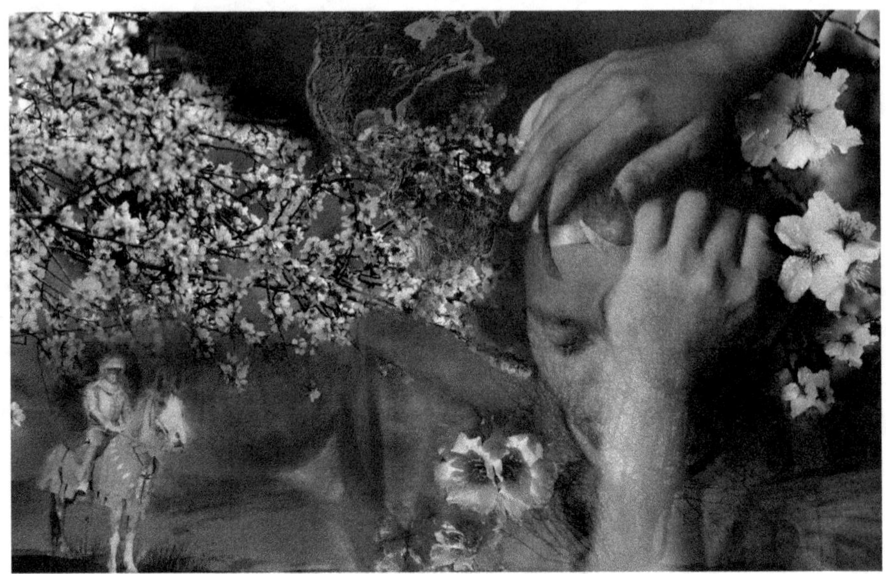

"Jeremiah" By Amanda A. Flowers

opinions stop your process or your progress. Some even have a fear of success; truthfully, this fear holds many people back from their destiny. Remember, you do not have the spirit of fear, but of power, love and sound mind.

Our daughter, Nichole, was working on a prophetic art piece in Photoshop on her MacBook. It was a very good art piece, one of her best ever. It was about fishing for men. She asked different people to pose for photos, swimming in their clothes under the water in our swimming pool. The photographs turned out great. She loaded them on the computer and had the final artwork nearly finished. That week her hard drive crashed and she lost everything. She was in tears. Sometimes the devil hits hard to destroy our best creativity. We need to pray, and ask for God's supernatural covering over us, our computers and other supplies. When a disaster strikes, we have to choose to go forward, and not let the devil win. He will bring us down, crush us, and destroy our hope. This usually means he is threatened by your work and he knows the potential power of it. He is seeking to destroy your destiny. Do everything to recover and move forward to the next project!

We are clearing new ground and making the road for the prophetic arts to find their place. Do not give in and lose heart. Clearing ground requires the removal of barriers in our way. It is back breaking work. Most of it is a spiritual battle. Ground is won when we intercede, and war in the Spirit while we paint or create. Get together with other artists or creative people and encourage each other. Trust the Lord for provision. Ask Him for supplies and watch Him meet your needs.

Remember Bezalel. God chose an artist to be filled with the Holy Spirit before anyone else because it is a high calling! All the arts need to be restored to the honor of the Lord. Do not devalue your efforts. They have eternal kingdom purpose.

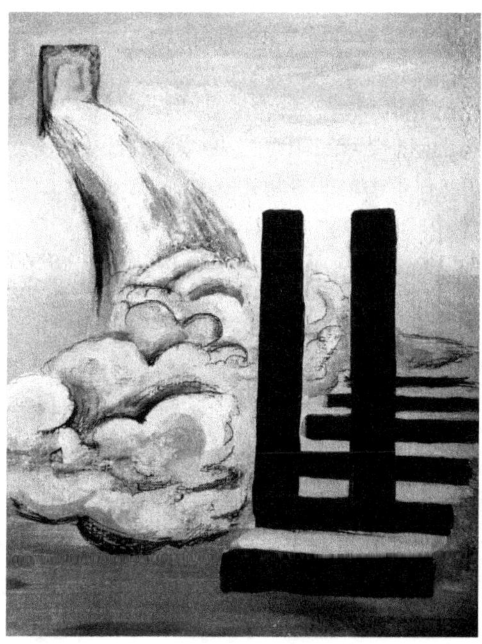

CHAPTER 12

RESTORATION

As artists, we need to be concerned with the stains that the arts have left from previous generations and cultures. Every object that was created to be an idol is an offense to the Lord. These objects brought curses on the land. We are sent to redeem the land through the blood of Jesus. He is retained in the heavens until the restoration of all things (Acts 3:19-21). We can cleanse the land, making it ready for our soon coming King! I believe that we can repent and bring a shift in the earth as we take communion and release the power of the blood of Jesus; particularly relating to objects of art made for the purpose of worship of false gods and regarding bloodshed on the land. Prophetic artists should be intercessors and understand how to cleanse the land from past idolatry. When you are in museums in various cities around the earth you can repent for idolatry and bloodshed.

To reclaim the arts we have to understand the process:

"See, today I appoint you over nations and kingdoms to uproot and tear down, to destroy and overthrow, to build and to plant." Jeremiah 1:10.

We start with the past, getting to the roots and tearing them out. A few years ago, my husband and I found Gwen Shaw's book called, "Redeeming the Land" (Shaw). The Lord took us on a journey of discovery and understanding that the earth was made perfect, before sin was introduced. Jesus was sent to atone for all things. The first Adam brought a curse to the people, and the land.

Jesus, the second Adam, came to reverse the curse. We can, through Jesus, repent for sins and idols that bring a curse to land. The Bible tells us that the land cries out for justice. Jesus is retained until there is restoration.

The Lord began to send my husband and I to places to repent on behalf of the sins of idolatry on the land. He may send you to a city, a museum, or ancient shrine to repent for the sins of idol worship in that place, (and sins of bloodshed like murder, abortion, or child sacrifice).

The land responds to sin and evil:

> *"They worshiped their idols, which became a snare to them. They sacrificed their sons and their daughters to false gods. They shed innocent blood, the blood of their sons and daughters, whom they sacrificed to the idols of Canaan, and the land was desecrated by their blood." Psalm 106:36-38.*

The blood of people and children who were sacrificed to false gods desecrates the land. Creation was made for God's glory and longs for cleansing and the restoration of all things and to go back to the holy, glory-state of the beginning.

> *"For the creation waits in eager expectation for the children of God to be revealed. For the creation was subjected to frustration, not by its own choice, but by the will of the one who subjected it, in hope that the creation itself will be liberated from its bondage to decay and brought into the freedom and glory of the children of God.*
>
> *"We know that the whole creation has been groaning as in the pains of childbirth right up to the present time. Not only so, but we ourselves, who have the firstfruits of the Spirit, groan inwardly as we wait eagerly for our adoption to sonship, the redemption of our bodies." Romans 8:19-23.*

Creation is longing and groaning to be liberated from its bondage of decay. It cannot be liberated on its own. It is waiting for "the children of God to be revealed." Who are they? They are those who know their sonship and authority in Christ. They are the ones who will intercede, repent and cleanse the land. They

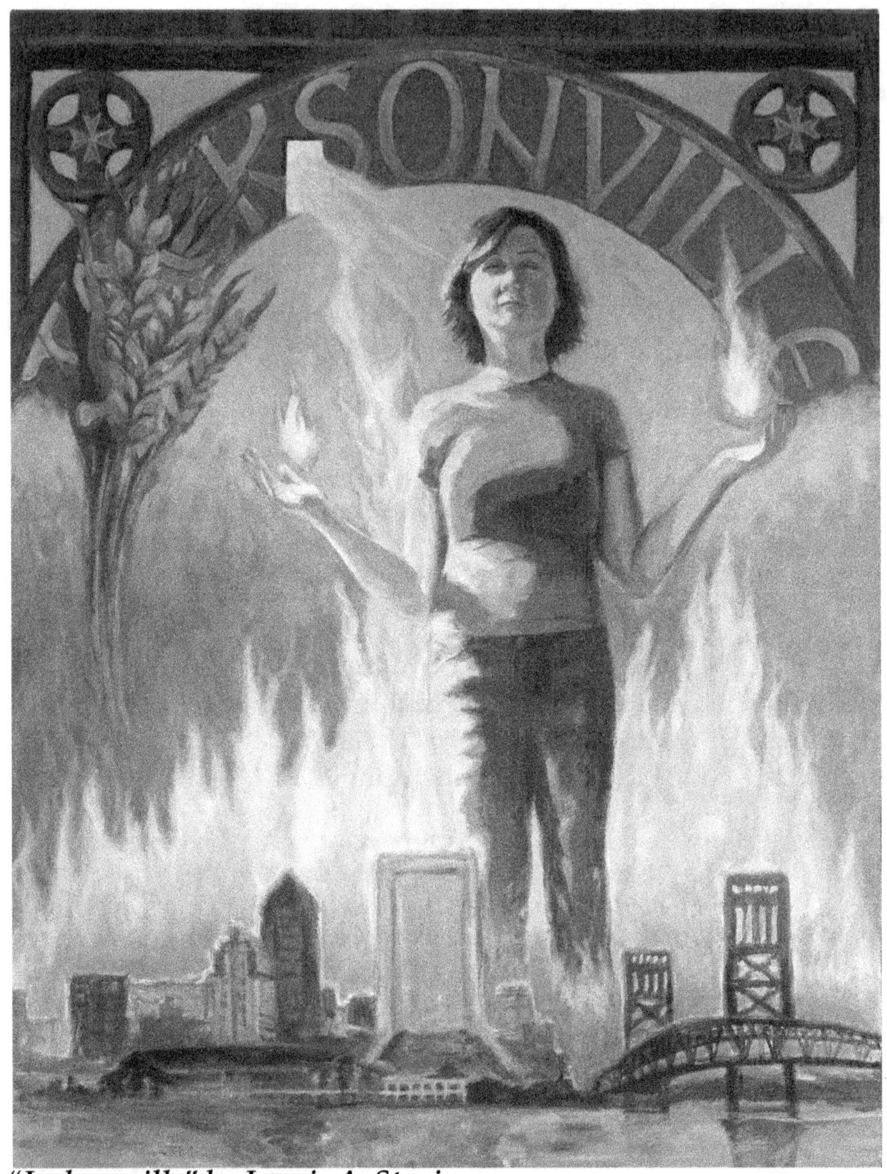

"Jacksonville" by Laurie A. Stasi

will bring low the mountains of evil. They will speak to mountains and they will move. Creation knows it can return to the glorious state it once had. It has been groaning for it because its DNA is wired for it. We can also return to the glorious state we once had in the garden, we groan for it through our "adoption to sonship." This will bring the redemption of our physical bodies. Our DNA was created for the glorious state of the garden. For the word says,

> *"And if the Spirit of him who raised Jesus from the dead is living in you, he who raised Christ from the dead will also give life to your mortal bodies because of his Spirit who lives in you....For if you live according to the flesh, you will die; but if by the Spirit you put to death the misdeeds of the body, you will live." Romans 8:11, 13.*

As we live by the Spirit we are able to "put to death the misdeeds of the body." This gives us ability to truly live. Even our mortal bodies will have life. This is not talking about our heavenly bodies or our spiritual bodies. It says that Christ will give life to our "mortal bodies." Moses was healthy even as a very old man because God gave life to his mortal body. We can have this same supernatural health here on earth, as we put to death the misdeeds of the body. As artists, we have to understand the full picture of what is possible as we walk and live in the Spirit.

Romans 8 goes on to say,

> *"For those who are led by the Spirit of God are the children of God. The Spirit you received does not make you slaves, so that you live in fear again; rather, the Spirit you received brought about your adoption to sonship. And by him we cry, "Abba, Father." The Spirit himself testifies with our spirit that we are God's children. Now if we are children, then we are heirs—heirs of God and co-heirs with Christ, if indeed we share in his sufferings in order that we may also share in his glory," Romans 8:14-17.*

We can "share in His glory," by bringing the glory to the earth, the fullness of the garden and the glory of heaven through the sacrifice of Jesus. As artists, we should also bring the glory through our art and creativity. Sonship also means we can operate in the gifts the Father has for us, gifts of creativity, and authority. We have the access code to the kingdom of heaven and can bring it, "On earth as it is in heaven."

When the Israelites crossed the Jordan into the Promised Land, they were told to:

> *"Drive out all the inhabitants of the land before you. Destroy all their carved images and their cast idols, and demolish all their high places." Numbers 33:52.*

God did not tolerate these false gods, even though they were only made of stone or wood. They had stolen the heart of His bride. He is a jealous God, and does not tolerate anything to be worshipped over Him. God is looking for people to partner with Him in cleansing the land of those created images:

> *"I looked for someone among them who would build up the wall and stand before me in the gap on behalf of the land so I would not have to destroy it, but I found no one," Ezekiel 22:30.*

God wants us to stand in the gap through intercessory prayer for the land. The sins of the people bring God's wrath, and His justice requires that He destroy it. In history, people created artwork/idols and God's judgment was brought against the people and the land. We, as His artist and priests, attend to Him, and lift the offering of repentance, sacrifice of Jesus' blood through communion, and thereby bring the washing of the transgressions of idolatry. The arts must be cleansed and restored to their former glory for the purpose of worshiping the Lord.

I have heard a Christian comment that we do not need to do this, that Jesus' sacrifice was enough. Look around. Does this earth look like heaven? We have a part to play to bring the glory.

The prophet Isaiah said,

> *"A voice of one calling: "In the wilderness prepare the way for the LORD; make straight in the desert a highway for our God. Every valley shall be raised up, every mountain and hill made low; the rough ground shall become level, the rugged places a plain. And the glory of the LORD will be revealed, and all people will see it together." Isaiah 40:3-5.*

As Christians artists and intercessors, we are preparing the way for the Lord's coming. The high mountains in the Bible were places they set up Ashterah poles, and idols to worship false gods and perform aberrant acts. We need to bring down these mountains and idolatrous art. We also need to cry out for the way of holiness.

> *"And a highway will be there; it will be called the Way of Holiness; it will be for those who walk on that Way. The unclean will not journey on it; wicked fools will not go about on it," Isaiah 35:8.*

What if we repented at every place of current and ancient idolatrous worship? God can send people to places like Stonehenge, the Mayan ruins, and prehistoric worship sites, or places where children were sacrificed to false gods. We can repent of the sins in those places. For example, when I visited a museum in Atlanta where they had ancient Egyptian stone gods on exhibit, I repented before the Lord for these idols. I took communion and declared the blood of Jesus cleanses idolatry. I declared that Jesus is Lord and King of Kings.

I went into another museum and found a display of pagan African masks worn by shaman who were high on drugs. The shaman wore the masks in riotous dances to call upon demonic gods. On display was a video of a shaman with a mask on performing his ritual; you could see him becoming delusional and then insane as a demon overtook his spirit during his wild ecstatic dance. I could feel the evil coming from this display. This video plays over and over in the museum, repeating the demonic incantation. In quantum physics, it was found that objects can contain or retain sound. What is released into them in the form of curses, false worship or witchcraft, is contained in them. We need to break off these curses through the power of the blood of Jesus.

Our spirits should grieve that these objects and videos are on public display. We have to pray, repent for these idols in our cities, and ask that there would come a day of their full removal and destruction. These arts gain extreme spiritual authority in an area, and promote demonic activity. The destruction of this stronghold is possible through the blood and power of Jesus and the authority we are given in His Name.

In this type of intercession, we actually stand before the Judge in heaven and ask for a hearing. In this place in the spiritual realm, we first repent of the sins of the fathers (Neh. 9:2) and the generations before us, and then plead our rights through the blood of Jesus. God makes a determination against the forces of evil, because Jesus paid for freedom and the restoration of all things. Jesus came to reverse the curse of the garden and mankind. We do things in the spiritual realm that others do not see, until they manifest a shift here on the earth.

Church Pierce wrote a prophetic word from the Lord:

> ""You comprehend and then you work with Me to fashion, form and bring to fullness My plan today-My will being seen in the earth realm. You can clear out anything that enters the atmosphere that I have given you to rule. You can understand anything you need to understand in order to take dominion over the space and land I have given you. The resources you need to accomplish My purpose, you can create. I am moving in your midst and My voice is alive all around you. Hear and see Me., and make Me a dwelling place in earth with you!" (Pierce).

God has given us authority and wants us to take dominion in the arts. We are in a battle to "Uproot and tear down, destroy and overthrow, rebuild and to plant," Jer. 1:10. First we uproot the past, and then we tear down and destroy evil in the arts. Then we can rebuild and plant new creative arts for the Lord's glory and establish His Kingdom. We want to fashion a footstool for Jesus as His resting place here on the earth. Let the earth reflect the beauty and holiness of heaven.

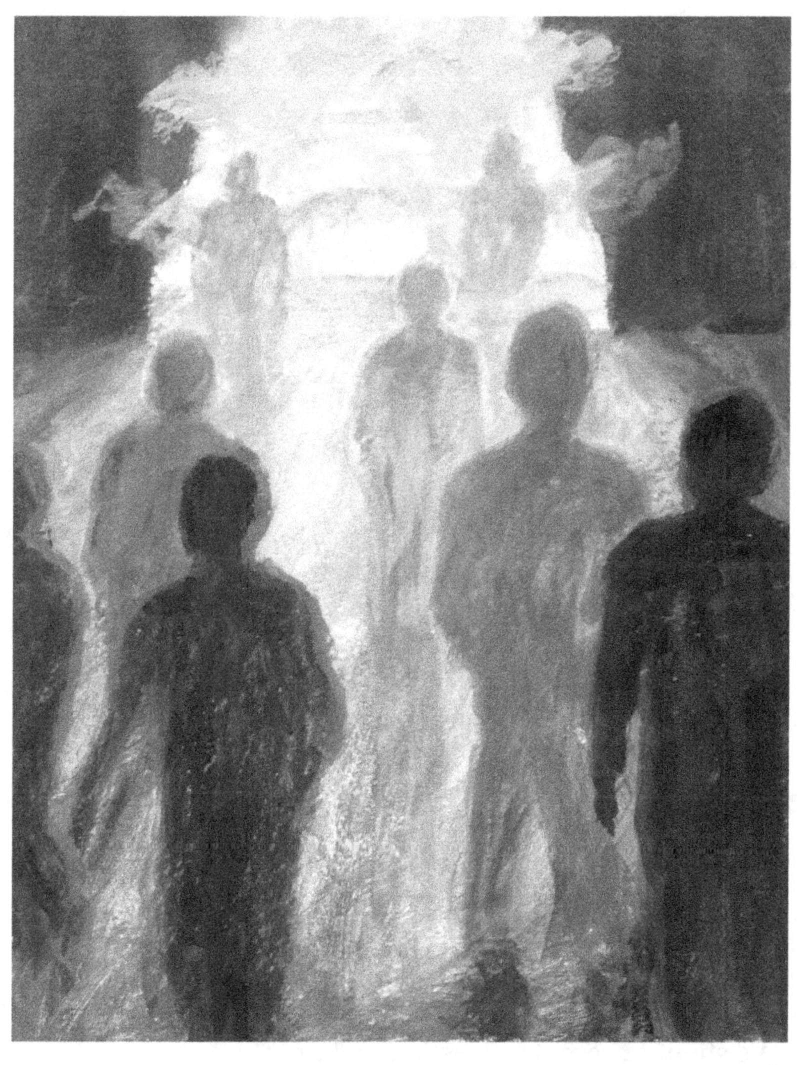

"Angels Among Us" By Laurie A. Stasi

CHAPTER 13
DYNAMIC ART GROUPS AND ART EDUCATION

When artists come together there is a synergy at work. The creative energy bounces between them, and they all grow exponentially. In history, when artists have come together and formed alliances, they were able to usher in a new creativity to move forward. When you study the Impressionists, they were a group of outcasts who fought against the tide to bring in the next wave. At first, the public and critics were hostile to them and rejected their work. But the young artists painted together, gathered at the café to discuss art, and supported one another. They were rejected by the Salon, so they launched the Salon des Refuses, or the Salon of the Refused. More people attended their exhibit than the regular Salon exhibit. Christian artists who band together can also fight against the worldly tide by banding together. We can usher in a move that goes against the culture. We should promote Christian and prophetic art.

When an individual goes alone against the stream, it is like swimming against a rip current. I live in Jacksonville, Florida, and when we first moved here I did not understand the danger of the strong rip currents in the ocean. They are a flow, which is very strong like an undertow current, but in a condensed area. It can suck people out away from shore into the deep sea. Every year people die from these intense rip currents, because they struggle and use all their energy fighting to swim against them. When artists go against the strong flow of society, or the normal church standards for art, there is a condensed effort against each of us as individuals. Many artists give up hope in the fight. It is difficult to survive when we go it alone.

In our city, there are rowing teams who practice on the St. Johns River. From my condo I can hear the coach's voice echo across the water as he follows the rowers in a motorboat, giving needed instructions. As a group they can move at a very fast pace, even against the current. This is how we can be effective against the current of our society. We must band together. We must hear the Holy Spirit's instructions as He directs our groups. Most visual artists work independently. We must realize the need for this group effort to move forward. It takes the teamwork and timing of seasoned rowers to utilize our strength effectively to develop the arts for God's glory.

INTERCESSION

Christian artists also need to come together to intercede and pray for the walls to come down that stop or limit the Christian arts from moving forward. Without this, I do not believe that progress will be made. In our church, I have a friend, Elaine Zink, who has been praying for ten years for God to usher in the arts. She saw a vision when she started, of a new road being established in front of the church. Elaine believed that when the road gets rebuilt in the natural, it would happen in the spiritual and the arts would come to church. Recently, that road was rebuilt and the city put in beautiful trees and plants in the medians, and widened the complete street. It was during construction that the church began the arts classes at our church.

God wants intercessors to pray, break the ground and prepare the road for His creative work in the arts. This is the first assignment of art groups; to intercede. In order to take back the mountain of the arts, we need to fight the spiritual battles and stand our ground. The devil does not want to give us this territory. Do not underestimate the power of prayer to pull down his strongholds.

CROSS POLLENIZATION

Artists banding together also creates cross-pollenization. In class, I watched another artist use different colors together and I challenged myself to experiment differently with those colors. I have grown by observing other artists' use of textures, or types of brush strokes. When they were experimenting with mixed media, I noticed what looked good, and what did not. We learn from each other. The reason why we copy master paintings is because we gain knowledge from them. We learn from their success. We can copy their lighting, their composition, and the delicate balance of their color scheme. When a group comes together we bounce ideas off each other constantly. We can ask, "What is wrong with the proportions of this arm in my painting?" and get direct feedback to fix our problem areas and grow quickly. We may get out of a rut when someone comes in with a new approach. We need to constantly grow in our art, and have others around for a quick critique, which speeds the creative process.

There is also great power in arts groups when we brainstorm together. We challenge each other to higher standards. It is amazing how much creativity is released when we bounce ideas off of others. This method is used in many areas, including advertising, business, and even counseling. As artists, we can come together and share vision from God. We can find creative ways to develop our projects, and see them come to pass. I love the flow of God's gift of creativity in these brainstorming meetings.

Groups can adapt and change art for a specific culture. Decades ago, Colon Valle was one of the first Hispanic woman who made it into Hollywood. She eventually decided to take the theater to the Hispanic people on the streets. She started The

Puerto Rican Traveling Theater group, with a home base in New York City. The group found that they could not wait for popular writers to start writing scripts that related to the Hispanic culture, they had to develop their own writers. They performed on a portable stage on city streets in Hispanic areas of cities. They went out to where the people lived, and performed plays and skits that connected with the people and their unique culture.

This group of Hispanics adopted an art form and changed where and how it was presented. Christians need to think like this, to adopt and change in order to be relevant to our audience. We need prophetic artists in every media, presenting a word from the Lord that may be concealed in a comedy skit, a play, a children's book, or adventure novel. This Hispanic group was able to band together and accomplish what one could not have done alone. Their message is still going to the streets.

BANDING TOGETHER IS ESSENTIAL FOR GROWTH

Years ago, when I lived in Illinois, I was part of an art guild. We gathered once a month to hear a speaker who presented on a particular topic related to art. Some evenings we had workshops with guest experts presenting valuable information. We exhibited regular shows in our gallery, which was part of a local museum. Some of the shows were juried with awards. We sent out press releases to our events. This was all very important for the growth of the artists. We grew together and learned about resources and competitions from each other. We critiqued each other's work, and the shows became incentive for constant productivity. The press releases forced us to take our art seriously. When we presented to the general public it expanded our exposure and community.

At Ponte Vedra Presbyterian Church there has been an arts group that has met for many years now. They have studio days every week for artists to come in, paint and have coffee together. Regularly, they have field trips and outings. They have themed exhibits in the "Bethel Galley," and the artists submit their artwork based on the theme for that month. They send out press releases to the local arts newspaper and invite the general public. Sometimes they have one person shows, by established artists. Their gallery is one hall of the church that leads to the administrative section. This hall is open to the public daily, and no additional staff is needed for the general public to come through and see the art. This church offers their artists important support. The artists grow in this accepting atmosphere of creativity. This ministry also draws people into the church. Ponte Vedra Presbyterian Church is an excellent model for a vibrant church ministry.

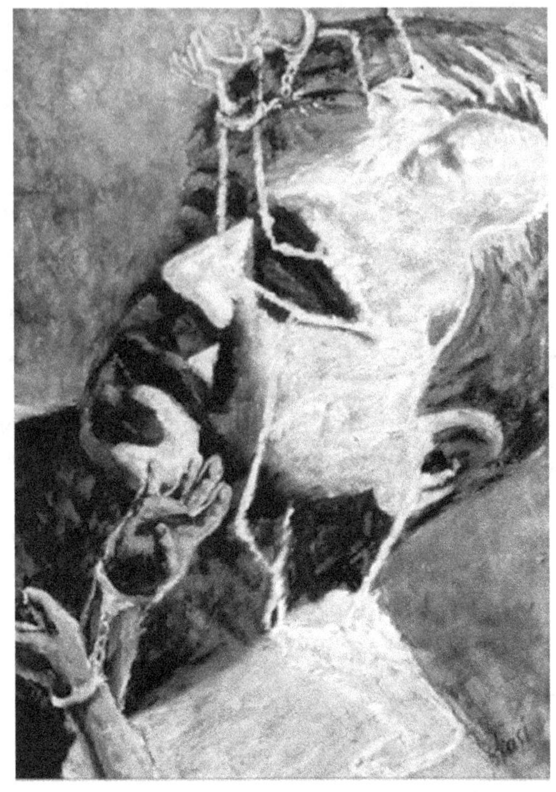

"Jubilee" By Laurie A. Stasi

Some who read this book may be called to start an arts group. You may choose to do a guild or a church group like Ponte Vedra Presbyterian. You need to be certain you are called by God to do this, because it will demand a lot of your time. It is a major commitment and you need to be steadfast as you birth your group. Just as the artists of the Bible, Bezalel and Oholiab who were told to train up the artists, you will need wisdom.

In Exodus 35, Moses asked the Israelites to bring material and stones for the tabernacle. The people responded; "everyone who was willing and whose heart moved them came and brought an offering..." It says that their hearts were moved. God can work on people's hearts to support artwork that is created for God's glory. I believe God would bless any church that promotes using the arts for the honor of the Lord. Another option for funding the arts groups would be for dues to be received by the artists in the guild, or charges for classes.

It is important to teach the essentials of creating excellent art. God wants the church represented through quality and professionalism. Also, encourage training and developing skills in secular education when it is needed.

Our church had a vision to start a community center in which we would offer classes such as beginning guitar, dance, graphic design, beginning acrylic painting, and drawing. Our church also occasionally offers dream interpretation, prophetic singing, and prophetic art classes. The vision is to reach out to the community through classes. A church with a very large campus can have a chance to utilize their unused space in the hours when many rooms sit empty. Doing these kind of classes help develop a presence in the community.

Many churches may feel called to teach about prophetic art. Artists need to learn the skill of hearing from the Lord. They need to develop knowledge in the prophetic. The Bible teaches so much about art, and the artists must take guidance from the Word. Churches can hold workshops, or classes to instruct artists. They can even offer creative arts conferences. Individuals who are interested in growing themselves in prophetic art, should try and attend conferences related to the prophetic, intercession, intimacy, and the arts. They need to pursue their growth in these areas and be accountable to the gift that God has given them.

We also need to develop prophetic art schools in which the artists should have some proven ability in their arts area to enroll. They can have specific tracks to develop talent, but also tracks to train in the prophetic. Having a worshipful environment in these schools would create a womb for artists to discover what God is speaking to them in their gifting. I have found several prophetic art schools on the Internet that have already begun and are expanding the Kingdom of God and taking back the arts for the Lord.

COORDINATE SHOWS TOGETHER, SELL YOUR ART

In my college class our teacher taught us how to put together press releases and have official art shows. It was a learning experience as we went through the steps to promote our art to the community. We learned how to hang the art professionally, and frame each piece. We had contact with the media, and invited our friends and relatives. Art that is stored in a closet will influence no man. For art to have an effect on society, it has to be made public. It must hang in homes, churches and offices. Groups can easily have regular shows to draw attention to the work God is creating through them. Once I learned the basics, I put together a traveling show of my art that I hung in different churches during lent. I put out press releases and local papers always picked up the story. I gradually learned how to interview, and how to give thought provoking explanations for the artwork.

Art groups can encourage the business of art, and the art of selling, if you feel God wants you to do this. Share tips on different web sites where you can sell your art. Some people have a lot of success at art fairs, others through local shops. God may have you learn the business of making prints and selling products like note cards. By banding together, you can walk through this process together and share information to help each other grow in art marketing and selling.

PROPHETIC ART ASSIGNMENTS

In any art group, you may want a section of the time devoted to develop the creative skills and teaching artistic technique. I will not cover those topics in this book because there are endless ways to learn watercolor, or oil, or calligraphy. Please do your homework and learn your art area. I am giving a few ideas in the area of the prophetic so that an art group would have something to begin with. It is good to have everyone listening to the Lord, and time to share what God is speaking to your members regarding art and creativity.

10 VISUAL ARTS INDIVIDUAL ASSIGNMENTS

These assignments are useful to help you grow as an artist, and to challenge you as a seer.

ASSIGNMENT 1: Journal. Keep a sketch journal, and a dream journal. Daily record what the Lord is telling you and showing you! Be faithful to see the interpretation. Paint the visions that He tells you to paint.

ASSIGNMENT 2: Soaking. Spend time in meditation to receive from the Lord. Sit in a prayer room, Spend time soaking and praying. Pray in tongues. Record what the Lord is showing you. "Whatsoever is true, whatever is noble, whatever is right, whatever is pure, whatever is lovely, whatever is admirable-if anything is excellent or praiseworthy-think about such things." Phil 4:8. Find things to think on, meditate on and get revelation from the Lord about these things.

ASSIGNMENT 3: Improvement. Ask the Lord where you need to improve your skills. He may tell you to take a class, to focus on drawing hands until you are able to do them without thinking, or to copy the masters. Maybe you need to draw people every day. He will help you improve your abilities; you must be faithful to work on particulars that need growth. Ask other artists for a critique, and then create assignments for yourself to improve.

ASSIGNMENT 4: Learn more about the prophetic. Buy another book on the prophetic and study it. Practice it. Go to a prophetic conference or take a class in the prophetic. Find opportunities to prophecy. Go to the streets and minister to people. Write out short prophecies and sketches for your loved ones.

ASSIGNMENT 5: Ask for the spirit of wisdom and revelation. Practice painting in the Spirit. Put on soaking or worship music, and let yourself feel the guiding of the Holy Spirit. Let Him lead you in your color choices and movements.

ASSIGNMENT 6: Illustration and design. Ask the Lord for Bible story to illustrate. Meditate and ask for a vision that illustrates His heart regarding the message, or let the creativity flow and do illustration guided by the Holy Spirit. The focus is an illustrative or design oriented piece of art work. Take special note of the colors, design and composition to make it stand as a good work of art.

ASSIGNMENT 7: Focus on one of the parables. Paint an abstract in the spirit, or make it design oriented. You could focus on the theme of the parable, for example "lost coin," and do a modern interpretation from the concept. What contemporary play can you do on the theme? Ask for guidance.

ASSIGNMENT 8: Paint out a prophecy that was spoken over you. Look at different styles of art. Paint in a style that you have never tried before. You can do several versions in different techniques. Make something in a style that fits your personality and you would love to look at every day. Hang it where you can see it and meditate on it.

ASSIGNMENT 9: Paint a prophecy for another person. Ask the Lord to reveal His love for them, their calling or a word in season. You may choose to do their portrait, and include layers or a background that includes prophetic images. You can also include a prophetic word in text or a verse for them.

ASSIGNMENT 10: Go through the types of prophetic art listed in this book and ask the Lord to give you a focus. Spend several weeks engaged in exploring that area for the Lord. Research and explore the highest quality work done in that area by other artists. Create a scrapbook or Pinterest for inspiration.

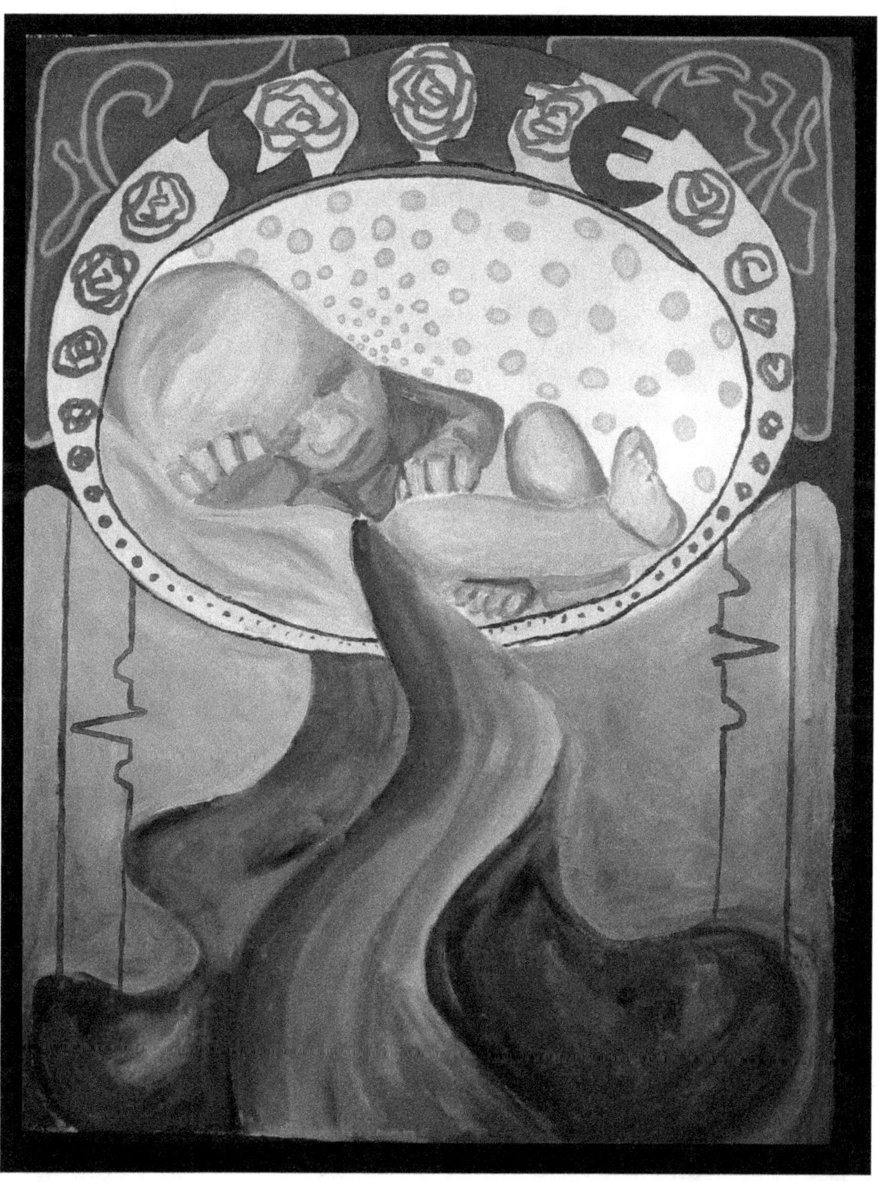

"LIFE" By Nichole A. Ryder

19 VISUAL ART GROUP EXCERCISES:

Remember to pray for wisdom and revelation and anoint each person in your group when you begin to meet together.

EXERCISE 1: The group should sit in a circle. Give each person a blank piece of paper. They sign their name and pass the paper to the left. Then each person asks the Lord for an image for the person's paper they have. They draw what they saw, (use markers, colored pencils, pen and ink, or anything quick). Do not use up the whole paper; leave room for more images. Then the same paper is passed left again, and another person adds a revelation they receive for the name on that page. Pass the papers to the left again. You end up with a montage of prophetic images for each person. Do this about five times. At the end, have each person explain what the Lord was speaking. This piece of artwork is now a very personal gift from the Lord.

EXERCISE 2: Teach your group from Kirk Bennett's book, "Deepening Prophetic Revelation through Meditation." Have the group meditate on the same verse. They should pray, and ask the Lord to show them how to sketch it. Give them time to work on their drawing or painting. End with each person explaining to the group what the Lord has shown them regarding the verse.

EXERCISE 3: Put on a worship track. Choose one song and have them paint or illustrate what revelation the Lord gives them. Version 2- Break up a song into sections and have the artists each work on a piece of the song. In the end, there are prophetic illustrations for the complete song. You may have one person pull it together as a worship video. The final product could be used in church.

EXERCISE 4: Art as intercession: Make a list of things that the Lord directs you to pray. Put on worship music, or have a prophetic musician come play, or go to a prayer room. Have the artists paint and pray out the prayer list. The act of painting is unified with our spirit praying. We are prophetically praying and painting. The very motions are prayer and worship. It becomes a prayer offering and rises to the Father like incense.

EXERCISE 5: Learning to use our sensory gifts of the prophetic: Divide your groups into pairs and have them "feel" and sense what the Lord is saying for the other person. Let them relax and take time with this. Pay attention to your senses. Second Part: Have a prophetic musician come play. Then ask your group what the music was saying prophetically. It is an experiment; there are no wrong answers when you are learning.

EXERCISE 6: Using prophetic art for evangelism: Have your team get a revelation for a person on the streets (in the mall, anywhere). Give them time to draw or paint it. It may be in the form of a card. If they are a poet, it may include a poem. Take your team to the streets and find the people the revelations connect to and minister God's love to them.

EXERCISE 7: Painting in the Spirit: Have your group spread apart in a room. Explain that we can paint in the Spirit, without any physical paint, we are painting in the spiritual realm. Put on worship music. It takes a group that it childlike and open to receiving from the Lord to loosen up and play with this. In one of the classes I taught, a woman saw a vision of a maypole (a pole with streamers coming down from the top). I thought we should come like children and play at the maypole. Each of us grabbed a streamer (in the spirit) and played together around the maypole, weaving in and out of each other. It was a fun, creative time in the spirit. The things we create in the spirit actually exist in the spiritual reality. We may see them in heaven someday. If you see a colorful maypole when you get to heaven, you will know where it came from. This vision may also have been connected to the first Protestant prayer prayed in our nation, here in Jacksonville, Florida on May 1, 1562 (On Mayday, when Maypoles were used in celebration). Later, our city held celebrations of the 450th anniversary of the Huguenots landing here, and the first prayer in our nation on May 1 in 2012.

EXERCISE 8: Do a lesson on unity in art, a collaborate painting: Read Psalm 133. Do a short teaching on abstract painting, giving examples. Show pictures of abstract paintings done in the Spirit (you can find some online) Explain that this is not about painting realistic images, just strokes or patterns. Put up a very large canvas. (a canvas drop cloth bought at the hardware store works great). Put on worship music, or warfare music. Everyone paints all over the canvas. No one can take ownership of his or her own work. Others may paint over each image or add to it. We die to self. Some artists have a hard time with this; they are too connected to "ownership" of their art. Try to add, and grow each other's strokes, someone may have a peach stroke, and other "feels" the contrast color needs to be along it, or boxed around it, or radiating from it.

Another version of this exercise is doing it with realistic images. Everyone asks for an image from the Lord and paints it on part of the large canvas. Then, each adds to the other's images, more color, and more detail. Unity in the piece happens when we surrender our work to others as led of the Lord.

Version 3: of collaborative painting: Have multiple canvases, each person gets a canvas for ten minutes, then pass the canvas to the next artist to work on. Keep passing the canvases until your time is done.

EXERCISE 9: Study the use of banners and using art to war. Listen and receive images and create banners designs together. Then put worship music on and war in the spirit. You might want to do batik of your images.

EXERCISE 10: Create and illustrate a book together. Ask the Lord for a topic, or a song, or Bible passage. Have everyone do an illustration, or have everyone use their cameras to take a creative photo that represents part of the project.

EXERCISE 11: Research creative worship together. (smallfire.org has some ideas and links) Put together a worship project.

EXERCISE 12: Create a monument or sculpture together honoring something God has done for your group, your community or your church. Ask the Father for revelation on the theme and materials. In the 1990's, when a new art museum opened in Elmhurst, Illinois, they wanted to install clay pillars as a memorial. I took my children to the event and we each sculpted a small clay tile along with dozens of other volunteers. My high school art instructor, Mr. Hartgerink, edited, fired and painted the tiles and the museum attached them to the pillars. They were diverse and a very creative memorial.

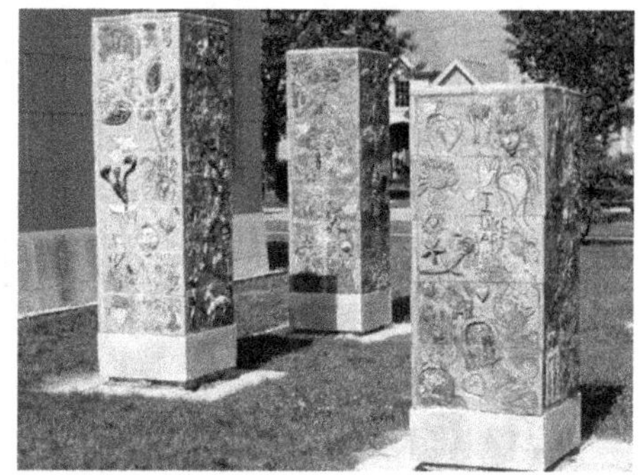

EXERCISE 13: Have each person in the group bring in images from magazines and spend time discussing the prophetic meaning of the images. Grow and learn prophetic symbolism together. Create a collage.

EXERCISE 14: Bring in source photos of animals. Have your group prophetically get pictures of an animal for each other or themselves. Give them time to sketch and paint their animal. Then have the group discuss the positive prophetic characteristics of each animal, as a prophetic word to each artist, revealing positive characteristics about them.

EXERCISE 15: Study together one of the Seer books, (James Gall)

EXERCISE 16: Discuss how to fight spiritual battles that artists face: fear, intimidation, and fighting against the religious spirit in churches.

EXERCISE 17: Learn the Biblical power of art through the Holy Spirit. Discuss how the world uses art to change societies, and discuss idols in America. Bring in photos of propaganda and analyze how Christians can use media to advance our causes.

EXERCISE 18: Study "You May All Prophecy," Steve Thompson

EXERCISE 19: Teach the process of Prophetic Painting. This is a guide, not a rule.

1. Revelation.

2. Research. Get photos to work from if necessary. Study the Bible verses that link with what the Lord is saying. Meditate on them.

3. Composition and layout from the vision or revelation. Sometimes you may use the rule of nines to help create a balanced composition.

4. Preparation of materials as led by the Holy Spirit. He may show you the size, and the materials to use. Prime the canvas, do a light sketch if necessary.

5. Set aside time to paint under the anointing. Give yourself several hours or days. Put on worship music, pray and immerse yourself in the Father's creative flow.

6. Choose your colors by the guidance of the Lord. Learn about color meaning and symbolism. Study color combinations that work, look at magazines and books. Be led by the Holy Spirit as you create, listen to Him guide you where to apply the strokes. In some visions, God is emphasizing the color (i.e. it was a navy blue horse). You must emphasize it in the painting also. In some visions, the colors don't matter; He may not even show much of the color and lets you have the freedom to express the color through your creativity.

7. Dialogue with Holy Spirit. Ask Him for areas to emphasize, for color creativity, and shapes to highlight.

8. Step back from the art piece. When you are too close, you lose judgment. You need to get perspective by looking at the whole piece subjectively. Keep contrast. Make sure you have light lights, and dark darks. Do not get muddy. Try to have a background, middle ground and foreground, when possible.

9. Discuss your piece of art with others. Many times other people have additional prophetic revelation to share. Ask for a critique, and be open to adjustments.

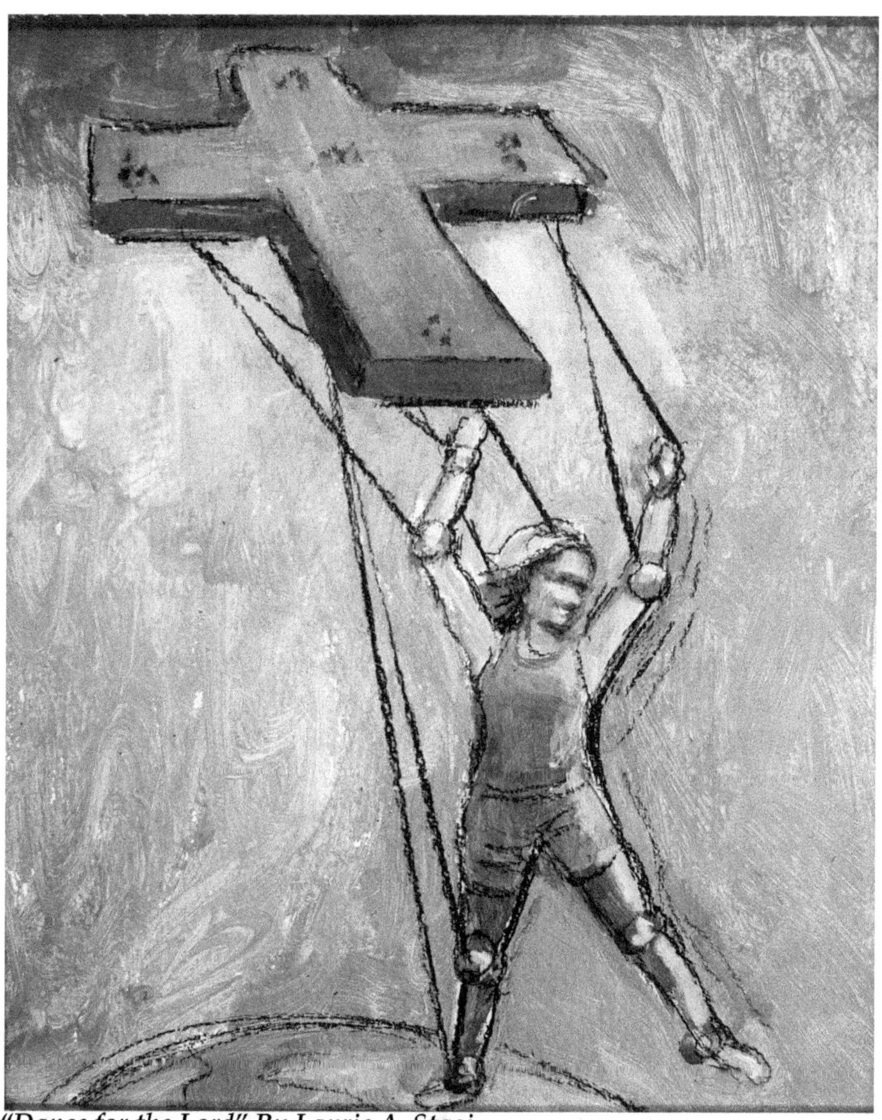

"Dance for the Lord" By Laurie A. Stasi

CHAPTER 14

24 BIBLE STUDIES

We need to dig deep into the Word of God and understand His scripture references related to the arts and being a prophetic artist. This is written to be used as a personal Bible Study to journal your responses, but may be used in a group.

BIBLE STUDY 1: Worship.

Read Psalm 95:1-7. What specific of types of worship are in these verses? How is your praise walk? Create a plan to broaden your personal worship time. Do you make time for the Lord? Do you practice all these types of worship? How can you be more thankful? Think of declarations to add to your worship time.? David was a worshipper at heart and lived it daily. It was one of the reasons the Lord called Him, "A man after God's own heart."

Read John 4:23-24. This teaches about worship in the Spirit. What does that mean? How can you improve your worship in the Spirit? How do you personally worship in the Spirit? What does it mean to worship in truth? These verses explain that God is spirit; why would that change how you worship?

Look at the Vows of worship in Psalm 61:8, Jonah 2:9, Psalm 76:11-12. What vows did they make? What is a vow of worship? How can you apply that to your personal private time and our art? Read Psalm 20:5 about the use of banners (art) in worship. In this instance, what was the reason they worshiped God? Banners often proclaimed a name or characteristic. What could have been on this banner in this circumstance? How can visual art be incorporated with our worship? What is its purpose?

Study 1 Chronicles 16:1-14. It is a chapter describing worship in the tabernacle. What does this tell you about worship? Their assignment was within the tabernacle, a place created by the artisans. What place does art have in the context of worship? How do churches incorporate art into their worship environment? How can you minister before the ark continually in your creativity? How can you lift up offerings through your creativity/art? What happens to you during worship? What happens to God? Think about what God has done and about His attributes and names. In what way can you worship His name through your art, writing, songs, etc.?

In 2 Chron. 20 worship was used to go into battle and it confused the enemy. Can you worship using your art and use it for war in the spirit? How would you go about doing that with your art?

BIBLE STUDY 2: How we hear from God.

Review the following verses, and the various ways you can hear from the Lord: 2 Tim. 3:16-17, 1 Kings 19, John 16:13-14, Jer. 33:3, John 10, Matt. 7:7, Job 33:14-18, Joel 2:28-29, John 5:19-20, Heb. 1:14, 1 Sam. 9:9, 1 Cor. 14:1, Dan. 6:27, Prov. 24:6.

Is it easy to hear God? How do you receive from the Lord? Why does God speak differently to different people? Can you grow in your ability to Hear Him? How?

See Prov. 8:17. What helps you find God (and hear from Him)? Are there seasons where you have heard God differently? Are there times when God is silent? What do you do then?

Hab. 2:1-3, what was the prophet instructed to do with his revelation from the Lord? Are you prepared to be a prophet using your art form?

BIBLE STUDY 3: God our Creator, Elohim.

Study Gen. 1- Gen. 2:3. Why did God create? Why did He create such variety (example, many colors, various flowers, people look different)? Do you think we have delegated authority to create (remember we are made in His image)? See Deut. 28 verses 5, 8, and 12. What do baskets represent? What are these verses saying related to the work of our hands? God also refers to skilled hands in Ex. 28:6 and verse 15, and 36:8, 39:3. Why do you think you desire to be creative? What happens to a creative person when they have no outlet for their creativity? Do you feel that the Father enjoys your creativity?

See Colossians 1:15-20. What place did Jesus have in creation? The Bible begins by revealing God as Creator. See Rev. 4:11 what characteristic of God's nature are they worshipping God for? How did God create? In Rev. 21:1, is God done creating?

When is our creativity an offense to Him? In 2 Kings 18:4, what happened to the bronze serpent? How do we know if what we are creating is pleasing to Him?

BIBLE STUDY 4: Bezalel

Bezalel was the first artist listed in the Bible. See Exodus 31:1-11. What gifts of the Spirit did God give him? Is skill a gift, or does it need to be taught? What was his purpose and assignment? Why do you think God chose him? What articles for the temple did they make? What artistic abilities were necessary for all the work (example: silver smithing etc.)? What other abilities were necessary to complete the work (example: self discipline)? Who assisted Bezalel?

Read Exodus 35:4-35. What materials were brought? Who contributed and how? What other skills do you think were necessary to coordinate hundreds of artisans and creative materials? Do you have other abilities in these areas? Verse 34 says God "put in his heart to teach." What do you think he taught? How important is it to pass along your knowledge of your art? What opportunities do you have to teach others your craft? Would it help if the body of Christ had a system in place to share creative knowledge and education? Is God conscious of quality craftsmanship? If so, how can you increase the quality in your craft?

Turn to 1 Peter 4:10-11. What guidance might this verse give as we create?

BIBLE STUDY 5: Restoring the Temple.

Read Amos 9:11-15. In what ways can you create a type of the "Tabernacle of David?" From this passage what elements would God want included in it? (Worship music, musicians, creative expression, prayer, visual images that are symbols of Jesus as was the lamp stand, etc.). Have you been to prayer meetings or churches that incorporate all of these elements? Would all these elements add to true worship?

God will restore from captivity (vs. 14). In what ways have you been captive and bound in your art and creativity? What has held you back? Have you suffered discouragement in your art? What would make you fruitful in your art? How do you take the mountains (the art world, media, arts, art education) and overtake them with sweet wine? What personal projects can you create that are a "tabernacle" to God? Are there group projects your group can do to bring together the tabernacle elements?

Read Acts 13:22. This tells how God felt about David. Why do you think God was pleased with David? How important is obedience to God? In what ways are you accountable to God for your art? Are you obedient? If you have not been, what can you do to create discipline to become obedient?

BIBLE STUDY 6: Symbolism of the Temple Articles and Ornamental Decoration.

See 1 Kings 6-7. It includes some of the images; ark, altar, cherubim, palm trees, open flowers, a woven chain, pomegranates, lilies, pillars, metal sea (basin) with gourd decorations, the base with bulls supporting it, panels with lions, bulls and cherubim, and wreaths. What is the symbolic meaning of each? Do they have personal meanings to you?

2 Chronicles chapters 2-5 include information on the temple construction. (Tabernacle information is in Exodus chapters 25-40 for further study). Looking at the main furniture pieces: altar, the water basin, the lamp stand, the table of showbread, the altar of incense, and the Ark of the Covenant. In what way does each represent Christ? Can you think of things that Jesus said about Himself that connect with these symbolic objects?

God loves to use symbolism, "It is the glory of God to conceal a matter, But the glory of kings is to search out a matter," Prov. 25:2. Much of what the Lord reveals in visions is symbolic. I think metaphor and symbolism are some of the love languages of God. What are some of the visions you have received from the Lord, and the symbolism meaning?

BIBLE STUDY 7: The Prophetic.

Read and discuss 1 Cor. 14:1-5 and Verses 24-40. What should you eagerly desire? How do you eagerly desire, what actions should you take on your part? In verse 3, what does prophecy do for people? What if you see or hear something negative from the Lord, do you prophecy negative over them? How do you turn a negative into a positive? In verse 4, what does it mean we *edify* the church? In verses 24 and 25, how do unbelievers view prophesy? Have you experienced the feeling of having your heart laid bare through prophecy? Journal or share that experience. Prophecy helps people believe in God. In verse

26, "Everything must be done so that the church may be built up." What if the church is not using the spiritual gifts, will it be built up? Verse 31, who can prophecy? To what purpose? See verse 39. Are you eager to prophesy? Do you practice your gift? How do you think you can grow in your prophetic gift? How will it affect your prophetic art?

Read Eph 4:11-16 Discuss the various offices/gifts. In verses 12-13, what are the purposes of these gifted individuals? God intends the Church to be more than it is now; He wants a mature bride. How will developing and growing people in their gifts help the Church? See Romans 12:4-8. We each have "different gifts, according to the grace given to each of us." In verse 6 it says, "If your gift is prophesying, then prophesy in accordance with your faith." Faith is part of the gift of prophecy. How is faith necessary to step out to prophecy? The Bible explains, "We see in part," sometimes that makes it difficult to prophecy. How much faith do you have to prophecy to someone or through your art? How can you increase your faith? What doubts and fears stand in your way?

I encourage everyone to read, "They May All Prophecy" by Steve Thompson to grow in the prophetic. If you are in a group, end the lesson by having everyone prophesy for everyone in the group. Activate everyone and encourage him or her to prophecy. There is grace to practice together so that we may be equipped to do it in other circumstances.

BIBLE STUDY 8: Dreams and Visions.

Look at Job 33:14-18. What does God communicate to us in dreams and visions? Can nightmares be from God? Do you think all dreams are from God? Do people realize God is talking to them through dreams? Turn to Joel 2:28-29. God will pour out His Spirit on whom? See verses 12-1, what needs to happen before God releases His Spirit? How important is fasting, repentance and consecration to your life? How do you live a consecrated life?

Consider Joseph and Daniel as examples of two individuals who were given a gift of dreams and interpretation. How were their gifts used? See Dan. 9:3, and Dan. 10:2-3. Do you think prayer and fasting played a part in Daniel's gifting? What happened in Daniel 2:17-18 when Daniel didn't know Nebuchadnezzar's dream? How were Joseph's dreams influential in his own life, and in the lives of the people in the land? What circle of influence do you have with your dreams? Have you used dreams in your art? Are individuals supposed to use all of their dreams in their creativity or art? What have been the most impacting dreams you have had for another person? Journal your and record your response.

BIBLE STUDY 9: Type and Shadow.

God loves to use types and shadows. Read Col. 2:16,17. The festivals and Sabbaths were a "shadow of things to come." What was the substance or reality? How many of the events in the Old Testament were a shadow of Christ (can you name some)?

Heb. 10:1 explains that the law was a shadow of good things to come. How do shadows relate to prophetic art? What is a shadow in relation to the real object? What are the visions we paint?

Romans 5:14 gives an example of a type. Who is the type in this verse? A type is an example, thing, or person in the Old Testament that corresponds to the fulfillment or antitype in the New Testament. There are many types of Jesus in the Old Testament. Moses was a deliverer who set his people free from slavery; he was a type of Christ. Can you think of other people who were types of Jesus in the Old Testament?

The tabernacle was a shadow of things to come, what did it predict? How can understanding types help in our prophetic artwork? Does God give you images in visions that reveal "types" of Christ or "shadows of things to come?" Give examples if you have some and journal about them.

BIBLE STUDY 10: Developing Intimacy, and love of Christ in our art.

Use the Song of Solomon to grow in intimacy in your personal walk. Read chapter 1 and consider how individuals are drawn to Jesus. Rate your personal relationship with Jesus. Are you hungry for Him like the bride, or are you waiting on the side like the daughters of Jerusalem? The bride cried, "Draw me after you." We can grow in our hunger by praying and talking to Jesus as the bride did. How did the Song use visual images to portray the love story? How can you use your art to portray intimacy with Jesus? Have you seen visions like in the Song of Solomon? What visions have been for your own personal intimacy with Jesus (not to be shared, but meant to be personal), and when are they something you have shared to edify others? How and why does poetry open our spirit to love? One of God's love languages is poetry and metaphor. How can we develop our understanding of these poetic devices? Have you seen paintings that looked like poetry? How do we capture that?

Years ago I painted, "Awake, O north wind, And come, wind of the south; Make my garden breathe out fragrance, Let its spices be wafted abroad. May my beloved come into his garden and eat its choice fruits!" SS 4:16. It specifically moved me in that season. Write down some image from the book of Song of Solomon that touches you in a deeper way and explain why. Could you use it in your art form?

BIBLE STUDY 11: Bringing the kingdom to earth.

Review the concept of Jacob's ladder in Gen. 28:10-22.

Are there places that are portals (see verse 16 & 17)? Jesus said to pray, "Thy kingdom come, thy will be done on earth as it is in heaven." How do you bring heavenly things to earth?

How can heaven be released through your art? How do you go up into heaven? Do you have angels that correspond from heaven? Have you ever found a place that felt like a portal to heaven?

The Jewish festivals are known as seasons of portals. Have you noticed increase in heavenly activity during the festivals? Look at Acts 19:11-12, "God did extraordinary miracles through Paul, so that even handkerchiefs and aprons that had touched him were taken to the sick, and their illnesses were cured and the evil spirits left them." When can objects bring the kingdom to earth? Do you believe God use your art in this way? Have you had experiences where your art or creativity brought the kingdom?

BIBLE STUDY 12: Soaking/Contemplative Prayer.

Meditate on the verses: Psalm 4:4, Matt. 11:28-30, Psalm 46:10-11, Psalm 37:4 & 7, Is. 40:29-31. Jesus told us to abide in Him. Take time to soak up strength from Him, as a vine branch draws strength and nourishment from the trunk and roots. Use a soaking CD and spend time soaking and meditating on being "One" with Jesus.

BIBLE STUDY 13: Holy Spirit and Tongues.

Bezalel was filled with the Holy Spirit. As artists we need to be filled and refilled.

Isaiah 32:14-15. How does the wasteland become fertile again? If we become spiritually dry, we need a fresh flow of the Spirit.

Acts 1:4-8. Jesus wanted His followers to have the Holy Spirit. What did they have to do to get Him? What do you think they did while they waited?

Luke 11:9-13. What does this say that you need to do to receive the Holy Spirit?

Study the gifts of the Spirit in 1 Cor. 12. In which gifts do you feel you are strong? Is the body complete without all the gifts? In your church, are all these gifts activated?

1 Cor. 14:1-5. What does this teach about the Spirit? What does it mean that we edify ourselves through tongues? How important is this gift to your work as a prophetic artist?

Isaiah 61:1-7. What were the results of the Spirit on Isaiah (and on you in your calling)?

Acts 4:29-31. What did the believers pray for? Pray to be filled, or refilled with the Holy Spirit. (We can always use more!)

BIBLE STUDY 14: Using Art to War.

Read Zech 1:18-20. The craftsmen were sent to battle to terrify the enemy who has assaulted Israel. Why would God choose craftsmen (and not warriors)? How can art be a weapon of war? How has art had an effect (negative and positive) in our society? How can you use your creativity to war in the spirit? What do you think horns represent? Our society uses visual arts and the media to launch media campaigns to advance causes. It is a weapon. (Think of some advertising campaigns that you feel have been effective and why). How can you use media to advance the Lord's messages you receive? Hitler used media to gain acceptance to further his causes. How can people be blinded through deceptive media?

See Joshua 4. The ark, a visual representation of covenant with God, (and His tangible presence), was sent ahead of the Israelites and it parted the Jordan River. Is there art that can remind you of your covenant with God? Can it have miraculous power to part the spiritual waters you face? The ark was also used to lead the march around Jericho (Joshua 6). Can certain art in media lead the battles of the Lord? What do you think the enemies of Israel thought when they saw the Ark of the Covenant? What did it do to the children of Israel? What did it represent to them?

Many people have said that it was the power of media and social media that won the last presidential campaigns. Do Christians use media enough? How can you use media to further the gospel and the prophetic message of the Lord? Do you need further knowledge to use media?

BIBLE STUDY 15: Use of Banners in the Bible.

Ex 17:15, why do you think the Lord is called "My Banner?" In Num. 2:2, what was the purpose of the banners? This demonstrates that you can have art that displays identity.

Ps. 20:5, what did they do with the banners in this verse? In Ps. 60:4, what do you think it means to unfurl a banner against the bow? How can you use art in this same way?

See Song of Solomon 2:4. What is our Beloved doing here? See Song of Solomon 6:4, what is the Beloved comparing her to? What do these banners represent? In Is. 5:26 for what purpose does the Lord use these banners?

Also look up and discuss: Isaiah 11:10-12, 13:2-3 18:3, 30:17, 49:22-23, 62:10-12, Jer. 50:2, 51:12, 51:27, Ez. 27:7. What spiritual impact did the banners have? What do banners proclaim or what identity do they portray? Do they reveal a battle strategy? In the time of war banners were used to signal the troops in the maneuvers of war. How can visual art do the same? Can you do these same things in your art?

BIBLE STUDY 16: Research Biblical color symbolism.

If you are in a group, have each person in the group research one color, finding verses in the Bible for their color (or if you are on your own, select several colors). For a quick search use Biblegateway.com. It takes just minutes. For example, I searched for "scarlet" and found that it was used on the curtains in the tabernacle (threads twisted with blue and purple). A scarlet thread was also tied to a bird in the process of cleansing a leper; it was the color of the cord (another "thread") hung from a window of Rahab the prostitute that protected her family. In Song of Solomon "her lips were like a scarlet thread," and "Though your sins are scarlet, they will be white as snow," in Is. 1:18. They put a scarlet robe on Jesus (a full robe of "threads"). We see a clear pattern of the meaning of the color scarlet. It is redemption, the color of Jesus' blood. It is the flow from the lips of the beloved, the song of redemption. It is His redemptive scarlet thread or cord that flows throughout the Bible, the flow of Jesus' blood. Look at the verses you have found for each color, review the symbolism in each circumstance, and the common theme of the color. Share or journal your findings.

BIBLE STUDY 17: Memorials, Altars, and Monuments

In Ex. 28:12, what were the memorial stones? What did they represent? Aaron wore these stones on his shoulders, what do shoulders represent? He wore them like we wear lockets with pictures of people in them. In the spirit he carried the children of Israel on his shoulders.

See Josh. 4:7-24, what was the purpose of the memorial? What did the stones represent? How did they carry the stones (verse 5)? In

Gen. 8:20-22, what was the purpose of the altar? How did God respond to the sacrifice? Are there some forms of art that are a vehicle for sacrifice? In Gen. 12:6-8 what was the reason for Abram's altars? Can you do art as an altar when the Lord appears to you? See Gen. 35:1-7. What was the purpose of this altar? See Gen. 28:16-22. Why did Jacob set up a pillar? What did it look like? What did he say to God at this memorial?

In Ex. 20:24-26, what did they use this altar for? Why do you think God wanted them to use stones without tools? God didn't want their body exposed to the steps, what does this say about the stone steps? In Ex. 24, Moses built an altar and set up 12 pillars. Who did they represent? They sacrificed and went up the mountain (verse 9-11). What did they see? Do our memorials (along with the sacrifice of Jesus) create an environment to come closer to the Lord?

In Joshua 22:10-34 the tribe of Reuben built an "offensive alter." What was wrong with it? What could have happened to them by building it? Why was it okay in the end? How does the intent of your art make a difference on whether it is offensive? Share examples of modern day memorials made by man.

BIBLE STUDY 18: Creativity and Imagination.

Review Eph. 3:20-21, what can God do? It says, "more than all we ask or imagine." How much can you imagine? Is all your imagination of good things? What if you imagine sickness? How big is your God? Do you have faith to believe in God's power to do the impossible? It says, "According to His power that is at work within us." What does that mean? See Heb. 11:1-3, what is faith? God can make something out of nothing, what can He do with your imagination and prayer? Look at Heb. 11:6. Do we please God, as prophetic artists, if we don't have faith? Why should we have more faith than others?

See Ezek. 13:1-9, there are those who follow their own spirit. What does this tell about our desires? We are made of body, soul and spirit. We need to follow the right desires and God led imagination. How can you tell if your flesh is leading you?

See 2 Cor. 4:4. Have you met people who have been blinded by satan? There is a lot of imagination in Hollywood that does not come from God. How can our imagination, illuminated by the light of Jesus have a positive effect in our society? What things can you imagine for the Lord to use to spread the prophetic Word of the Lord? Review the chapter in *Shadow Painter* on Creativity and Imagination. What limits do we need to put on our creativity and imagination? What possibilities do we have when linking our faith to our God-led imagination?

BIBLE STUDY 19: Serpent on the Pole.

Study Numbers 21:4-9 to discuss healing art, like the serpent on the pole. Why were there snakes? What did the people have to do to be healed?

See John 3:14-15. People in the Old Testament looked on the snake and were healed; whom do we look on to be healed? Can your art bring Jesus' miraculous healing and release the kingdom and glory? Has God given you images that represent Jesus, but in another form, like the snake?

See Isaiah 53:5. If we present the good news, that Jesus' wounds heal; does it matter if we speak it, or tell it in a painting or writing? Is it truth either way? Can it release faith in either form?

In 2 Kings 18:34 why was the serpent on the pole destroyed? Why did God have them make it in the first place? In Acts 19:11,12, what physical objects were used for healing? How did they gain power? How can objects become anointed? When can your art heal? Is it wrong to desire that art be used to heal? In the world there are miraculous pieces of art, weeping statues or paintings. Do you believe they are all from God?

BIBLE STUDY 20: Biblical Symbolism.

See Matt. 13:10-17. Did the disciples understand the symbolism in Jesus' parables? Why did Jesus speak in parables? Who may understand the "secrets?" What does it mean that some people's hearts were calloused? Are there things we present through our creativity and art that people will not understand? In verse 15, "Otherwise they might see with their eyes, hear with their ears, understand with their hearts and turn, and I would heal them." When people do understand the symbolism, what change does it have in a person? What great potential is possible when we use God-inspired symbolism? In verse 16, we are blessed because our eyes see and our ears hear. Have you met people who just don't "see" or get the message? Is it worth arguing with them?

In Matt. 7:6 it says, "Do not give dogs what is sacred; do not throw your pearls to pigs. If you do, they may trample them under their feet, and turn and tear you to pieces." In light of this verse, are there some things we create we should keep within the church? Why does God's message seem confusing in our dreams? "It is the glory of God to conceal a matter; to search out a matter is the glory of kings," Prov. 25:2. In this verse, how can you understand God's language better and search out meanings for symbols that God presents to you? (There is a book listed in the appendix, *Understanding the Dreams You Dream* that is helpful in interpretation.)

Do a short search on the internet for conceptual art. What concept is portrayed in the art? A concept is the strongest base for your art. In prophetic art, God initiates concept. Journal examples of revelation and the symbolism and concepts you have received from the Lord.

BIBLE STUDY 21: Having the "Mind of Christ."

See 1 Cor. 2:4-16. The apostle Paul stressed that the message was not just in the preaching, but the demonstration of the Spirit. In verse 10, who reveals the things God has prepared for us? You need to be in tune with the Holy Spirit. In verse 11, how do you know the thoughts of God? How do you understand what God speaks to you (vs. 12-13)? People without the Spirit do not understand the things of God, but calls them "foolishness." What do the verses 15-16 reveal about how the Spirit guides you?

Read Col. 3:1-2. How do you seek the things above, not on the things that are on earth? How do you abide in Christ? What does it mean, to have the mind of Christ?

Col. 3:5-17. How does your negative walk affect your intimacy and abiding? What things help your spiritual walk and help you abide (verse 16)? Verse 10, how do you put on the new self? In John 15, the parable of the vine and branches, see verses 1-11. To have the mind of Christ you need to abide and remain in the vine. What happens to the vine when you don't abide? In verse 7, what happens when you do abide/remain in Jesus? What is the fruit God wants produced in you and your creativity? Verse 9 says to remain in Jesus' love. How do you think you are able to stay in that place of love? Can prophetic artists create when they don't abide?

BIBLE STUDY 22: Creative, Manifold Wisdom.

The word Wisdom in the Bible also was used to mean skill or creativity. Explore Proverbs 8. This chapter explains a lot about Wisdom, and here Wisdom is personified as "she." In verses 17, how do you find wisdom? In 18, 19, and 35, what are the benefits of wisdom? In 22-31, when did wisdom begin? What does verse 30 show when it says, that she (wisdom) rejoiced and delighted in the world and mankind?

Turn to Exodus 31:3-5. What is the purpose of Wisdom? What other gifts link with it? (example: knowledge). See Ez. 28:12-19, satan corrupted his wisdom. What did he do wrong? How is it a warning for artists?

In 1 Cor. 2:6-16. What do you think is the hidden wisdom? Why did they not understand it? In verse 9, "Eye has not seen..." God has great things in store for us that have not been released before. How does God reveal things to us (vs. 10)? How do you get wisdom? Solomon prayed and asked for wisdom, what was the fruit of wisdom in his life? What part does this creative wisdom play in your creativity? How does God inspire you or when do you get that "spark" of instruction from Him?

BIBLE STUDY 23: Performance Art.

Study the prophetic actions performed in Ezekiel 4. What symbols and actions did God use? What were their meanings? Do you think the people clearly understood? Was it easy for Ezekiel to carry out his assignment? What was most difficult for him? The Lord commanded Ezekiel to eat a mixture of grains made into bread for 390 days. Can what you eat be a prophetic action? Has God asked you to eat anything in particular or not to eat? What was the symbolism of what he ate (see verse 13)? What symbolized the nations?

Read Ezekiel 5:1-6. What prophetic actions, (performance art) was Ezekiel asked to do in these verses? Discuss each action and meaning.

Research a current performance art exhibit in today's society. There are a few good videos on YouTube (but be cautious, some may be offensive). Review the section in *Shadow Painter* on performance art. Have you done performance art? You may want to ask the Lord for a performance idea to work on, if you are feeling called to do this. Ask for a practice assignment!

BIBLE STUDY 24: Installation Art

The Lord set up the temple with particular instruction for object placement. Review the Placement and meaning of: The Altar (Ex. 27:1), Laver (Ex. 30:18), Table of Showbread (Ex. 25:23), Lampstand (Ex. 25:31), Alter of Incense (Ex. 30:1), Art of the Covenant (Ex. 25:20) and Mercy Seat (Ex. 25:17). These furnishings had symbolic placement in the Temple. They portray the progressive steps in the Christian walk, growing into intimacy with the Lord beginning with our salvation, symbolized with the altar of sacrifice. It is here where we first met Jesus and understood His sacrifice. Review the objects and what you believe it represents in your spiritual journey. Placement was extremely important in the message the Lord revealed.

When we do art, placement can also be symbolic. Do a quick Google search on Installation art images. What one modern art exhibit interests you? Was there symbolic placement? What was the concept? My friend created a prayer room, and the Lord told her where to place the objects. Have you thought of any type of installation art? Be open to hearing from the Lord regarding this type of art. Record any leadings of the Holy Spirit about doing an installation.

Ask the Father for guidance in your projects! In 2 Peter 1:19:19 we read,

"And we have the word of the prophets made more certain, and you will do well to pay attention to it, as to a light shining in a dark place, until the day dawns and the morning star rises in your hearts." I pray that you are a light breaking the darkness in your city! God gives revelation to us through the Holy Spirit. He brings a new day and a revelation of Jesus, our Morning Star, to our hearts and our creativity. May He guide your art projects.

CHAPTER 15
SEEING AHEAD

What is the future of Prophetic Art? In this section I have listed a few areas I felt the Lord was speaking about, and included what others have prophesied.

COFFEEHOUSES

One thing the Lord has shown me in dreams was art ministry in coffee shops. It was a creative place where Christians and non-Christian can gather and share creative ideas. In one dream, there were Christians with the gift of the prophetic, ministering to others. The Lord wants this kind of creative social place and there are many Christian coffee houses already doing this type of ministry. There are poetry nights, art exhibits, comedians, contests, even prophetic coffee houses where people gifted in the prophetic, give prophetic words from the Lord to the audience. There is an emotional need in people to connect with others and find a place of belonging. The bar in the T.V. show "Cheers" was a place for broken people to connect. God wants to show His love in a similar type of creative environment where people can hang out together and meet their social, spiritual, and creative artistic needs.

PROPHETIC OUTPOURING

The prophetic will be released in great measure, and the secular world will take notice. Joel 2 tells us that there will be an outpouring:

> *"I will pour out my Spirit on all people. Your sons and daughters will prophesy, your old men will dream dreams, your young men will see visions. Even on my servants, both men and women, I will pour out my Spirit in those days." Joel 2:28-29*

Christian artists will flow with revelation from the Lord. The secular world will not be able to comprehend or understand the accuracy and power of the revelation received from God. There will be paintings depict events that will happen. There will be ministry using the prophetic arts. God will be glorified and worshiped through the arts as never before.

What is coming has never been birthed on this earth. There is definitely no earthly demonstration to compare it to. We will only have the Spirit-led imagination of God to guide us down this trail of exquisite beauty and supernatural delight. As we value Him and His gifts, He will reveal the treasures in heaven.

ALTERNATIVE CREATIVE WORSHIP

God wants to release freedom and creativity into the church. Many churches have become disconnected from the culture. Modern technologies are available to bring the colors, lights, sounds, and images from heaven into our worship. It is not about entertainment! It is about releasing true creative worship to glorify the Father. This is attractive to many in our generation, and draws them to the vibrant intensity of passionate love for the Lord. Churches that allow for this freedom are free the chains of religious tradition that is a bondage that limits talent and the prophetic gifting.

There is an organization that promotes creative alternative worship, you might want to see some of their photos or read about their projects. They are found at www.smallfire.org. They state:

> "Alternative worship is intensely concerned with creativity. Partly, this is because reinventing worship requires it; but more because of a belief that creativity is essential to human wholeness and should be offered back to the Creator in worship. Since we are made in the image of a creator God, we are all creative – but life, and often sadly the Church, conspires to tell us that we are not, that we have nothing worth offering. Alternative worship offers people the chance of creative expression in worship. Not just the team making things to be admired by the congregation, but the congregation making things as worship, to be admired by the team."(Collins)

The organization Beyond Church, in the UK, creates ten art related worship events, each year, which are opened to the general public. For instance, they created a beach hut advent calendar, revealing one decorated hut for every day during advent. Each hut is an installation art worship piece, for the glory of the Lord and to inspire and stimulate discussion about God.

God wants creativity used by Christians to stimulate new thought, to draw the community to Him, and to deepen our worship. He wants to restore art to the Church in full reconciliation to express Christ so that God will be glorified in the fullness of all His expressions.

APOSTOLIC WORSHIP

This generation now understands our part in bringing heaven's proclamations into our church services through the prophetic. John Dickson writes:

"Apostolic worship means worship that engages every believer and goes forth into the atmosphere and into the community to establish God's will on earth as it is in heaven. Greek apostolos means "One who is sent out," so apostolic worship means worship that goes forth to establish God's will on earth.

"This kind of worship includes speaking forth in intercession and prophetic declaration what God is saying in the midst of worship over specific problems and areas of warfare in a community, city, region, state or nation." (Pierce 20)

As artists, we take part in this new move of God by making prophetic declarations through our artwork in the worship setting. We may "see" a prophetic declaration for our city or region, and paint it to release the kingdom of heaven or create a focus of prayer on that topic. God may have an artist paint someone stomping on a snake or dragon, to show that the Lord wants to destroy the spirit of Leviathan over your region. The painting unifies vision in making proclamations and releases what the Lord is speaking for that season. There is great power in unity of the body as we catch the vision together and stand against evil.

"Again, truly I tell you that if two of you on earth agree about anything they ask for, it will be done for them by my Father in heaven. For where two or three gather in my name, there am I with them." Matt. 18:18,19.

In unity, we release the kingdom, and the Lord's glory. This also establishes the Lord's government here on the earth.

John Dickson writes:

"What the head is thinking, the Body should respond to in its worship. If the Lord is celebrating, His body should be celebrating. If He is warring, we should be warring. This is how it is in heaven; a sea of individual worshippers who, when joined together, synergistically bring forth the awesome experiences we read about in the book of

Revelation. Whatever God is doing, His worshippers in heaven respond to it in their worship." (Pierce 30)

By operating in this apostolic worship, we are not swinging blindly in the air against the enemy. We become like trained marksmen, who view their target through a high-powered scope, the prophetic. We can see clearly where to aim our powerful weapons of warfare that are mighty to the tearing down of strongholds. In this last generation, we will be a mighty force, as the Lord releases special keys to help us war and worship in the Spirit.

TRANCES

There will be artists who will be able to paint during a trance. They will look at the painting later, and wonder who painted it because they were entirely in the Spirit's peace while they painted. This is a wonderful place of total surrender to the Lord and letting Him use you entirely.

THE LIGHT AND GLORY

> *"Arise, shine, for your light has come, and the glory of the LORD rises upon you. See, darkness covers the earth and thick darkness is over the peoples, but the LORD rises upon you and his glory appears over you. Nations will come to your light, and kings to the brightness of your dawn." Is. 60:1,2.*

The darkness is going to get darker, sins will abound. But the light will become brighter, the light of the glory of God on His people. It is interesting to note that light is made up of the full spectrum. Creatively, I think we will be able to bring the beauty of the color and spectrum from heaven better than ever before. The spectrum is also a rainbow, a promise of His covenant, as the Lord brings His glory to the earth.

OVERFLOW

One word I have been given is "overflow." This is when the arts extend over their normal boundaries and into other art areas, creating a creative crossover. Imagine having dancers on a stage performing without music. There is grace and beauty demonstrated in their talent, but something is missing. The music magnifies the splendor of their performance. We could not even imagine having all dances performed without music. Right now, there are arts areas that need to work together to form a unity, in new combined forms of creativity. They will come together and be so much more than they are now.

I remember a poet that spoke at an event. He had incredible talent. He created a score of music that went with the rhythm of his spoken words. It was done in a way I had never seen before. Even the way he enunciated his words had a sound and beat that was unique. Four instruments joined in as he recited his work, creating an incredible drama. The musicians responded to his words and overlapped as if they were having a conversation. It made an indelible impact on me.

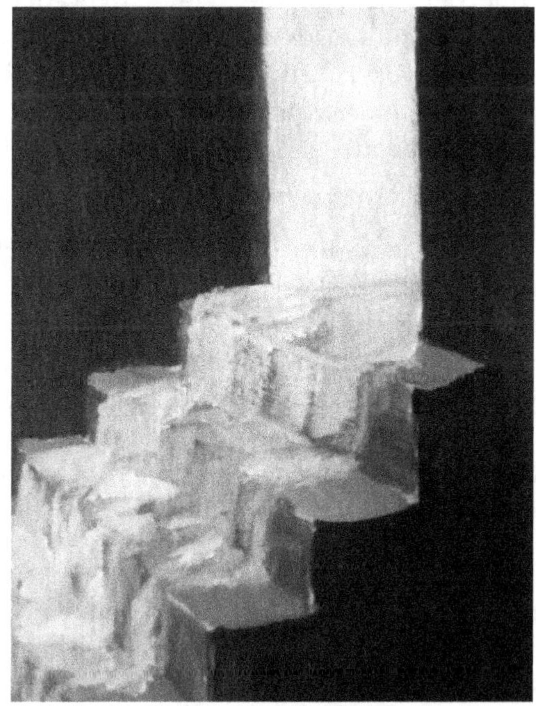

"Heavenly Flow" By Laurie A. Stasi

God wants an overflow of creativity, because He is creator and wants us, in His likeness to let our creativity flow. There have been imaginary lines around the different arts areas. My daughters attended an arts magnet high school and there were different tracks for all the arts. Once a year they had an "Extravaganza," and in all freedom the artists would create routines together. Dance overflowed into painting, with music, and video. It was very impressive. Unfortunately it was with the world's standards and perversions. God wants the arts to overflow together to worship Him.

Jesus said that He wants us to be one even as He and the Father are one. To be one, we need to demonstrate creative oneness and unity. The results will be amazing and breathtaking. No one performer is the "star." Everyone has to die to self, in order to let others overlap on their work. Doing collaborative pieces are very difficult for visual artists, because it takes compromise and an understanding that my work can be painted over by someone else. Visual artists are accustomed to being isolated "lone rangers," working alone in their studios.

Years ago, in our arts class, we worked on a collaborative painting together. We unrolled long rolls of paper and hung it along the walls. We wore old paint clothes, and splattered and painted like Jackson Pollock. I was bothered when someone painted over areas I had created. To work together, pride must be broken and self-sacrifice is required. Training artists in "overflow" means they must come to an understanding with one another, accepting compromise and unity.

This creative overflow can be achieved through small teams composed of different arts areas; poets, musicians, dancers, drama, writers, etc. on each team. They could spend pressure cooker time together, called incubation, and bounce ideas off of one another. Creativity breeds creativity. The challenge would be for them to find new ways for the arts areas to overflow into each other, and present a unified presentation together. The goal is to have a performance that is creatively inspired by God, using their talents in unity. To say the word performance does not mean this is for man's approval, but for God's glory. The outcome would be many small performances by multiple teams. The purpose of these teams could be extended to outreaches, churches, and other higher forms of art.

LEVITICAL ART

Recently the Lord has emphasized the Levitical purpose in prophetic art. I have heard of several other artists mentioning the same theme. Levitical pieces are paintings in the church, for the church, and for the Lord. They are also integral to worship. David brought poetry, music, visual images, fabrics, light, dance, beauty, design, scents, and colors all together to worship the Lord. It was creative prayer, praise, and worship as an offering. I am sure this is part of the reason David was considered a man after the Lord's own heart.

As Levitical priests and artists we can focus the worship through a prophetic vision of what the Lord is saying for that meeting. Just as priests ministered unto the Lord, these Levite artists will minister for the glory of the Lord and assist in worship and sacrifice.

David called for the donation of materials for the temple. The Israelites were very generous. Then David prayed:

> *"LORD our God, all this abundance that we have provided for building you a temple for your Holy Name comes from your hand, and all of it belongs to you....keep these desires and thoughts in the hearts of your people forever, and keep their hearts loyal to you. And give my son Solomon the wholehearted devotion to keep your commands, statutes and decrees and to do everything to build the palatial structure for which I have provided." 1 Chron. 29:16, 18-19.*

In this verse, David wanted the people to always remember the creation of the temple and its purpose. He asked the Lord to keep the desires and thoughts (of the temple) in the hearts of the people forever.

The Hebrew interpretation for 'desire' is yester, which means: form, framing, purpose, framework, pottery, graven image, man (as formed from the dust), purpose, imagination, and device (intellectual framework). The Hebrew for 'thoughts' is "machashabah: thought, device, plan, purpose, invention."

To pull this together; as people of God and prophetic artists, we are supposed to remember and desire the temple and its form, its beautiful sculpture, sturdy framework and complex purpose on earth and in heaven. Have it in your imagination, thoughts and heart forever! The temple model should be the framework for the artwork you create. Let your imagination focus on God's temple images. Let your creative plans be like the temple, in beauty and in intent. Always point to Jesus in the subliminal or overt message, just as every part of the temple was a foreshadowing of Him.

In understanding these truths, the Lord showed me a vision. The framework and beauty of heaven released through imagination is like delicate candlelight of a pearl candelabrum. It glows with the light of revelation. It is beautiful and it is decorated with pearls of great price. This is wisdom, a gift to dig for, to seek at great expense. If you look at pearls closely, they are luminescent and reflect colors. The hues are so delicate, and pearls are formed in layers, like revelation upon revelation we receive from the Father, building the gift of the prophetic. This is the multicolored wisdom of Ephesians 3.

In a previous chapter, I used a quote from Todd Bentley about the building blocks in the invisible realm that were the framework of creativity. God wants us to dream, or vision with Him and prophecy for the heavenly things to materialize in the natural realm, (Bentley). We can see and imagine the creative things in the heavenly kingdom as a frame or an image of what God wants to release, and we create that idea or object by calling it, prophesying, and decreeing it. God then establishes it.

Chron. 29 also says, "keep these desires and thoughts in the hearts of your people forever, and keep their hearts loyal to you." The love the temple and laws (expressed creatively through the arts and our talents) and the supernatural creativity we get from heaven, needs to be bound to our hearts as the Jews bind them on their foreheads. There is a cautious reminder connected with this: "and keep their hearts loyal to you." It is easy to become disloyal with this great gift. The power of creativity has enormous potential for the kingdom, or for evil. We must pledge our hearts to the Lord's will, in total loyalty as knights who carry a great treasure.

FROM THE MODERN PROPHETS:

In the remainder of this book I am including some quotes from modern prophets because the Bible says we all see in part. By pulling together revelation from the Body of Christ, we are able to get the big picture. This will help us on the prophetic path that the Lord is revealing.

CREATIVE MIRACLES AND ART

Shawn Bolz has been a forerunner in miracles and prophetic creativity. Below are various excerpts from his prophecy regarding art and the link it has with miracles:

> "I looked in the Spirit and I was in an art gallery looking at a masterpiece. I knew it was a picture that had not yet been created yet. I could feel that God longs to partner to artists on the earth to bring forth new masterpieces that will once again bring enlightenment. . .I heard the Lord say the old phrase, 'A picture is worth a thousand words, and these pictures will be worth a thousand sermons.'
>
> "I had an encounter again in a place that I call the store house of heaven. . . the room of creative miracles. In this place I was looking at aisles and aisles of body parts all destined to creatively grow on someone who was missing

them here on earth! In this same area of creative miracles though, I could see that the same power that would create a limb or internal organ is also the same power that will release creative art projects, new sounds, scientific breakthroughs, and inventions! This is amazing that it takes the same virtue and power to heal as it does to be creative; furthermore, we have the same access to bring forth renaissance projects as we do to bring forth healings!" (Bolz).

There is a wonderful connection between the creative miracles, and creativity in art. Artists will begin to understand this and will see both manifest in their lives! The same faith it takes for a creative flow is the same faith it takes to manifest an amputated arm to re-grow. Both are released from the Father's creative storeroom in heaven.

Rick Joyner prophesied in an article, "The Weightiest Matter," about the art move that is coming motivated by love and high worship:

> "There is an anointing coming upon artists that is even greater than that which was given to Bezalel for building the tabernacle of Moses. . . the greatest masters of all will be
>
> now. . . The more pure the love, the more pure and powerful the art will be. These are gifts from God to His Bride, and they will touch her in profound ways to draw her heart to Him and be used to express her heart for Him.
>
> "The truest art will always come out of the highest worship, and will be high worship. This is why, at the end of this age, the most creative gifts the world will have ever seen will come from the Church. These will be a part of the garment that she will wear, and what she wears will reflect what is in her heart. She will see His glory, she will reflect His glory, and she will produce glory in all that she does. Glory will be her garment, and it will be alike a train that follows after her. . . there will be a whole new revelation of

> the coming wedding feast. The greatest joy of the creations will be to see the Creator's joy in His Bride. . .These gifts will also both draw and equip the Bride for her highest purpose—her union with the King. It will begin to draw the nations to the feast." (Joyner) used by permission.

JoAnn McFatter also prophesied about the creativity that God will release. We need to see it with faith and receive it in fullness!

> "But we are at the dawning of an age of creativity such as we've never seen before, for it will be Holy Spirit driven. . . God wants to overshadow us with that God-seed idea. His treasury room in Heaven is FULL, waiting to be accessed by you! There are so many different things such as books, paintings, inventions, architecture, business strategies, patents, music—the list goes on and on—just waiting for ones who will open their mind and spirits to receive it from Him. . .The creativity is above all that we have seen or heard up to this point in history. He's saved the best till last" (McFatter).

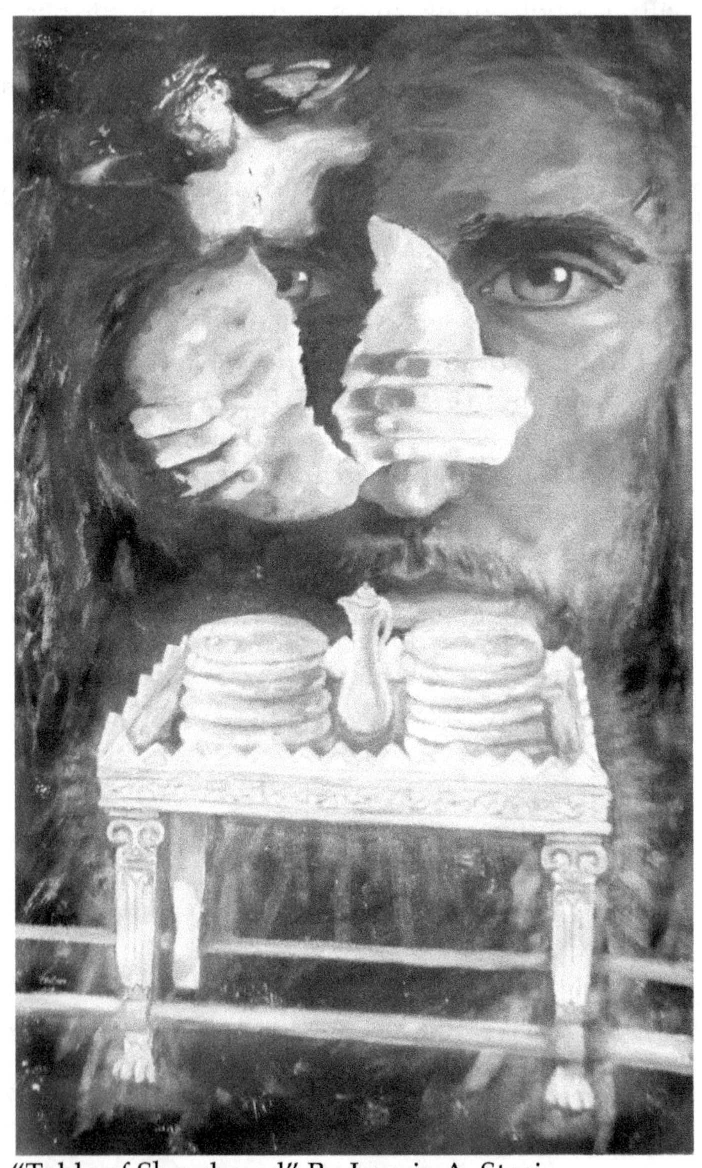
"Table of Showbread" By Laurie A. Stasi

IN CLOSING

God has immeasurable love for you. He created you with your gifts and talents. He is tugging at your heart, asking you to use them for His purposes, and for the prophetic mission of bringing His voice to others. He wants to share His love through you. Will you be His vessel? Will you be a prophetic prophet in the arts?

Step into the Lord's creative realm and run with what He gives you! Be faithful in your calling. Be diligent in proclaiming His words, visions and prophecies. Stay close to His heart in everything you do, and release His heartbeat in your words, colors, music, actions and creativity. Let it be a love-song from Him to others, and from your heart back to His. Search the unfathomable mysteries of His wisdom, imagination and creativity. It is a treasure beyond earthly value. The fear of the Lord is the beginning of wisdom, and when you find wisdom, you will find Him, for He is wisdom and our Creator.

> *"I advise you to buy from me gold refined by fire so that you may become rich, and white garments so that you may clothe yourself, and that the shame of your nakedness will not be revealed; and eye salve to anoint your eyes so that you may see." Rev. 3:18.*

The end time church is encouraged to become holy and dressed in white. It is also told to, "Anoint your eyes so that you may see." It is very important in the last days that you have eyes to see. God wants you to have spiritual understanding in these days, and He is offering a gift of spiritual vision. Ask the Lord for more insight into His realm. Seek and you will find! It is necessary to overcome the attacks of the enemy in these dark days. Your hunger will release the heavenly realm into your life. It will let you proclaim the Lord's banner, or warfare messages for the last day church. "Set your mind on things above, not on things that are on the earth," Col. 3:2. God wants you to be one with His thoughts, to have the mind of Christ. To truly "see."

Fight for Lord's purposes for all of the arts to be redeemed in our generation. Aggressively take the arts from the secular world, and bring them back to the glory of the Lord. He wants you to be led by Holy Spirit, guided by His revelation. Climb Jacob's ladder and access the kingdom and bring it to earth.

The Lord is eager for His creative bride to be adorned and breathtaking, and the operating fully in the prophetic. He longs for her fullness in every area. When you create for Him, listen for His tender heartbeat and the beauty of His soft voice and seek His revelatory guidance. Honor your Creator, your King of Kings with your creative talents. Let your love for Him flow through your gifts to Him as a beautiful, delightful offering.

"I keep asking that the God of our Lord Jesus Christ, the glorious Father, may give you the Spirit of wisdom and revelation, so that you may know Him better. I pray that the eyes of your heart may be enlightened in order that you may know the hope to which He has called you, the riches of His glorious inheritance in His holy people, and His incomparably great power for us who believe," Eph. 1:17-19.

WORKS CITED

Bentley, Todd. *Ignite the fire Conference.* Grand Rapids. Aug. 23, 2007. Prophecy.

Bolz, Shawn. "The Renaissance Spirit is Being Released." Identity Network. Expressions 58. Sept. 07, 2007.

Castillo, Joe. *The Word Becomes Flesh.* Dec. 14, 2010. Performance. Web.

David E. Bresler, PhD, Lac. *Academy for Guided Imagery.* Web. 2011.

Garibaldi, David. *Incredible Christian Artist David Garibaldi.* Oct. 24, 2011. Performance. Web.

Hughes, Ray. *Decree – Quotes. June 26, 2011.* Web. Mar. 2013.

Jeanne-Claude, Christo. *The Gates.* Feb. 2005. Fabric Panels. New York City, NY.

Maxwell, John. "The Leaders Edge." Quoted in *Enjoying Everyday Life* By Joyce Meyer. July 24, 2006.

Joyner, Rick. "The Weightiest Matter" by Rick Joyner. *MorningStar Prophetic Bulletin #55.* Used by Permission. Aug. 2007.

McFatter, JoAnn. "The Lost Art of Creativity." *White Dove Ministries.* Mar. 3, 2008.

Pierce, John Dickson & Chuck D. *Worship As it is in Heaven.* Ventura: Regal. 2010. Print.

Shaw, Gwen. *Redeeming the Land.* Jasper: Engeital Press, 1987.

Sherwood Pictures. Sherwood Baptist Church, Albany, Georgia.

Encyclopedia Britannica, *Conceptual Art.* Web. Mar. 2013.

LeWitt, Sol. "Paragraphs on Conceptual Art", *Artforum,* June 1967.

Tobias, Cynthia. *The Way They Learn.* Tyndale House Publishers. 1994.

Zink, Paul Sr.. Jacksonville, Florida, July 28, 2013, Sermon.

ARTWORK

I have included artwork by myself and my daughters Amanda A. Flowers, and Nichole A. Ryder. You can view our artwork in color on the web page: *www.shadowpainter.org* or my Facebook page, *The Shadow Painter.*

Please email comments, corrections or suggestions to: stasiart@gmail.com or visit www.shadowpainter.org

APPENDIX

RECOMMENDED READING:

"Art and the Bible," Francis Schaeffer

"Can you Talk Louder God?" Steve Schulz, (hearing God)

"Deepening Revelation through Meditation," Kirk Bennett

"Dreaming with God," James Goll and Bill Johnson

"Facing the Wall," Don Potter (a book about worship)

"Possessing the Gates of the Enemy," Cindy Jacobs (intercession)

"Practicing the Presence," Brother Lawrence (intimacy)

"Redeeming the Land," Gwen Shaw (intercession)

"The Beginner's Guide to the Gift of Prophecy," Jack Deere

"The Supernatural Power of a Transformed Mind," Bill Johnson

"The Final Quest," Rick Joyner

"The Glory Zone," and "Glory Invasion" by David Hertzog

"The Lost Glory" David Markee

"The Prophetic Ministry," Rick Joyner

"The Prophet's Dictionary," Paula A. Price, PhD (for interpretation)

"The Seer," by Jim Goll.

"The Supernatural Ways of Royalty," Kris Vallotton

"The Way they Learn," Cynthia Tobias (about learning styles)

"Understanding the Dreams you Dream," Ira Milligan (my favorite for interpretation)

"When Heaven Invades Earth," Bill Johnson

"Worship as it is in heaven," John Dickson & Chuck D. Pierce

"You May All Prophecy," Steve Thompson

www.ingramcontent.com/pod-product-compliance
Lightning Source LLC
LaVergne TN
LVHW010056110826
845155LV00028B/364

* 9 7 8 1 8 8 8 0 8 1 8 5 5 *